Nolia Fisherman around Chilika Lake

A Socio-Economic Study

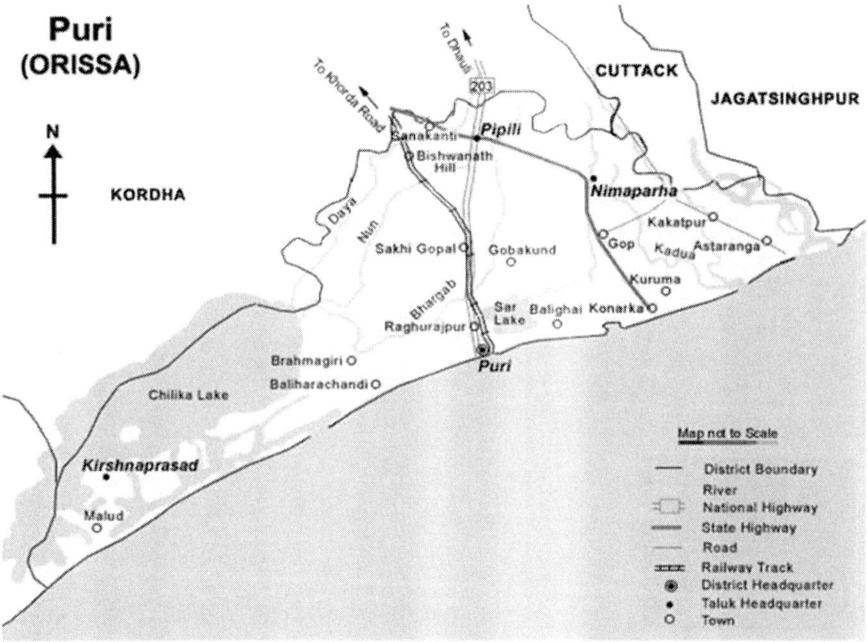
Puri
(ORISSA)
N
KORDHA
CUTTACK
JAGATSINGHPUR
To Khorda Road
To Dhauli
203
Sanakanti
Pipili
Bishwanath Hill
Nimaparha
Daya
Nun
Kakatpur
Gop
Kadua
Astaranga
Sakhi Gopal
Gobakund
Kuruma
Bhargab
Sar Lake
Balighai
Konarka
Raghurajpur
Puri
Brahmagiri
Baliharachandi
Chilika Lake
Kirshnaprasad
Malud
Map not to Scale
District Boundary
River
National Highway
State Highway
Road
Railway Track
District Headquarter
Taluk Headquarter
Town

Nolia Fisherman around Chilika Lake

A Socio-Economic Study

Geetanjali Panda

Delta Book World
New Delhi - 110002

Nolia Fisherman around Chilika Lake: A Socio-Economic Study

by Geetanjali Panda

First Published in 2022

ISBN: 978-81-955519-4-1

Published by

Delta Book World
G-4, Prahlad House
4832/24, Ansari Road
New Delhi - 110 002 (India)
Tel.: 011-47072321
E-mail: deltabookworld@gmail.com

Laser Typesetting : Aarati Computers, Delhi

PRINTED IN INDIA

Acknowledgement

It would not have been possible to complete this work without the good will, support and encouragement of a number of persons. First of all, I express my sincere thanks and gratitude to the Nolia people of Puri district.

I am also thankful to the following organizations for allowing me to elicit information related to my work:

- NBC, Bhubaneswar
- Anthropological Survey of India, Kolkata
- State Achieves, Bhubaneswar
- Directorate of Census Operations, Bhubaneswar
- Marine Fisheries Department, Puri
- CDA Office, Balugaon and Bhubaneswar
- B.D.O. and A.F.O. of Krushnaprasad Block, Sarpanch of Arakhakuda
- Villagers of Arakhakuda, Pansapada

I express my sincere thanks to my well wisher Madam and guide Prof. Sabita Acharya, Vice-Chancellor of Utkal University, Vanivihar, Bhubaneswar for her steady encouragement, able guidance and supervision in carrying out this research and preparation of this work.

Geetanjali Panda

Preface

Nolia Fisherman around Chilika Lake is a socio-economic study of fishermen communities living around Chilika lake, the major thrust of the present work.

The justification of this study has been very clearly outlined in the introduction. The discussion of the conceptual frame work and the review of the literature have been vividly mentioned to provide the basic information of the work. The aims and objectives of the study are also clearly mentioned.

In order to make the work proceed in a smooth manner, a few working hypothesis in the Chapter-I have been formulated and used. As the work is based on empirical data collection, I have also mentioned about the limitation of research while collecting data from the people and finally mentioned about the establishment of the rapport which ultimately facilitated my data collection. The second chapter goes with the title "Coverage of Study" which describes about the district profile of Puri highlighting with Demographic features as well as the Nolia, the fishing communities and their interethnic relations. It also describes the geographical location of the study area, road and communication, flora and fauna, climate, rainfall, census analysis and the important institutions like social organization, economic organization, religious organization and political organizations.

The third chapter mostly delineates the study "Social Structures" with specific reference marriage, family, kinship, religious practices. It also describes about the lifecycle rituals. In fourth chapter, the "Religious activities are discussed". I try to analyze in chapter fifth about the "Economic Organisation" which includes the techno-economics of Fishing along with the functions of Fishing. This chapter also includes an important part which is very essential for fishing i.e. Navigational ethno science. In the sixth chapter, "Political Organisation" which mainly highlights the leadership pattern of Nolia (fishing caste) people and a comparative analysis of present politics and traditional politics. Chapter seven deals with the "Women Empowerment" is clearly analyzed.

Chapter eight has included Sponsored development activities in fishing village: An evaluation in the factors like educational, fishing, environmental, income and activities of NGO etc. The chapter nine presents "Impact of modernization on coastline culture and changing scenario. In the last chapter, I discuss about the conclusion, findings and testing of supposed hypothesis.

Contents

List of Tables

Abbreviations

ANM	-	Auxiliary Nurse Midwife
APO	-	Additional Programme Officer
BCG	-	Bacillus Calmette-Guérin
BDO	-	Block Development Officer
BPL	-	Below Poverty Line
CDA	-	Chilika Development Authority
DPT	-	Diptheria Pertussis &Titanus
FEO	-	Fishery Extension Officer
GAIS	-	Group Accident Insurance Scheme for Fishermen
GRS	-	Gram Rozgar Sevak
IAY	-	Indira Awas Yojna
IBM	-	Inboard Machine Engine
ICDS	-	Integrated Child Development Scheme
ICZMP	-	Integrated Coastal Zone Management
IGNOAP	-	Indira Gandhi National Old Age Pension
NRLM	-	National Rural Livelihood Mission
MBPY	-	Madhu Babu Pension Yojna
MGNREGS	-	Mahatma Gandhi National Rural Employment Guarantee Scheme
MT	-	Million Tone
NABARD	-	National Bank for Agriculture and Rural Development
NAMP	-	National Anti-Malaria Programme
NWFF	-	National Welfare for Fishermen
OBM	-	Out Board motor Engine
OMFRA	-	Odisha Marine Fisheries Regulation

ORMAS	-	Orissa Rural Development and Marketing Society
PDS	-	Public Distributive System
PENCODE	-	People Employment and Need based Community Development Organization
SRS	-	Savings-cum-Relief
PFCS	-	Primary Fisherman Co-operative Societies
PRA	-	Participatory Rural Appraisal
RRA	-	Rapid Rural Appraisal
SGSY	-	Swarnajayanti Gram Swarozgara Yojna
SHG	-	Self Help Group
SNP	-	Special Nutrition Programme
STEP	-	Support to Training for Women Empowerment Programme
T.T	-	Titanus Toxoid
UAA	-	United Artist's Association
UGUP	-	Upgraded Upper Primary School
VLW	-	Village Level Worker

1

Introduction

This book is based on micro-perspectives of the coastline culture of fishing communities living around the Chilika Lake. Chilika Lake is situated in Odisha and is spread across Puri, Khordha and Ganjam districts. It flows into the Bay of Bengal and covers an area of over 1,100 kms. Fishing is among the oldest and most crucial forms of livelihood for inhabitants of the coastal regions of India since ancient times. The marine ecosystem along with the naturally found resources of the surrounding environment have aided in securing a source of income thereby supporting and producing many protective habitats. Nearly nineteen lakh traditional fishermen responsible for around 70 percent of India's marine catchers spread over 2,000 coastal villages. They form an important part of the country's total population. Unfortunately, their way of life has not received adequate attention from social scientists.

The fishing community is quite unique when compared to other productive communities like farmers, industrialists, technology servants or servicemen etc. The Fishermen group of Arakhakuda, a peripheral village of Chilika Lake call themselves 'Nolia' because their traditional attire consists of Noli (ring) worn in the nose and ears.

The book focuses on the cultural practices of these communities, their life style, socio-cultural involvements, economic and political systems, administrative structure and cultural ecology. In addition to these aspects, the origin and development of their religion, worship pattern, observation of different festivals, their traditional beliefs and practices are also detailed. Because the socio-economic aspect of any community is directly linked to its educational, political background, and extent of development in that geographical area, these factors have also been analyzed. The book also covers their social structure, economic organization, political systems, and women's position in the society, women empowerment and their role in decision-making processes.

The culture studies explain the technology and process of catching, grading, drying, branding and selling of fishes through both traditional and modern ways. The ways in which the traditional people used navigational ethno science in past while catching fishes are also studied. It is also found that new generation people have neither the knowledge of science nor do they practice their traditional knowledge. The changing economic lives due to different environmental factors are also covered. The reasons for decline in catching of fishes affecting their economy are also studied.

Several studies have already been conducted in the society to focus on their economic life, changing role of women, changing technology, various development programmes and on the alternate livelihood patterns adopted by fishermen. But the book provides the above contexts in combination with social, cultural, economic and political aspects of society in today's changing scenario. The consequences of damage done to the traditional fisheries and their ecology through commercial sectors, hurdles and imperfections in fishing and marketing activities, the increasing hardship in fish vending, alienation and marginalization of the fishing folk in Orissa, the changing scenario of their traditional culture because of intrusion of various NGOs and Government officials are the main problems of the fishermen society. So the author's concern is to attract the eyes of planner and Government to plan the future development of Nolias according to their present requirements and necessities.

Concepts and Theories

There are two types of sociological theories – Macro and Micro theory. Macro theory focuses on the society as a whole and aims at establishing the general features and characteristics of the society. It is basically looking at the society as a whole or looking at the bigger picture. On the other hand, micro theory focuses on the creators of the society. Micro-theories are small scale, like looking through a magnifying glass where the individuals who have developed a particular type of society are focused upon.

Micro-perspective is seen as one of the defining characteristics of anthropological approach. A famous one-liner of Clifford Geertz states 'anthropologists do not study villages; they study in the villages'. The micro research tends to be more explicit about the general and abstract properties of the units under observation. The social aspect of micro-perspective explores the role of meaning, ambiguities and contradictions of social life, patterns of society and underlying logics of social behavior, 'The interpretation of narratives of ritual and symbolic behavior' (Kalb,1996).

Tylor was the first anthropologist to provide a scientific definition of culture. He in his book titled *Primitive Culture* (1871), defines culture as that complex whole which includes knowledge, belief, art, morals, laws, customs and any other capabilities and habits acquired by man as a member of society to its individual. According to Malinowski, Culture is the total way of life and it includes all the mental, social, and physical means which makes its course. In other words, according to Malinowski, Culture may be defined as a system of derived needs and an organized system of purposeful activities (Behura, N.K.).

The coastline culture entails the culture of coastal areas. Coastal India spans from the Southwest Indian coastline along the Arabian sea from the coastline of Gulf of Kutch in its western most corner and stretches across the Gulf of Khambhat and through the Salsette Island of Mumbai along the Konkan and southwards across the Raigad region and through Kanara and further down through Mangalapuram or Mangalore and along the Malabar through Cape Comorin in the southernmost region of South India with coastline along the Indian ocean and through the Coromandal Coast or Cholamandalam coastline on the South Eastern coastline of the Indian subcontinent along the Bay of Bengal through the Utkala Kalinga region until the easternmost corner of shoreline near the Sunderbans in Coastal East India.

The people along coastal India exhibit vast diversity among an underlying commonality as a result of its coastal topography. They are different with respect to their language, clothing, lifestyle, beliefs, faiths etc.

The common elements of the people of coastal India includes cuisines that consists of agrarian and coastal products and clothing that involves long flowing drapes with bare midriff for both men and women suited for humid and warm climate. Throughout coastal India, women wear drapes or '*Saree*' in various styles. In the western corner of the coastal belt, drapes are called as 'Dhoti' for men and '*Chaniyacholi*' for women and towards the Southern regions the drapes are called as '*Lungi*' or '*Mundu*' for men and '*Veshti*' for women. Women experience relatively more role in the coastal social system as compared to non coastal peninsular Indian societies and enjoy significantly more prominence. All this can been visualized when viewing the types of festivals and rituals they perform like Durga Puja, Kali Puja etc. where the female power or 'Shakti' is worshipped.

The word fishing is not new in human civilization or Anthropology. It has its beginning from the dawn of human civilization. Fishes evolved in the Devonian era, 395 years ago. It was called the age of fishes. Amphibians evolved from fishes and moved onto land. The climate was very warm and often dry. During this period plants became common and wide spread. Several new types appeared including ferns, club mosses and the earliest seed plants (Galley Press, 1975: 34-35).

History of Fishing

Fishing is an ancient practice that dates back to at least the beginning of the Paleolithic period about 40,000 years ago. Isotopic analysis of the skeletal remains of Titanium man, a 40,000 year old modern human from eastern Asia, has shown that he regularly consumed fresh water fish. Archaeology features such as shell middens, discarded fish bones and cave paintings show that sea foods were important for survival and were consumed in significant quantities. During this period, most people lived a hunter-gatherer lifestyle and were, due to necessity, constantly on the move. However, where there are early examples of permanent settlements such as those at Lipinski viz, they are almost always associated with fishing as a major source of food.

The ancient river Nile was full of fish; fresh and dried fish were a staple food for most of the population. The Egyptians had specific tools and methods implemented for fishing which is found reflected in the early drawings and papyrus documents. In India, the Pandyas, a classical Dravidian Tamil Kingdom, were known for the Pearl fishing as early as 1st century BC. Their classical Seaport Tuticorin was known as deep sea pearl fishing. The Paravas, a Tamil caste centered in Tuticorin, developed a rich community because of their pearl trade, navigation knowledge and fisheries. Ancient Greek is a reflection of low social status of fishing.

For centuries India had a traditional practice of fish culture in small ponds in eastern India. Significant advances in productivity were made in the state of West Bengal in early 19th century with the controlled breeding of carp in bundhs. Fish culture received notable attention in Tamil Nadu (formerly the State Madras), West Bengal, Punjab, Uttar Pradesh, Gujarat,

Karnataka and Andhra Pradesh. Odisha initiated fish culture through establishment of Fisheries Department.

The primitive races living in Stone Age, prove without a doubt that the first men to attempt the capture of fishes by means other than their bare hands were those in the hunting stages of civilization. The devices employed by the prehistoric men who first turned their attention to this art were the same ordinary and self-made equipment that they previously used during chasing and hunting animals in the forests and plains. Little by little as experience increased and skill advanced among the various tribes, modifications of the original weapons were devised to increase their efficiency under specially encountered conditions when pursuing prey with peculiar advantage for escape, something that is not possessed by animals that run on land. The tribals used the weapons like the spun and harpoon (James Hornell, 1950: 1).

The Laccadive Islander still has much of our primitive prehistoric ancestor in his make up; he goes to his fishing with a sense of enjoyment, which is seldom the issue with his mainland brethren, who are too often led to poverty stricken and circumscribed lives in crowded and unsanitary villages. His freedom is born from sporting live fishes that furnishes him with keen enjoyment when he puts himself to sea in his graceful little sewn-plank boat in search of the elusive flying fish; to attract the fishes from greater distances, huge torches made of bundled coconut leaves are burned, the light brings the fish around the boat. In such situations, nearly 100 to 150 fishes are caught. In other parts of the world spearing and harpooning of fishes are common but not in Bengal or New Guinea (Ibid, 1950, 1950: 10-12).

In the Indian rivers, with an exception of those of Malabar and Bombay where the natural condition are unfavorable, the hilsa occupies an analogous position like that of Salmon in British stream. When the floods of summer set in with the coming of south west monsoon and the melting of the snows in the Himalayas, the river, rushing headlong into the sea in spate are crowded with great shoals of hilsa coming from the sea to spawn. The breeding ground have never been located with any exactitude certainly they are far upstream, for multitudes of unspent hilsa are met with a longway inland, frequently scores and even hundreds of miles beyond the farthest tidal influence. In Indus, Knaveries and other river of same length the hilsa await eagerly by the river side population.

There are different trapping devices used for marine water fishing and fresh water fishing. The people of Bengal, Odisha and Ganjam use different traps. In the study of Eastern Europe there are examples of two groups i.e. middle oniester and the earliest Neolithic group. Another is at Soroki where is no evidence of fish bones or of any fishing equipment from any of these site unless some of the microlithic blades could have acted as inserts on fish spear, as was suggested for Soroki (Ruth Tringham, 1971, 51-53).

The importance of fishing is amplified through the variety of devices that have developed in the present times including fish hooks, traps, seine net, dugout, boats and paddles. This is seen in Mesolithic of Europe. The Mesolithic fishermen adorned themselves with ornaments though at a notably lower order of complexity making do with perforated teeth, Shaea pebbles, ember lumps and the like (Graham Clark, 1977: 76, 136).

The fishermen communities are important in all stages of culture. Capture fisheries have two types–small scale fisheries and large scale fisheries. These two types are traditional and mechanised. The fishermen communities belong to lower strata of society. In China and Korea they are victims of prejudice and oppression and socially designated as very lowly in Japan. In Africa the Somali leave fishing to "The midyan and other disposed groups". In Mauritania the fishing activities are conducted by Imagine, a low status coastal group. The school dropout rate is highest among them. The relations among the crew members are important in fisheries due to interdependence and importance of each worker. In traditional fishing women's role cannot be neglected. They manage the household as well as help with the fishing activities. They are engaged in unloading, drying and freezing processes and also selling fish on the street and from door to door by usually carrying the fishes in large baskets on their heads (Joshi, V.P. – 67).

Mitra in the course of describing the fish and its trading in the Lake gives the origin of commission agents in the following terms, "Initially the merchants in order to avoid the large establishments utilised the service of some of the fishermen to collect the catches from the fishing grounds and bring them to assembly points near the rail heads. These men gradually gave up fishing and took to the profession of commission agents. At present there are 272 commission agents for whole Lake, who work about 4 per cent of fishermen population." (Mitra, 1956).

The fish population shows a decline. The influence of refugee, fishermen, intensified fishing in in-shore and off-shore water, use of nylon nets, catching of fingerlings and over exploitation of prawns in the near shore waters are causes of the downward trend (Sahu, p.1-8).

Fisheries development occurs through cooperation, cooperation is ultimately the main group instinct which enables fishermen to live together, work together and help together in times of strain and stress. The history of modern world is, in fact the history of cooperation, for its lack would have deemed social, cultural and economic progress impossible. W.C. Alec, A.E. Merson, R.W. Gerard and other many scholars emphasized on cooperation as more natural than competition. Therefore World Bank emphasized on Fishery Cooperatives for the development of this sector (Joshi, p 18-19).

The unorganized fishing sector uses approximate labour-intensive technology. It has established a permanent relationship with nature. Fishing is done as a household enterprise, undertaken in pursuit of a livelihood leading to a culturally conditioned way of life. The people of the coastal belts fish primarily in the using small craft and simple gear of relatively low capital intensity. Their fishing operations are skill- intensive, fisher folk have an intuitive understanding of coastal aquatic milieu and the fishery resources in it. The traditional ecological knowledge and skills are passed from generation to generation. They are linked to locally oriented market networks. The internal driving force of the fisher folk is towards sustainability. The sensitivity of fisher people towards the health of the marine environment helps them check over exploitation of the resources as it disrupts the ecological system and in turn, their economy (Sahu, 2009).

Historical Perspective: History of Fishing People in Odisha near Chilika Lake

1) Pre Independence Period
2) Post Independence Period

Pre Independence Period:

During British rule, Lake Chilika was under the control of Jagir Mahals. The 'fishing sairats' (fishing grounds) in Chilika were leased out by the notable owners such as Raja of Parikud, Khallikote and Palur, and the Zamindars of Puri, Cuttack and Khurda. The fishermen used to obtain sairats by playing 'salami' as license fee for a particular period. The period is confined to sunia of each year.

Even in recent past fishing is seen as profession of low castes. Other castes are more dependent on agriculture for their sustenance. The traditional fishing communities enjoyed the right of fishing throughout the year by paying the license fee. The non-traditional fisher person used take loan only for their personal consumption.

Post Independence Period:

After independence and with the introduction of Zamindari Abolition Act during 1953, the fishery sairats came under the control of Anchal Adhikari. In the year 1959, Chilika came under the Revenue Department. The revenue authority issued license to the people for fishing. The socio-economic condition remained unchanged even after independence, so to help in their economic upliftment, cooperatives were formed in every fisher villages. The cooperatives comprised of traditional fishing communities as members only and were named as Primary Fisher Persons Cooperative Society. An apex society was formed at Balugaon as Central Cooperative Society. Besides this there is a provision of working capital for buying fishing implements to its affiliated primaries and marketing of fish procured by the primaries. This helped the people for a certain period to come out of the web of middlemen and earn a fair price for their catch. The practice of obtaining lease from government and sub lease to its primaries continued till 1991.

There is also an indirect war between fishing and non fishing people over the fishing rights in Chilika Lake. The Lake was slowly being taken by non fisher persons and the anti social elements. In 1981, the government made a rule that allowed fisher person either by caste or profession or person exclusively dependent on pisci culture as profession to become a member of primary societies. The non fishermen were also given some opportunities (CDA, Banaja).

There are numerous references of fishing in ancient religious Hindu epics of such as the Puranas, Smritis and the Ramayanas. In Kautilya's Arthasastra, written between 321 and 300 BC references to fishing industry, fish processing and fish eating are found. The references to the fishery legislation inscribed in Ashoka's Pillar Edit V, dates back to 246 BC, Gupta's (1908: 10) report on fisheries of Bengal refers to fishing castes. Hutton (1931) also mentions about them. References to sea fishing are also available from Gazetters (Webster, 1911, O'Malley, 1908, 1914) of the coastal districts of Bengal. Hornell (1922, 24 a, b) mentions sea fishing and discusses fishing methods and fishing gear in the Ganges.

Fish Production

Chakraborty, Nair and Balakrishnan (1973) in their article examined the characteristics of marine fish production in India. India produced annually approximately 0.7 million tonnes of marine fish. Total production figures as well as landings from individual fisheries varied widely over the years. At present, there is an increase in resourcefulness and specific efforts are being made to produce higher yields. A study of these figures has assumed importance for a proper understanding of the resources of important fisheries. The quarter wise catch figures of important fishes have been studied and indices showing their seasonal and regional occurrences have been constructed and discussed.

Srinivasan (1981) while discussing the status of marine fisheries of Tamil Nadu drew attention to the problems faced by traditional fishermen because of increase in competition from mechanized boatmen following the prawn boom. He cautioned that if the pace of trawling continues unabated, the Madras coast may also experience the diminishing return which has already set in on the West Coast. The author also stressed the importance of diversified techniques in maximising production and improving the productivity of artisanal fishermen. Further, the author has suggested that the present system of financially helping a few big boat owners should be changed to favor a large number of small boat operators.

Saxena (1984) studied the management aspects of shrimp fishery with particular reference to India in 1984. According to him, the Indian shrimp fishery after 1975 experienced a decline, which has been substantiated by reduction in catch per unit effort. In the light of the decline of the Indian shrimp fishery, three types of tools to maximize production have been suggested:

(i) an exhaustive techno-economic survey should be undertaken to study the production, processing and marketing costs, margins, practices, channels, etc. along with the socio-economic conditions of the local fishermen in order to provide alternative employment opportunities and financial compensation,

(ii) the type of management tools must include regulatory measures and

(iii) more encouragement of shrimp culture.

Subha Rao (1986) made a study to examine the trends in the total fish production of Andhra Pradesh and compared the same with all India fish production at different points of time. Andhra Pradesh was lagging behind in the long term trend of annual growth of fish production than that of India as a whole during the period 1961-81. The catching pattern with reference to percentage distribution of different species in different years showed a declining trend in most cases. The common feature in all the species was heavy fluctuations.

Sathiadhas (1997) studied –

(i) the production, trend and variation in catch composition of marine fish over the years,

(ii) the economics of different craft-gear combinations in marine fishing operations,

(iii) the marine fish marketing problems to determine price ranges of different varieties and to assess the share of fishermen and middlemen in consumer's rupee in Tamil Nadu.

The author used both primary and secondary data. Data on costs and earnings of different craft-gear combination and price of different varieties of fish including handling and transportation charges at various points of the marketing channel, collected by direct observation at selected centres. The study revealed that –

(i) both mechanised and non-mechanised sectors are important to increase the fish production,

(ii) motorization of country craft helped the fishermen to improve their living condition,

(iii) catch per unit effort of trawlers is continuously declining in Tamil Nadu,

(iv) lesser the number of intermediaries in the fish marketing chain, higher is the share of fishermen in the consumer's rupee.

Devaraj, Sathiadhas and Reghu (1998) in their paper reviewed the marine fish production in the state vis-a-vis the potential yield, assessed the economic performance of trawlers and motorised gillnetters, analysed the distribution pattern of marine fish in the internal market and the performance of marine fishery exports, evaluated the capacity utilisation of processing plants and suggested policy measures for improvements in production and marketing of marine fish.

Dibakar Naik (2001) made a study on trends in marine fish landings and marine fish marketing in different maritime districts of Odisha during 1996 to 1999. He has given his findings that marine fish production in Odisha has increased from 38.70 thousand tonnes in 1980-81 to 133.46 thousand tonnes in 1996-97 and it declined to 121.08 thousand tonnes in 2000-01. On an average the State has recorded a growth rate of 8.86 percent for marine fish production during the last one and a half decades. Marine fish marketing in Odisha is carried out by a large number of intermediaries forming a long chain of market channels. In short, five or less number of intermediaries form the market channel for the marine fish in Odisha. In the existing marketing system the fishermen's share has decreased by the extent of 22.20 - 26.76 percent owing to the increasing middlemen in the market channel.

Marketing

Singh and Gupta (1983) conducted a study on marine fish marketing, and fisheries development in India in the year 1983. They pointed out that transportation facilities available for moving fish are very inefficient in India. Due to inadequate transportation, no fresh fish is available in potential markets located far away from the landing centres, whereas surplus fish at harbours is being sent to fish meal plants. Further, it has been observed that the catches of certain varieties like sardines and mackerels are caught in large quantities during the fishing season which results in a surplus at the producing centers.

Kalavathy (1985) studied the organisation of fish marketing in Madras Fishing Harbour in 1985. She identified different marketing channels and means of transportation for different species of fishes. While studying the role of women in marketing, she did a case study for each role that women are specifically involved in, i.e. women as auctioneer, retailer, and trash fish wholesaler. She concluded that the mechanisation benefited some categories of fish marketing women operating at Madras Fishing Harbour by generating higher incomes or new earning opportunities. It also perhaps aggravated income disparities among fisherwomen.

In a small landing centre, the marketing of fish is fairly decentralised and a higher percentage of women are engaged in fish marketing. In a large landing centre, marketing is more centralised, offering fewer employment opportunities but higher profits for those women who have managed to stay in the business.

Sathiadhas and Panikkar (1988) made a study on market structure and price behaviour of marine fish in Tamil Nadu. They concluded that fish marketing in Tamil Nadu is still under the clutches of middlemen. Of the 25 varieties of fish covered under the study, the percentage of marketing margin in consumers' price for 20 varieties which constitute 90 per cent of landings worked out at more than 40 per cent.

Panikkar and Sathiadhas (1989) studied the fish marketing system prevailing in Kerala, the price structure, seasonal and spatial price variations, marketing margins of commercially important varieties of fish and the share of fishermen as well as middlemen in consumer's rupee. The study revealed that due to lack of infrastructure facilities the supply of fish at the landing centre is highly inelastic which would often result in disposal of fish at throwaway prices during heavy landings. The involvement of a number of middlemen in the marketing chain adversely affects the interest of both fishermen and consumers. Fishermen's share in consumer's rupee varied from an average of about 40 per cent for cheaper varieties of fish to about 65 per cent for high priced varieties. There has been a marketing expenditure incurred by fishermen in recent years.

Bennett and Rogers (1992) conducted a study about a person who was into fishing trade who used a bicycle to trade fish in Sri Lanka. The authors spent a day following the activities of the bicycled trader. They studied the composition of fish bought and the expenditure incurred for preservation and other marketing fees and the profit earned by the trader in one day. This case study highlights some of the marketing problems faced by bicycled traders selling a perishable commodity like fish –

(i) the distance and the time taken to travel from home to the fish market,

(ii) the importance and unpredictability of consumer preference,

(iii) loss of quality due to poor storage,

(iv) the variability of demand, both for fish as a food and for individual species of fish.

Sathiadhas and Panikkar (1992) attempted in this paper to discuss the marketing margins, and producer's and middlemen's share in consumer's rupee for commercially important varieties of marine fish in Madras region of Tamil Nadu, India. For this study, Pudumanikuppam, a major mechanised landing centre as primary market, Chintatripet as wholesale market and Pattalam, Chintatripet, Saidapet and Adapalani (all in Madras city) as consumer markets were selected. Data on landing, wholesale and retail prices of selected varieties of fish were collected 15 to 20 days in each quarter during April 1984 to March 1985 following the marketing channel.

Salagrarna (1997) explained the experience of a firm established in 1996 in Odisha dealing with marketing of dried fish. The firm (oriental dry fish industries) engaged in hygienic fish processing into high quality products in order to get high price than that of traditionally processed fish. The firm marketed its product in the North-Eastern region since the market price in that region was more than three times the price elsewhere. But the firm took risks such as:

(i) high transportation costs,

(ii) uncertainties in transporting to the distant markets through hilly terrain,

(iii) delays in getting payment for the products and

(iv) dealing with prevailing instability and tension in the area due of rampant terrorism. The experience led the firm to search for other markets, as it is essential to cater to local markets before dealing with distant markets that seem lucrative but loaded with risks.

The Department for International Development (DFID) conducted Post-Harvest Fisheries Project (1997) an awareness programme on fish and fishery products at Hyderabad in August 1996. The programme brought together 12 producer groups to discuss problems and prospects in production and marketing of value-added products. In the programme three major problem areas were identified, which needed to be resolved–

(i) lack of awareness on the part of the consumers; the inability of small producer groups to undertake market promotion at an appreciable level;

(ii) the inability of agencies of specific areas in creating and sustaining market demand in spite of fluctuation of catches; and

(iii) lack of awareness of quality control measures, and laxity in observing them if known. The problems identified by the programme prevail even today in several parts of the country during the marketing of fishery products. It implies that sustaining market demands are interconnected with consumer awareness of different fish products and proper application of quality control measures. More efforts should be put forth in these directions.

Chand and Nityananda Das (2007) have given an account of basic requirements for an organised Fish Market. They have specified the essential infrastructure needed for an organised market. It has been suggested that in order to make the entire fish marketing system successful, apart from having an organised fish market, right marketing strategies are essential. For this process to work correctly, identification of consumers' needs and nature of demand for products and services is necessary.

Devadasan (2003) has stated in his study that India has a good potential to increase its hold in the international fish market by exporting value added fish products. It has been concluded that most of the currently used market channels are not suitable to trade value added products. Anew and an appropriate channel would be called the 'super market chain' will procure products directly from the source. Appearance, packaging and display are all important factors leading to successful marketing of any new value added product. The retail pack must be clean, clear and crisp to make the contents appear attractive to the consumer. The customer must feel confident by looking at the package in order to be inclined to experiment with a new product launched in the market.

Fishing Technology

Kurien and Mathew (1982) have studied the impact of technological changes on fishing. According to this study there are huge regional variations in the species-mix of the marine resources in the country. The nutritive values of all species of fish are almost the same but market demand and prices for various species vary. There is direct impact of mechanisation on fish production in quantitative as well as qualitative nature.

Krishna Srinath (1988) conducted a study on the efficiency of the technology based on the perception of fishermen of their present and future status in relation to their living conditions prior to motorisation. The study was conducted in Vypeenkara during August-October 1985. Data was collected from 50 units out of 115 motorised crafts through an interview schedule. Information on personal variables, impact of motorisation and the living standards and projection for future, aspirations and facility satisfaction as assessed qualitatively by fishermen themselves were collected. From the study, it was concluded that motorisation can be instrumental in bringing about significant changes in the living conditions of fishermen and their outlook and inculcating the spirit of unity and cooperation among them. The fishermen in general felt that their status had improved as a result of motorisation and were more optimistic about their future. Kemparaju (1994) conducted a study on the drift gillnet fishery of the state Goa during the period 1985-88. It was found that the drift gillnet fishery during the period from 1985 to 1988 in major centres showed a steady improvement indicating its continued importance in the exploited fishery of Goa despite the noticed fluctuations. It was also observed that in the small-scale fisheries sector, the drift gillnet fishing was significant as it exploited highly valued fishes such as seer fishes, tunas and sharks. Thus the drift gillnet fishery had better development prospects in the state.

Mahesh V. Joshi (1996) studied the factors affecting the mechanisation of fishing crafts and the impact of mechanisation on marine fish production and income and the standard of living of fishermen's households. He also studied the hazardous effects of mechanisation and foreigner's deep fishing in Indian Ocean and identified the problems of small fishermen. The main findings of his study were:

(i) there is direct relationship between fishing mechanization and employment opportunities. It was also observed that the average earning of crew member households in mechanised fishing were substantially higher than those of non-mechanised fishing. Mechanisation and higher wages were co-related to each other.

(ii) Generally fishermen may borrow from the commercial banks, fish merchants, money lenders, relatives' and friends. Co-operatives failed in providing credit to the fishermen. Finance is the main obstacle in fishery development.

(iii) The variable cost per trip for a trawler is higher than the O.B.M. boat. The cost of fuel is a single prime item in the case of trawlers. The salary of crew members is high in mechanised boats.

(iv) All the fishermen have strongly unanimously and aggressively opposed for deep fishing permission to the foreigners.

(v) It is found that arrangement of maintenance of mechanised boat is very difficult compared to non-mechanized boats.

(vi) Mechanised boat owners have more income and a relatively higher standard of living as compared to non-mechanised boat owners.

(vii) It was observed that there was a serious problem, limitations and litigations of mechanisation. It badly affected the small fishermen. There was an issue unstable stock because of exhaustion of fish stock due to mechanisation. It affected the employment. There were problems of fuel, finance, maintenance, repairing, higher costs, etc., due to mechanisation.

(viii) Contribution of the Government and co-operative institutions for finance was very negligible. Fishermen preferred loans from fish merchants, friends and relatives. Banks were also one of the sources of borrowing.

Krishnan; C.K. 2003 has examined the recent trends in mechanisation of Malabar fishery sector. He has studied the operating cost of trawlers fitted with in-board engines using diesel as fuel and out-board engines using kerosene for ring-seiners. He worked out that the average cost of operation per day for a ring-seiner unit using out-board engine run by kerosene was between Rs.5000 and Rs.6000 and for diesel leyland in-board engines came down to Rs.2000. In view of this, more and more active fishermen were attracted towards the introduction of in-board engines.

Fishery Resources

George (1973) made a remark that for successful exploitation of the marine fishery resources, it is most vital that we should have an absolute knowledge of the resources. In India over centuries, marine fisheries exploitation has been in the hands of backward and conservative people. So modern developments in fisheries have had no impact on them, it is only in recent years that a change in attitude has taken place. At present marine fish landing in India has attained the number of almost a million tonnes. It is possible to step up this production several folds. For this, considerable planning is required. Very large numbers of mechanised fishing vessels are required, besides landing and berthing facilities for them. Adequate quantities of ice, water, fuel, oils, etc. need to be set up. All these require high financial investments. For making such investments a thorough knowledge of the available resources is necessary. Many countries have produced fishery atlases that give all the information of their available resources. In India, the production of such an atlas is required and for this efficient and thorough studies of resources are required. The explorative surveys done so far are inadequate and everything needs proper planning.

James (1988) elaborated in their article that pelagic resources play a key role in the overall marine production in India. Marine fish production from the Indian seas has shown considerable increase during the last four decades. The bulk of the catch is oil sardines and mackerels, but these species show characteristic wide fluctuations in abundance as well as distribution compared to other fishery resources.

Finance

Discussing on the role of Financial Institutions in the promotion of fisheries sector, Pathak (1997) indicated that the availability of adequate and timely credit is the most crucial input for increasing the fish production and export. He also mentioned that NABARD had so far sanctioned more than 5200 fisheries schemes with total refinance assistance of Rs.4037 million and the disbursement of credit for fisheries has increased at a compound annual growth rate of 36.7 per cent in the last ten years, when the aggregate assistance provided to all the scheduled banks reached a level of Rs. 1071.7 million in 1995-96 from Rs.133.5 million in 1985-86. Thus the bankers contribution could best be realised from the fact that out of the total marine fish landings of 2.469 million tonnes reported in 1992-93, more than 28 per cent of the catch was from those boats that availed bank's credit facilities. In future, the bankers will take up fisheries programme and can invest over Rs.8000 million by the end of Ninth Five Year Plan and the seafood export would have a business of three billion US dollars in the international markets.

Price

Senthilathiban and Selvaraj (1992) conducted a study on the price spread of some of the commercially important fishes in Chidambaranar district in the year 1989 and 1990. Four landing centres were randomly selected and data on landings, auction price, marketing costs and marketing margins were collected. The collected data were analysed to find out the variation in mean retail price of different varieties of fishes and the relationship between retail price and the net amount realised by the fishermen. The study revealed that–

(i) the fishermen's share in consumer retail price was above 60 per cent for all the important fish varieties in the selected fish landing centres,

(ii) there was a positive correlation between the retail price and the net amount realized by the fishermen at one percent level for almost all the fish varieties,

(iii) the fishermen got a better share for those varieties having high consumer preference,

(iv) share of marketing margins accruing to retailers varies from 14 to 23per cent.

Socio-economic and other Sectors

Tewari, Acharya and Singh (1997) described the findings of a macro-level study and a participatory appraisal study of demographic characteristics of fishing communities in India carried out in the context of the project "Strengthening of research and training in population and development dynamics of rural fishing communities". The marine fishing fleet, marine fisher-folk population, marine fish production, coastal environmental problems, and perceptions and views of the fisher-folk were outlined. Findings indicated that production increased along with the increase in the number of fishermen and boats. However, overexploitation, deterioration in environment quality, fall in catch per unit effort, high price of fuel and equipment, and high labour and service charges were detrimental to the rate of growth of fisheries. It was concluded that proper management of resources and judicious exploitations were necessary.

Srinath Krishna (1988) made a study on the food consumption pattern and nutritional status of a marine fishermen community in Vypeenkara, Cochin during the year 1982-83. She conducted a survey by selecting 150 households and the particulars regarding total quantity of food bought every week and the frequency of consumption were collected through interview schedule. She concluded that the major problems encountered in the development of fishermen community was low nutrient intake of the fishermen. The high percentage of malnutrition of this particular community mainly attributed to two factors namely low purchasing power and non-availability of nutritious foods and other vegetables in the coastal areas. Lack of alternative sources of protein mainly resulted from low purchasing power. She suggested that the most important step in the upliftment of the community was to increase the purchasing power by increasing the income from fisheries and introducing supplementary occupations, so that at least the requirements for protein and calories were met.

Hansen (1996) presented that small pelagic comprise almost half of the world marine fish catches, which were once considered mainly for the reduction industry. Now, based on the increasing demand for fish for human nutrition, new efforts to increase the uses of these small fish for consumption are being developed. An examination was also carried out using improved methods of handling and preserving the fish, which may provide nutrition and food security to the world at large.

Punekar gives a detailed account of socio-cultural life of 'The Sonkolis of Bombay' – fishing caste communities of Bombay coast. She throws light on how the fishermen of Bombay retain their traditional culture inspite of the impact of urbanisation on them. It is principally a community study based on detailed observation of the culture and lifestyle of the Sonkolis and is rich in empirical content.

Klausen (1968) in his Kerala fishermen and the Indo-Norwegian Pilot Project, makes a detailed analysis of the effects of techno-economic aids on the fishermen of Kerala belonging to two different religious sects but living in two neighboring coastal villages. In his study, he sees the social behavior of fishermen as a continuous process of choice.

Different papers have been contributed by various scholars are attached to Anthropological Survey of India on the study of fisher folk residing in different coastal states of India. Most important among them are – The Nolia of Puri and their sea fishing organisation (Mukherjee, 1968) comparative study of fisher folk: coastal West Bengal and Orissa (Mukherjee, 1970) Marine fisher folk of Andhra Pradesh, a preliminary exploration (Razek, 1970), Marine fisher folk of Gujrat: Preliminary exploration, (Hazra 1970), fisherfolk of Phuleswar and their sea-fishing organization and report of a preliminary survey (Mukherjee, Ray Chaudhuri and Maitra (1969). Small fishermen in Tamil Nadu by Selvaraj (1975) is another valuable monograph on fisher folk culture.

Mathur (1978) gives detailed analysis of fishing activity of the Mappila fisher folk of Kerala and their profound knowledge of the marine environment and cosmology. He also describes how the economy of fishermen is inter-woven with the socio-cultural milieu. Mathur's study seeks to test a set of specific hypothesis correlating fishing as an occupation and development of a fishing caste even among casteless Muslims, fishing as a hazardous endeavor and development of rituals and beliefs to cover personal risks of uncertainty and the like. Raychaudhuri (1980) in an intensive field investigation of a transient fishermen community assembled during winter at Jambu Island in the Bay of Bengal within 10 kms from shore, gave the social background of these fishermen, their knowledge of the topography and marine environment trade and economic network, conflict and cooperation among them.

Firth's (1941) study of economics of Malayan fishing industry is regarded as a pioneering work in this field. He elaborated his ideas in the book Malay Fishermen: their peasant economy (1966). He gives the sociology of fishing and economic organisation of fisher folk as a constituent of peasant economy. Like Thomas M. Fraser's (1966) study of fishermen of South Thailand, Firth's study is a longitudinal study. The same fishing community and changes taking place in its social life were studied first in 1940, then in 1947 and again in 1963. The recent study of Frazer Junior (1962) was analysis of the Malay fishing village as a part of dual economies.

Warrier (1987) in his survey of fisher folk in Madras city has studied their socio-economic condition. The study shows that for fisher folk, sea fishing is more a way of life than a mode of occupation or business. The study reveals discrepancies in the supply of mechanized boats by cooperatives to the fishermen. Sila Tripathi in his study has emphasized the use of navigational ethno science for the fishermen people of Sonepur, Odisha. Kurien (1984) has analyzed the economic backwardness of Marine fishermen and inequalities in the assets held among them. He has pointed out that these fishermen are exploited by the fish traders who buy their fish at lower rates. Kurien (1985), in his micro analysis of marine fisheries sector in Kerala, has helped us to understand the fish-economy of the state better. He has examined the problems and trends of catch, distribution and marketing of marine fish and the impact of technological changes on fishermen. He has studied their literacy, health conditions, housing and population growth. He has advised the State Government to provide livelihood security to the fishermen.

Sarkar (2009) in his study of Sunderban fishermen has drawn attention towards four important things about fishermen:

1. They continue to resort to super naturalism like ritualistic pujas to appease duties as a means of fighting against big uncertainties in fishing.
2. Mechanization of fishing gears has brought about a big change in fishing economy and resulted in class formation among fishermen.
3. Fisher-women are engaged in dry fishing, fish vending and net mending.
4. Fishermen are largely indebted and they fall victims to exploitation by middlemen working as linkage between active producers and final consumers. Jayaraman (2008) on the basis of his study of a number of fisher-women self-help groups of the two maritime districts of

Tamil Nadu has concluded that contrary to the common beliefs and misconceptions, poor women are actually quite credit worthy, honest, trustworthy and bankable.

Baral (1996) has thrown light on gradual changes taking place in the life of fisher-women of South Odisha. Boys and girls hailing from fisher families are going to schools and colleges; they are now inclined to drifting away from their traditional beliefs and practices and are seizing new other career opportunities. Both fisher men and women with respect to their traditional occupation have diversified and their political participation as compared to the past has increased. Fisher-women have begun to move towards an equal social stature but it is still a long haul (Paramanik, 1993).

According to a United Nation's report, women perform 2/3rd of the world's work, receive only 10 percent of the world's income and own only one per cent of the total worldly assets. The transformation of fisheries sector, mainly brought by mechanization, has engendered multi-faceted changes in the role and contribution of fisher women.

If we look at India's scenario, there are about 0.5 million fisher households located along coastal India and a total of 3 million fishermen residing there. The average number of sea going fishermen is 282 in a coastal village. Out of the 1.2 million fisher folk in post-harvest sector, women occupy a considerable proportion of more than 0.5 million (Sathiadhas et. al., 1998). They play a significant role in the pre and post-harvest operations in capture fisheries while their presence is conspicuous in all the stages of culture fisheries. Their role in household management is far higher than that of the women in other sectors. Majority of the labour force in the pre-processing and processing plants of shrimp are women. A greater proportion of the workforce in export oriented processing of cuttlefish, lobsters, and finfish varieties is occupied by women. In Tamilnadu, women engage themselves in seaweed collection in addition to the traditional jobs of fish curing, marketing, net making and prawn seed collection. Salt-pansare another major sector, which employs a lot of women in Tamilnadu, where the ratio of women to men is 4:1. In Andhra Pradesh, the main occupation of women include collecting fish, and mollus can shells in addition to their contribution in fish drying, curing, marketing, shrimp processing and net making. In West Bengal, fishermen spend only little time in actual fishing and engage themselves in net making, which in other states is dominated by women. Women from communities other than fisher folk carry out fish drying and curing. In Maharashtra women play a major role in fish marketing and supervising fisheries.

The entire fisheries economy revolves around Mumbai. In Gujarat women mostly do the handling and processing activities. In Lakshadweep, particularly Minicoy, the major fishery products known as masmin, riha and akruof tuna are produced mainly by women. However, the overall structural changes in the marine fisheries sector brought about by mechanization, extensive use of ice in local markets and export oriented development efforts have removed a good proportion of women from income generating sectors of fish drying, curing, dry fish trade and net making.

After independence a numbers steps have been taken by the government of India as well as state governments for the development of weaker section of society. In the last two decades both government and voluntary organizations have paid special attention to the problems of fisherwomen, who have suffered several kinds of disparity and deprivation. Fisherwomen, being victims of both backwardness and gender discrimination, are struggling to find space for themselves (Gulati, 1984).

Thus, all the studies pertaining to fishermen conducted so far either in India or abroad, has treated fishermen as a community. Most of them are community studies, covering various facts of community life though the same aspect of community life has not attracted the attention of all the researchers equally. Some have given greater attention to economies of fishing, while others have concentrated on the technology of fishing. Some have concentrated on the rituals and beliefs of fishermen. But most researchers have viewed fishermen not as an isolated community but as a part of the peasant society and the wider market system. While some studies have sought to portray the social life of fishermen at a given point of time, others have tried to unfold the face, degree, direction of changes taking place in their social life over a time span. Most studies however are descriptive, ethnographic and only few of them pose specific hypothesis or seek to fit the ethnographic data in a theoretical framework. About the Puri district fishermen especially Nolia with unique problems and features, a few comprehensive and systematic study on fisheries development and their social problems have been carried out till date. The ensuing study is a humble effort to fill up the gap in research.

METHODOLOGY AND RESEARCH DESIGN

Anthropology is famous for using a variety of methods of data collection. These methods follow a numbers of techniques which are not only scientific but also very practical and effective during fieldwork. The uniqueness of anthropological research lies on the fact that researches beautifully combine several techniques of data collection in a single research project yet strike a reasonable balance among all of them so that the data collected yields good result.

Observation- Observation is a method that employs vision as its main means of data collection. It implies the use of eyes rather than of ears and the voice. It is accurate watching and noting of phenomena as they occur with regard to the cause and effect of mutual relation. Observation is defined as "a planned methodological watching that involves constraints to improve accuracy" (Ahuja, 2001).

There are different types of observations but in this study but author followed only two types of observation – Participant and Non-participant observation. In participant observation it has been followed a plethora of activities and invested emotionally, interacting with people and actively joining their different actions and it affected the author's observations. The author sympathized with tragedy and may not have recorded its impact upon their fellow members. Fishing trip acted as a participant observation but during the preparation of an important religious ceremony, the author formally took interview of the important participants and recorded the ritual charts actively engaging in the ritual like a non-participant observer.

In the field study both types of techniques are employed for data collection, participant observation techniques used for study of life cycle ritual, at the time of different fishing activities like net, boat repairing etc. On the other hand study of market, their kinship structure and leadership pattern is studied through non-participant observation.

Schedule

Schedule is a form containing some questions or blank tables, which are to be filled up by the researchers after getting the requisite information from the informants.

In the field census schedules were used for the purpose of village census survey, their social structure, collecting data on household income, different types of occupation, fishing group, and studying how fishing group lived in their day to day activities, their income and expenditure patterns and how these differed from non-fishing groups etc.

Interview

It is a verbal questioning. Research interview is prepared and executed in a systematic way, it is controlled by the researcher to avoid bias and distortion and it is related to a specific research question and a specific purpose. According to Pauline Young "Interview may be regarded as a systematic method by which a person enters more or less imaginatively to the life of a comparative stranger". By interviewing, one can enter deeply into various situations and realize the significance of interview. Different semi-structured questionnaires were prepared and used as tools for research.

(a) Unstructured / Structured

- An unstructured interview means it is flexible. There is no prior indication of the specific issues on which the questions are to be asked.
- A structured interview on the other hand is based on structured interview guide which is little different from the questionnaire. In reality it consists of specific points and definite questions already prepared by the interviewer. In this the interviewer is expected to act in a neutral manner effecting the same impression to all respondents.

Standardized interview - The respondents are expected to choose one of the given options as the answer. The un-standardized interview is one in which the responses are left open to the respondents.

Individual interview - This one in which the interviewer interviews only one respondent at a time while in group interview, more than one respondent are interviewed. Personal interview is one to one usually conducted face to face or over the telephone but a non-personal interview taken through questionnaires via computer or other mediums.

Group Discussion

Various group discussions were arranged between the fisherman and the researcher. Group discussions were arranged among the SHGs members, Anganawadi workers, school children and village committee members. These discussions were useful in finding out the different aspects of fishery and how their social lives are inter-related with economic life. The schedules models were also used for this purpose.

Sampling

A sample is a portion of people drawn from a larger group of population. It will be representative of population only if it has same basic characteristics of the population from which it is drawn. So our concern in sampling is not about what types of units will be interviewed/observed but with how many units of what particular description and what methods need to be chosen.

According to Manheim (1977: 270), "a sample is a part of the population which is studied in order to make inferences about the population which is studied in order to made inferences about the whole population" (Ahuja, 2001).

Two types of sampling–

a) Probability

b) Non Probability

Probability sampling remains the primary method for selecting large, representative sample for social science and business researches. Some forms of probability sampling are random sampling, stratified random sampling, cluster systematic sampling, multi stage and phase sampling.

A large population cannot be studied in entirely because of constraints like its size, time consumed, no accessibility, limited time, lack of large amount of funds needed for such a huge project and population scattered in a very wide geographical area. These reasons make sampling necessary. I have taken 250 families of Arakhakuda region which has a population of 5000. Here I used stratified random sampling as method of sampling.

Case Study - The case study method is useful for exploring and analyzing any incident. Case study is a method of examining specially and in details a given situation in all its aspects pertaining to the particular study.

It is an intensive study of a case which may be an individual, an institution, a system, a community, an organization or even the entire culture. Yin (1991: 23) has defined case study as "an empirical inquiry that investigates a contemporary phenomenon within its real life context, when the boundaries between phenomenon and context are not clearly evident and in which multiple sources of evidence are used", case study is not a method of data collection rather it is a research strategy or empirical inquiry that investigates a contemporary phenomenon by using multiple or sources of evidence. It is a qualitative analysis.

Becker 1989 has said that the research design of the case study is similar to those of main stream social research. The main points common in case study and other methods pertains to sampling (persons, groups, organizations and whole culture), planning data collection (through open interview, narrative interviews, observation, documents), planning data analysis (devising concepts to be analyzed, determining category and developing typologies, formulating hypothesis etc.) and giving interpretation in the report (integrating logical argument).

The case study method is in this research used to study the systems of marriage and divorce of the fisher folk, the belief of God and their judicial system, the people who are directly benefitted by the governmental programmes along with those who are not benefitted by any programme. In case of women empowerment, the case study of a woman who struggled a lot in her life and then become successful with examples from their society are explained.

PRA/RRA - Participatory Rural Appraisal (PRA) is a shortcut method of data collection. It is a methodology for action research and utilizes a range of techniques. It involves local people and outsiders from different sectors and disciplines. Outsiders facilitate local people in anlysing information, practicing critical self awareness, taking responsibility and sharing their knowledge of how to plan and to act in life.

Rapid Rural Appraisal (RRA) and Participatory Rural Appraisal (PRA) are often used in literature. The difference of RRA & PRA is as below:

Rapid Rural Appraisal (RRA)

In RRA information is collected and elicited and extracted by outsiders. In other words people go to rural areas obtain information and then bring it back to process and analyze. The information is owned by outsiders and often not shared with rural people.

Participatory Rural Appraisal (PRA)

In Participatory Rural Appraisal information is owned and shared by local people. Outsiders go to the rural areas and facilitate rural people in collection, presentation and analysis of information by aiding them. The information is owned by rural people but actually shared with outsiders.

Quantitative Method- Statistical techniques is used as and when required. This central tendency (mean)is used as a method of data analysis.

Census- Census is very necessary for the holistic study of a group. The census forms helped me to analyses the demographic structure, age, sex structure, economic structure, age at first marriage, different types of family and marriage and educational standard of the fisher folks. From the census analysis I obtained the statistical data and graphs of the village which helped me to analyses the village people as a whole.

Photography- It is another method to know about the various situations of fishermen and their lifestyle. The different photographs of different situations provide a lively picture of the fishermen society. In the study photos of SHG meeting of women, their marriage rituals, catching of fishes, their market, the different types of net and boat, their traditional deities along with their festivals, village roads, village sanitation, house pattern, village Sarpanch, the fish drying place etc. were taken.

Research Design- It is the conceptual structure within which research is conducted and it constitutes the collection, arrangement and analysis of data. Research design is the system of outline of the ways in which a particular research will be carried out. In a research design, the investigator makes a distinction between the empirical phases of the interpretive phase. The first phase deals with the collection of data and second one with findings which is categorized by nature of data, theoretical approaches and conceptual model of the researcher.

Black and Champion (1976: 76-77) have given three important functions of research design. These are:

- It provides a blueprint.
- It limits boundaries of research of activity.
- It enables investigation to anticipate potential problems.

Phases in Research Design:

The research process proceeds in four phases as under:

- Specifying the problems/ topics to be studied
- Framing Research design
- Planning a sample to use (probability or non-probability or combination of the two)

- Analyzing the data and preparing the report

These are given in a diagrammatic form as below:

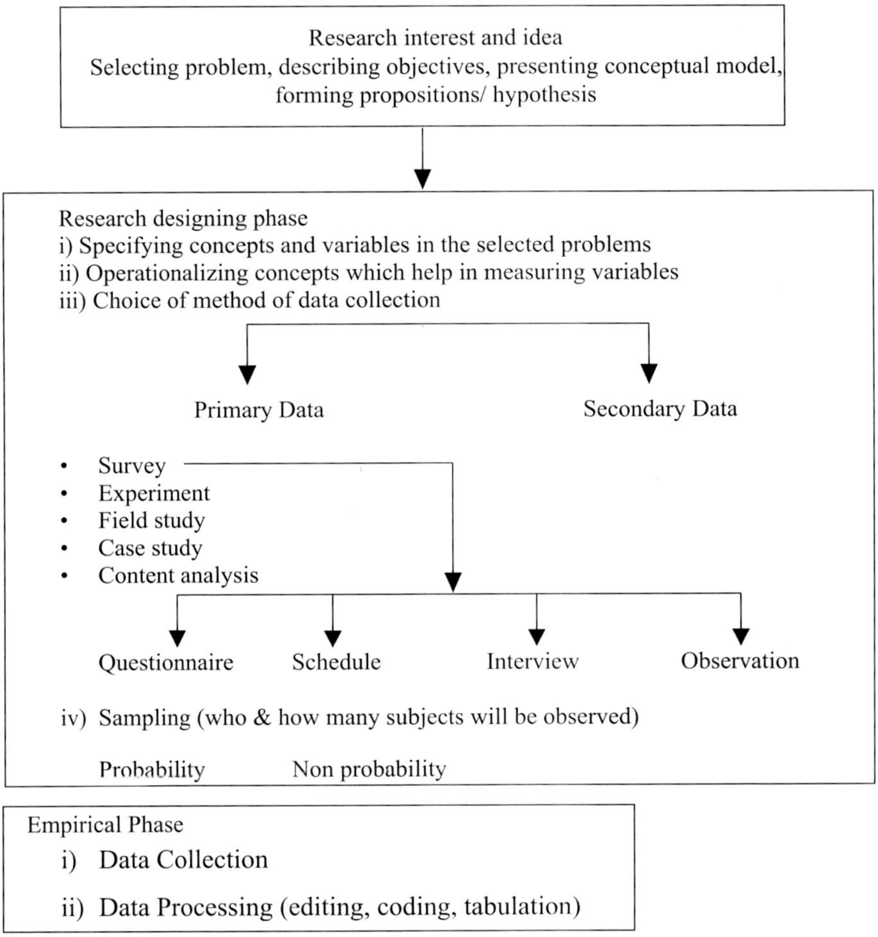

The Research is both exploratory and descriptive type.

Objectives

- To study the profiles of coastline culture, their socio-cultural life style, their situation in Odisha including topography, settlement pattern, ecology and administrative structure etc.
- To know about the social institute - specifically structure of family, patterns of marriage, kinship system and inter-personal relations and networks existing among Nolias.

- To study the traditional economy, occupational vis a vis modern economy, whether they are adopting Catching, grading, drying, branding and selling of fishes that's done by Nolias.
- To enquire about the use of Navigational Ethno-science in catching of fishes now and then.
- To study the traditional political organization as well as modern political system including the extent of women empowerment specifically in Nolia society.
- To access the extent of success after the implementation of government policies, plans and programmes for the development of Nolias in Chilika Lake.
- To evaluate the impact of modernization and change on coast line culture of Chilika Lake in particular and Odisha in general.

Working Hypotheses

The following tentative hypotheses are taken from the findings of the study- Coastline Culture of the Nolias of Chilika Lake.

- There is a narrow gap between coastal cultures vs. other cultures in Odisha.
- Major roles played by women in economic activities do not enhance their traditional position in Nolia society as compared to male members.
- There's been no relative improvement of quality of life of the Nolias even after adoption and application of modern technological devices.

Limitations of Research

- A large variation in the name of net as there is a confusion between Telugu and Odia name.
- No access to the financial records of the fishing people was one of the critical limitations.
- Unawareness of the primary respondent on the price, quantum and SHG actively working are the major factors.
- Fluctuations in the data personally collected with the data resourced from Block level, fishery department.

As a student of Socio-cultural Anthropology, the first-hand information is the basic requirement for the researcher to understand their way of life.

So my foremost aim is to establishment a good rapport with the people that may enable me to collect data very easily. The key informants who helped me a lot directly/indirectly are as Kailash Chandra Behera (40+) school teacher; Bipin Kumar Behera (21+) a student; Pradipta Behera (28+) a worker of NGO; Laxmi Behera, Jayanti Behera (Anganwadi workers) and Bulei Behera (58+) the organizer and Mahila Samiti member.

2

Coverage of Study

Chilika: The Study Area

About Chilika Lake :

Geographical position	Latitude – 19 28" to 19 54" N
	Longitude – 856" to 8508" E
Water spread Area	In Summer – 906 sq. km
	In Monsoon – 1165 sq. km
	Average water spread area – 1065 sq. km
Depth of Chilika	During Summer– 0.47 to 2.4 mts
	During Monsoon– 1.73 to 3.7 mts
	Average – 1.5 mts
Length of the outer channel	35 kms
No. of Lake mouths at present	2
Total Area of the Island	223 sq. km
Total No. of canals and rivers that discharge water to the Lagoon	10 Nos.
Number of Types of fish available	158 species (131 Marine and 27 Fresh fishes)
Fish Landing per annum	4,000 to 6,000 MT

(*Source: Fishery Department, Balugaon*)

About Arakhakuda Village:

Name of the village	Arakhakuda
District	Puri
Block	Krushnaprasad
Panchayat	Arakhakuda
Primary Health Centre	Panaspada
Police Station	Krushnaprasad
Population	4500- 5000
Caste-wise Household Distribution	Nolia

Contd...

Caste-wise occupation	Nolia(s) - fishing
	Brahman - Pujas, Religious Services
	Barik - Hair dresser
	Dhoba - Washing clothes and fishing
	Gauda - Milk seller

Odisha is situated in the North-eastern side of the Indian peninsula with a coastline of 480 kilometers (8 per cent of India coastline). It is surrounded by the Bay of Bengal in the east, West Bengal in the North east, Jharkhand in the North, Chhattisgarh in the west and Andhra Pradesh in the south. Accordingly to the census of 2001, the state has a population of 37 million, which grows at a rate of 1.5 per cent per annum. A quarter of the population is constituted by various tribes who inhabit the hilly interiors of the state. Of the rest of the population that has been divided according to the prevalent caste system, nearly 54 per cent of the state's scheduled caste population (SCs) resides in the coastal districts. As Odisha is primarily an agrarian state, 76 per cent people of the populous are engaged in agriculture. However, the state's dependence on its primary sector has resulted in extreme vulnerability to several natural disasters like droughts and cyclones. The cyclones that have struck the coastal areas time and again are a major setback to the state's economy, and the fisheries sector is always a prime causality.

The six maritime districts of the state are Balasore, Bhadrak, Kendrapara, Jagatsinghpur, Puri and Ganjam. These districts cover 14.5 per cent of the total land area in the state. There are 641 fishing villages situated along the Odisha coast. The total fisher folk population of the state during the year 2005 had 4,50,391 people in 86,352 households of which 41 per cent resided in Balasore, 15 per cent in Jagatsinghpur, 13 per cent in Bhadrak, 12 per cent in Puri, 10 per cent in Ganjam and 9 per cent in Kendrapara respectively. If we narrow down the numbers further, of the 1, 21,282 people engaged in marine fishery activities, 74,980 persons are full time fishermen, 34,315 people are part time fishermen and the remaining 11,987 are occasional fishermen.

The coastal regions of Odisha have a unique feature where a number of diverse ecosystems co-exist and aid the fishing reservoirs in housing a wide range of fishes. The different types of beaches, lagoons, estuaries along the coast give rise to numerous reformations in fishing and post-harvest practices, allowing income generating opportunities for lots of people.

The vast and dream like Chilika Lake is situated on the east coast of India. It is the largest brackish water Lake of India with estuary features is a welcoming ground for millions of migratory avifauna during the winters, every year. It is one of the hotspots of bio-diversity in the country and some rare, vulnerable and endangered species listed in the IVCN Red list of threatened animals inhabit the Lake area for at least some part of their life cycle. It was designated as a Ramsar site by the Government of India in 1982 owing to its wetlands that carry international importance. Sites with wetlands that carry unique properties and are found only in rare sites across earth have been named Ramsar sites under the convention of wetlands treaty signed by UNESCO in 1971. Chilika is also included in the list of wetlands selected for intensive conservation and management by Ministry of Environment and Forests, Govt. of India (Peter Deva Sundaram, M, 1948-1952).

Chilika Lake covers 1/5th of the total area of Sadar Sub-division. It is a basin into which the rivers of southern delta empty themselves. In the west, it is flanked by Khurda hills; in the east it is divided from the sea by a belt of sand and a group of stumpy islands formed over the years by silt deposits. A small opening of 2-300 yards connects its water with the sea and brings in the sea tide. The Lake accumulates rain water and is fresh and salty in summer. The soil of Chilika is colloquially called 'Nunia' which translates to salty. There are certain metals mixed in the soil that create the flavor when tasted by humans. The saline sources penetrate the upper layer of the soil and result in a bluish white appearance of the lake. The salt present in the soil may or may not be suitable for cultivation, depending on the amount of substances present. The villages on the banks of the lake practice salt cultivation according to their suitability (Maddox, S.L. 1890-1900 A.D., Vol. I).

The state's proximity to the rich shrimp grounds of Bay of Bengal (northern side) as well as the existence of a broad continental shelf in the Northern Zone ensures that fisheries are characterized by a high proportion of commercially essential species like hilsa, pomfrets and shrimp. However, large stretches of the coastal area (around 40 per cent of total coast) have effectively become a 'no-take' area (forbidden for fishing or other activities) as a result of several conservation measures and this remains the most significant issue that fishermen confront.

The rights of traditional fishing communities have been in the limelight in the recent years because of rapid commercialization and its adverse effects on many fisheries. But there is not much that can be done to tackle this problem because technological advancement is needed for the dynamically developing market driven world fisheries and there is a dualism of technology and traditional fishing in the budding marine economy. Along with the highly organized sector using massive inputs, the subsistence and decentralized forms of economic organization in fisheries remain resilient and dynamic, particularly in the developing economies of Asia. Artisanal fisheries provide approximately 25 per cent of the global fish catch and about 40 per cent of the fish used for human consumption.

Chilika Lake is the largest brackish water lagoon of India, situated in the eastern coast of Indian peninsula. A wetland like Chilika Lake is a major income source for fishermen, the dominant ethnic group of that area. The lagoon remains a vital lifeline for more than 200,000 people residing in 141 villages. Their main occupation is to catch fish in the Lake and the neighboring Bay of Bengal (Acharya, Sabita, 2000).

The lagoon is a highly productive ecosystem rich in fish and other marine resources. It gives occupation to more than 200,000 fisher folk who live in and around the Lake. But traditional fishing techniques like Janao, Bahano, Dian, and Uthapani and Daudi that used to be famous are gradually being abandoned. The area of Lake varies between 1165 and 906 sq. kms. Chilika is situated in $19^{0}28'$ and $19^{0}54'$ North latitudes and $85^{0}05'$ and $85^{0}38'$ East longitudes. It extends from south corner of Puri and Khurda districts to the adjoining Ganjam district of Odisha.

The village Arakhakuda comes under Krushnaprasad Block of Puri district. Both the Lake and the village are well connected by Satpada. Chilika is 60 kms from Puri and 100 kms from the Bhubaneswar airport. Approaches to the fish Landing centre and improvement of village roads especially for those fishermen villages in the inaccessible areas have been undertaken by the Government. Ferry services carrying vehicles and people are in operation between Satpada and Jahnikuda, benefitting more than 70,000 people living in Krushnaprasad block of Puri district in particular and drastically reducing the distance between Puri and Berhmapur. The villagers around the lake face problems like the lack of drinking water and various health problems due to poor sanitation facilities. The CDA is implementing infrastructure development programmes like renovation of village ponds, construction of fish landing jetties, construction of village community centres, providing solar street lighting systems etc., in villages in and around Chilika Lake. Alternate income generating programme through value addition for the poor fishermen like fishfed preparation, advanced dry fish techniques, preparation of fish and prawn pickles etc. are promoted in the surrounding villages. The Lake is divided into 4 natural sectors based on salinity and department i.e. southern zone, northern zone, central zone and the outer channel. The village Arakhakuda is under the outer channel of Chilika Lake. A new license arrangement has been introduced by the Revenue Department in early 1990's effectively changing the traditional rights, handing it over to the investors of prawn farming. The introduction of prawn culture, gheri and bund fishery in 1991 has led to changes in the process of hydrology and sediment transportation. This was largely due to the implementation of split bamboos and zero-mesh nets, encircling the culture area, which prevented free sediment flow. The inflow of heavy discharge of silt has changed the lake bed and resulted in rapid growth of macrophytes. Authors like Mitra (1946) and M. Peter Dava Sundaram (1948-52) have described the physiology of Chilika and the cause of change in salinity of the water. The change of economy has also changed the productivity of Chilika and the life of traditional fishermen (Ghosh, A.K. 2003).

Geographical Location

The study was undertaken among the Nolia people of Arakhakuda village of Puri District. The Arakhakuda village is a large village having approximately five thousand (5000) populations constituted in a total of 1117 households. There are 2291 males, 2284 females, and 484 children. The village is divided into seven Sahis. They are Laxmi Narayan Sahi, Mangala Sahi, Majhi Sahi, Bhagabat Sahi, Harijan Sahi, Nua Sahi and Hara Chandi Sahi.

Whenever they observe any festival or in case of any dispute in the village, the entire villagers acts in a combined spirit. The village has two major Sahis i.e:

a) Laxmi Narayan Sahi (Mangala Sahi and Majhi Sahi)

b) Bhagabat Sahi (Hara Chandi Sahi and Nua Sahi)

They call Laxmi Narayan Sahi as "badabhai or Nolia sahi" and Bhagat Sahi as "Sanabhai or Khola Sahi". The village is at a distance of 55 kms from Puri. It is connected by road. The village is situated at an inferior site, adjacent to Jadupur on the Puri-Sata Pada road. It is 5 kms from Brahmagiri. The village is situated in19.79 latitude and 85.63 longitudes. Arakhakuda is 90 kms from the city of Bhubaneswar.

Roads and Communication:

The road to Arakhakuda is very approachable. A pucca road connects the village to the Brahmagiri-Satapada main road which is wide enough for both two and four wheelers. People mostly use two wheelers, but they also cover the distance by foot to communicate with neighboring villages, and to go to Brahmagiri block. The village is well connected, with buses and trucks plying from Puri.

But the roads inside the village are Kaccha i.e., made of hard mud. In summer and winter the roads are full of fine dust particles. But during the rainy season the roads become muddy and slippery. Most of villagers own cycles or two wheelers for commutation purposes.

House Pattern

In this village, some of the houses are pucca with cement sand tile roofs. Some houses are thatched. Most of the houses have one or two living rooms and a kitchen. Only few people have constructed more than two living rooms. All the houses are placed in a linear fashion and have common walls of partition. The houses are square shaped and almost regular-looking. The village is densely populated. The houses have two entrances, the main entrance faces the road and the other one is in the backside of the housc towards the Chilika Lake. The net used to catch fishes is hung or woven in front of house. All the houses are North and south facing but some face the east direction.

Flora and Fauna:

We find animals like cows and goats of different colors, ducks, hens, roosters, dogs, buffaloes and different types of snakes.

The flora and fauna of the village include trees like drumsticks, mango, bamboo, coconut, banana, papaya, guava, brinjal, cashew trees, and marigold flower etc.

In the beginning of summer, the fields present on the entrance of village are filled with ripe cashew. The paddies are grown in rainy season. The main source of livelihood for the villagers is fishing. Fishing is banned from May to June15 every year because of government rule.

These are the common fauna found in the Arakhakuda village-

- Rangban (Indian shot)
- Gangasiuli (night blooming Jasmine)
- Hibiscus Rosa Sineris, Chinchamba
- Gulab (Rose centi folia)
- Hara guava (Indian balsam)
- Broad leaned water lily
- Padma (rose colored lotus)
- Kayin (blue water lily)
- Simli (red-cotton tree)
- Bombax mala baricum
- Sunflower (Surjamukhi)
- Wood - Sal (shorea robusta)
- Panas - Artocurpus Integrifolia
- Sisu - Dal bergia Sissoo
- Gambhari - Gmelina arborea.

Forest Types and Vegetation

The forests found in Puri range from dry or evergreen to semi-evergreen unlike forests found in other parts of Odisha. The presence of Sal (Shorea robusta) is found in different parts of the area. The Arakhakuda Gram Panchayat falls in the Puri district, so majority of the forests are full of Sal Orkonga (Xylia cylocarpa).

Birds - The Chilika Lake forms an abode for numerous species of migratory and other birds. The names of the common birds are peaf owl, (pavo cristatus) red jungle fowl (Gallus gallus), red spurfowl (Gallowperdia Spadicea), black patridge (franco Linus francolinus), common grey quail (cotur mix conurnia). The ground birds are generally found in the forest. In winter every year, many indigenous species of birds, flocks of ducks and plenty of strange and unique birds visit Chilika.

A very common animal seen in the villages of Puri district is Godhi or monitor vizard (varanus monitor).

Total Livestock-

Cows-485

Bulls-9

Goats-198

Ducks-4500

Poultries-11740

Climate and Rainfall

The climatic condition of the village is the same as the rest of Puri district. Arakhakuda village is situated in Krushnaprasad Tahsil in Puri district of Odisha state.

From March to May, the temperature continuously rises and May is the hottest month. The mean daily temperature in a month is 31.9^0 C. With the arrival of monsoon, by the middle of June temperature drops in this area. December is the coldest month and the daily minimum temperature in the month is 17.1^0 C (62.7^0 F). Humidity is generally high throughout the year. Winds are fairly strong in the village in summer and monsoon seasons. The wind speed drops post monsoon and in winters.

Landscape Elements

On one side Arakhakuda village is surrounded by water and on the other side it opens to the main road. The entrance of the village is with strewn with different plants like Kaju, Eucalyptus, Alacia, Casuarina, Kia, Cactus etc. Villagers fulfil their fuel wood requirements from the small forest. Specific villagers have private Kaju and Coconut plantations. There are three ponds managed collectively by the Panchayat. The village is 20 kms from Satapada.

Fishing Caste Communities

Society and Culture

The communities thriving around Chilika are fishermen communities. People belonging to SC communities are Keuta, Kandara, Tiara, Nolia, Khatia etc. The people of Arakhakuda village (Krushnaprasad block) belong to Nolia community. All the fishermen communities are Odia whereas Nolias are Telugu speaking people. In this village, the people come under SCBC but they are claiming the status of SC people.

Keuta: More than 60 percent of the fishing population are Keutas who are considered to be the successors of the original fishing families and are superior in class among all other fishing communities residing in Chilika. They are also known as Kaibartas and have been divided under different endogamies gr. i.e. Dhibara, Niari, Machhua, Siuli, Kedar, Girigiria and Nauri. These people generally fish in deep Chilika only with nets (casting net).

Nolia: They are Telugu immigrants mainly from Andhra Pradesh, Tamil Nadu and their neighboring states. Nolias are good swimmers and are extremely hard working. They can work for hours together in an open boat swamped at sea. They do fishing both in deep sea and Chilika Lake with drag nets (bhidajal).

Tiara: They fish in the shallow lake area. Tiaras use buja, tata for catching underdeveloped fishes and prawns. These people do not use nets.

Kandara: This is the second largest community in Chilika. They do fishing in shallow areas by using dhauli, tata. They generally do not use nets for fishing.

Khatia: In ancient times, Khatias used to hire lower caste persons for fishing activities and earned their livelihood. But since the last 30-40 years they have themselves started fishing in shallow and deep areas of Chilika. They use large nets for catching fish and prawns in deeper parts of the Lake.

Origin of the Fishermen Group (Nolia)

The fishermen of Arakhakuda migrated from coastal Andhra Pradesh and settled near the mouth of Chilika Lake about 200 years ago. The settlement place was one of the sand dunes called Arakhakuda. At present this place has developed into a large village.

The fishermen of Arakhakuda are originally Telugu speaking fishermen. According to Sangam Literature, this fishing tradition goes back a thousand years. According to the villagers they were called Nolia in Odisha due to their tradition of wearing golden rings in their ears. The Nolias have been divided into two types – Jalary and Orderloo. Jalaries are exclusive fishing groups who fish in the sea with nets and boats whereas Orderloos (bahania) are those who work as laborers in the ships and help with loading and unloading. L.S.S. O'Malley mentioned that the fisher folk of this location have their origin links with the Kaibarta and Kandara castes and also the Telugu fisher folk who had been invited in the 2nd half of 18thcentury by the ruler of Macchagao Basudev Mangaraj to settle at the mouth of the river Devi to serve him as pirates.

W.W. Hunter in his Odisha, mentioned that "Along the shore are little fishing communities, who get a livelihood by means of travel nets, one end pulled towards the shore by one man and the other end by a commrade upto his waist on the surf. But the fish caught are small. A more profitable trade is dragging with a big net inside the sea. Two large boats go out a couple of miles, and travel towards the beach with very strong nets cast in about 20 feet deep sea.

The Chilika Lake has been separated from the Bay of Bengal by sand dunes named Sipakuda and Baranakuda.

The fishing communities especially the helmets of boatmen belong to Telugu Settlements from Madras cost. They speak a different language, observe different customs and festivals, follow different Gods than those with agricultural profession and here I noticed that the boating villages along the whole coast upto the Devi river and even around it, consist of similar Telugu speaking colonies from the south. There are indistinct remnants of the aboriginal races and although their separate origin is forgotten they are excluded from Hindu commonwealth. They have a lot of customs and scruples that are religiously observed by the Hindus. There is a little village on the sands of Puri, which although situated within the holy precincts, denies the villagers entrance into the great temple of Jagannath".

Malley mentioned about the name of village Arakhakuda. We wrote that "the Noliyas are a caste of fishermen and boatmen who have migrated to Puri from Madras. There are two sub castes called Jaliya and Khalasi. The former are fishermen, while the latter work on sea-going vessels; some dig earth, pull pankhas and carry loads. The rule among them and among the Kumuties is that a man should, if possible, marry his first cousin. A widow may remarry and the groom may be her first husband's younger brother. The son inherits any property the family may have but if there are no sons, the property is becomes community property. Noliyas profess to be followers of Ramajuna and worship Baruna, the Hindu Neptune, with offerings of flowers and sweet meals before launching a boat or casting a net. They are found in Puri, Nuagaon, Arakhakuda, Manik Patna,

Khirisahi, Sahadi and Ramlenka". The village name Arakhakuda has been found in directory of 1886 (W.W. Hunter, 1872, p.20-31, L.S.S. O' Malley, p.84-85).

Infrastructure of the Village

Mahila Samiti	Two numbers (02)
School	Three numbers (03)
Youth Club	Three numbers (03)
Cooperative	Three numbers (02)
Temple	Three numbers (08)
Electricity	Available
Communication facilities	Boat, Bus
Types of Road	Metal
Water sources	Tube well, pond
Fuel sources	Wood from village forest
Nearby Markets	Balugaon, Puri, Satapada, Krushnaprasad
Available Foods	Rice, fish

Ethnic Composition/Interaction

In Arakhakuda village different caste people like Nolia, Brahmin, washerman (Dhoba), Milk man (Gauda), Barber (barik) and untouchables are found. The Nolias are greater in number than any other castes. The other caste people live at the outskirts of the village. Nolias need the help of other caste people for their daily activities.

The Nolias are dominant group in the village and they depend mainly on the fishing. The Brahmin people are dependent on deity worship and the priesthood work. The Milk man community lives by supplying milk. The washer man community lives by washing the Nolia clothes from time to time. The harijan people are richer, so the Nolias take their help when need arises. But they look at harijans as inferior according to caste. Interaction always occurs between these caste groups. Besides that they always maintain some restriction between them. The people are normally prohibited from visiting harijan and Muslim families.

Dress and Ornaments

Dresses, hair styles and ornaments are common to all societies and communities. But all these groups do not dress up similarly. Nor do they match hair-styles or ornaments. Important factors of divergences in these respects occur because of cultural background, economic condition, and the level of modernization.

Therefore, Odia and Telugu girls living in the village wear different types of dresses. Economic condition is also a related factor. Rich girls wear costly and more fashionable dresses than poor girls. Education is also another factor. A girl of poor family studying in a high school or college would differ from her mother and other elderly women of her family and village with respect to her hair style. Rich women wear gold ornaments while poor women, though fond of such ornaments, are not able afford them. The following discussion on dress, hair style and ornaments of fisher women would give a fair idea about their economic condition, educational background and also about the values and customs of the fisher women community.

The traditional dress of a fisher man is related to his occupation. He dresses himself up in such a way that he feels comfortable while catching fish in the high sea. He wears a small piece of cloth to cover the lower part of his body, while the upper part of his body remains bare. However, he wears a cap of conical shape. This cap has two functions. Firstly, the cap, because of its conical shape, has the aerodynamic function of cutting through the pressure of the sea wind. Secondly, inside the cap there is a small chamber in which the fisherman keeps a matchbox and some *pikka* (country cigarette) made of tobacco leaves. The fisherwoman wears *saree.* While the lower part of one portion of the *saree* touches her feet, the other portion of the *saree* falling down from the left shoulder is tied around her waist. The style of wearing the *saree* is helpful in properly covering most of her body. This also helps a mother to carry her baby when she goes out for selling fish. The baby is placed inside the bag like fold formed in one portion of the *saree,* while the other portion of the *saree* is tied round the waist.

Fisher women are fond of wearing *sarees* of different colors. Their favorite colors are green, red, pink and blue. They rarely wear white or yellow *sarees*. Sometimes they cover their head with a part of the *saree.* In ancient times, wearing a blouse was rare. However, in course of time many Fisher women have started wearing blouse, particularly while going out. When they work inside the house, they do not feel comfortable wearing a blouse. But most of them while going to a nearby market or a town, wear a blouse. Only a small number of fisher women wear petticoats. Young boys and girls have begun to wear modern dresses. While the school going boys wear half pants and shirts, the college going boys wear full pants and shirts. Full pants and shirts are also popular among other fisher women youths. They may not be educated or employed but they wear full pants and shirts when they go to the town, market or to a government office. Similarly young fisher women girls have developed fascination for modern dresses irrespective of their educational background. They wear frocks and *salwar-kamij*. The educated young girls also wear inner garments. From their clothes one has an idea about the educational and economic background of fisher women. Those fisher women who have better educational and economic background dress themselves better than other women. Similarly, there is a difference between the dress of the school going girls and girls who are not studying. An uneducated fisher girl may be wearing a frock or *langawani,* but generally she is less conscious of her dress than an educated girl. An old man is content with a small dhoti. He rarely wears a shirt or a T-Shirt. Fisher women are fond of using ornaments. Only a few of them can afford to buy gold ornaments as most of them are poor. They generally use ornaments made of silver. Generally they apply earrings and nose rings. Many of them wear chains made of colorful beads. Hardly anybody wears a gold necklace. Some old women wear silver anklets (known as Khadu) around their ankles. They also use glass bangles of different colors. Few of them possess gold bangles.

Tattooing is common in fishing folks, both men and women. A Fisherwoman tattoos her name or the name of her husband on her right hand. She believes that after her death she will not be punished by Yama (the lord of death), if she has done the name tattoo in her hand. Some fisher women tattoo a black spot on the center of their forehead. Tattooing is a very painful process. It is done with the help of a pin, and a black powder. In case of a child the pain is less. But many young women go for tattooing only after marriage so that they can tattoo the names of their husbands. However this practice has considerably decreased in course of time.

Religious Organization

Religious beliefs or concepts of the nature of supernatural forces differ from society to society and from people to people. In circumstances of miseries or sorrow, religion helps us to achieve psychological adjustment and peace of mind. Religion plays a role in rationalizing and justifying the ultimate group ends. It acts as an agent of social control by providing reward for the good and punishment for the bad.

The Nolias are very religious by nature. They celebrate many festivals and observe many rituals. The main Gods and Goddesses they worship are Budhima, Masani Chandi, Bali Harachandi, Gangadevi, Semanchal, Shiva, Bishnu and Krishna. The village has two temples-Laxminarayan temple and Bhagabat temple. These temples have different priests, who are Brahmin by caste. But their Gramdevati and Masani Chandi are worshipped by their own caste priests. They believe the Masani Chandi and Budhima are very angry and furious Goddesses. So the Nolias always try to satisfy them by sacrificing animals and doing pujas and melas etc. They observe different festivals like Holi, Diwali, Dusshera, Chaiti Ghoda Dance, and Makar Sankranti. They also observe some rituals that are associated with fishing. During every festival Nolias sacrifice animals and birds. Some rituals and festivals are done by their own caste priest called Manari. In Nolia Society women are strictly prohibited from doing deity worship. Only male members are allowed to do it. Nolias are devotees of the Goddesses. The Functionaries who offer worship to their deities reside in the village. The people are highly religious in nature. They are also superstitious to a great extent.

The main reason behind worshipping different gods and goddesses is to have a bountiful catch while fishing and return home safely. Many Nolias also worship and offer sacrifices for prevention of diseases and swift recoveries in case anyone falls sick. While some of these gods/goddesses are worshipped throughout the year, some worshiping is specific to fisherwomen. In general, the religious beliefs and practices of fishermen are related to sea and fishing.

With advent of modernization, they are getting slowly attracted to the 'great tradition' of the state. However, there are no clear signs that may suggest that they will discard their traditions in the near future. Like other castes, the fisher folk worship the important Hindu gods like Shiva and Vishnu and believe in the philosophy of the Hindu religion. They go to the nearest Shiva and Vishnu temples during important festivals; they also undertake pilgrimages to important temple like Simanchalam. Another important temple much revered and visited by them is the Jagannath temple at Puri, Odisha. Besides the important Hindu gods, innumerable local deities mostly Ammavaarus (Mother Goddess) are worshipped. Among local deities, the village deities who differ from village to village hold an important place of worship. The most important andcommon deity of Telugu fisher folk among local deities is Gangamma or Harachandiammavari. The goddess is mythologically associated with Lord Shiva. Even though she is the personification of the river Ganga, the same goddess is referred by all the fisher folk of Odisha as a sea goddess. This belief originated from the fisher folk of north Odisha who traditionally practiced fishing in the tributaries and deltas of the river Ganges. Gangamma is worshipped in most fishing rituals. She is believed to protect the fishermen and bless them with good catches while at sea. The festival of Gangamma is celebrated with sacrifices of goats and chickens. Puja is conducted by offering flowers, coconuts, bananas, wine, vermilion, some leaves of date palm, sandal wood, incense sticks or ghee threads and four pieces of red flags. Makara Sankranti is one of the important festivals celebrated in mid January. The fisher folks worship their ancestors and Gangamma, the goddess of the sea. It is believed that if this festival does not please the ancestors it may lead to poor turnout during fishing and illness among family members. Makara Sankranti is the festival during which the rich as well as the poor cook meat. Kartika Poornima is another important festival celebrated in the month of November and December.

The Nolias observe a special festival called '*Chaita Parab'* on full moon day in the month of *Chaitra* (March-April). During the festival they worship Goddess "Baseli" on an improvised horse, made with a painted wooden head and bamboo frame covered with cloth. A man gets into the empty bamboo frame and lifts the wooden horse with straps hung from his shoulders. Holding the reins of the horse in his hands he dances to the tune of drums and mahuri, an indigenous musical instrument. This is known as Ghoda nacha or horse dance. The people also observe Asta prahari. During this period the fishermen usually do not fish. Thus, the festivals are observed not only to signify the cultural life of the community but also help in conserving diverse aquatic species.

Economic Organization

Economic Organization is a type of social action. It's a combination of various kinds of human services and non human goods and services. The primary occupation of Nolia people is fishing but these days, they have adapted to different types of economic activities. They practice both marine and fresh water fishing. In past their economic conditions were very bad but now the economic condition is improving. They have no cultivable lands to cultivate any type of crops, so the people in the lean season engage themselves as laborers in nearby cashew fields and some women collect firewood to sale in the nearby market. They always spend more than their income for which they live in deficit budget which always affects their economy. Majority of their income is exhausted in food and drinks.

Market is a common place where buying and selling of different commodities takes place. There are many shops in the village that fulfill villagers' daily requirements. Their main market is known as Bramhagiri market.

Different types of green vegetables, fishes and various agricultural products are available in the market at affordable prices. Besides, villagers also depend on Puri's market.

Political Organisation

Arakhakuda village has two distinct types of political organizations. One is traditional and the other is modern political organization. The traditional organization comprising elder members of the village is called the village committee. For internal disturbances like disputes over fishing, marriage, or any other affairs, the villagers approach the village community. To help solve cases relating to thefts, disputes relating to property or murder, the people approach the Grampanchayat. A leader always possesses characteristics that differentiate him from others. The leader of Arakhakuda possesses characteristics like being economically strong, honest, having organizing capacity, positive attitude for doing hard work, etc.

Polling System

The polling system helped the villagers to get acquainted with the democratic practices and procedures maintained throughout the country. The prevalent system helped to consciously, nationally, socially, politically and economically alert them to their rights and duties.

In a family dispute, there are two parties: one is the sufferer and the other is gainer. The sufferer arranges a meeting in the village. He calls upon the entire older clan to give him justice. There is no particular time limit of the meeting. It may commence in the afternoon or in the evening. Both the parties obey the decisions that come out of the meeting.

Among Nolias, succession and inheritance of name, clan name, lineage, headmanship, priestship are patrilineal. Generally the males are owners of houses and other material possessions. After the death of the parents, any wealth is inherited by their son.

Relation with Neighbours

The villagers in one village are of one particular clan. They marry among their relatives and therefore all the villagers are relatives of each other. The people are very quarrelsome in nature, especially the womenfolk. They do not get along with each other. But the males somehow manage and are seen playing cards during their leisure times.

Language

The Nolias were mainly Telugu speaking people. The Arakhakuda village is divided into two major Sahis– Laxminarayan Sahi and Bhagabat Sahi. The Bhagabat Sahi people are the original Telugu Nolias who speak their native tongue. Other Sahi people who have migrated from Paradip and Kujanga speak Odia fluently. However the language barrier has adversely affected and inconvenienced the numerically few Telugu Nolias and they have started speaking in Odia and observing Odia festivals.

Leisure Time and Recreation

During the off season the Nolias get leisure time to enjoy. The male members play cards, listen to radio and watch television. The young boys play different types of games like cricket, football etc. But Nolia women are always occupied, and they don't get any time to enjoy. Rarely if they get time, they watch television, collect firewood, collect drinking water for cooking. The girls put on mehendi in leisure time, play Ludo, sew dresses etc. The people drink a lot and sometimes the Telugu nolia women also join them.

Food, Nutrition and Health

Food is a basic requirement of everyday life and nutrition is crucial for good health. Economic status of any family dictates their food intake quality. Among Nolias, only the richer families can afford to purchase different edible vegetables from the market. Generally the Nolia people take three meals in a day. They take watered rice, chuda or mudhi as their breakfast. For lunch they take rice as a compulsory item along with a fish curry. Telugu Nolias do not follow any restrictions when it comes to food.

But the Oriya speaking Nolias observe many restrictions on *Sankranti*, *Purnima* and Monday. They do not take non vegetarian food. In spite of government aids, lack of nutrition and malnutrition are found among people as a major problem. This has occurred because they do not eat fruits or vegetables and take meat and fish as their staple diet. This paves way for many ailments that they suffer on a regular basis like back pain, diarrhea, anemia, measles, Vitamin A deficiency, (which causes blindness) damage of liver and kidney (due to excess drinking). They strongly believe that some diseases are due to supernatural spirits and others are the wrath of malevolent beings. Previously they cured diseases with the help of sorcerers or Manari. But now they believe in modern medicine. Arakhakuda village does not have a hospital or a specialized doctor. In case of any emergency people take medicine from the village medicine store without consulting a doctor. The shopkeeper uses his own knowledge of medicine to suggest drugs to everybody.

3

Social Structure

Life Cycle Rituals

Life cycle rituals are an array of rituals that mark in the life of a person, stages and steps that he goes through from birth till death, roles that he performs over time, his social position and relationship with fellow humans, cultural experiences associated with his biological destiny: birth, reproduction and death. These ceremonies make way for basic distinctions to be observed by all groups of people whether young or old, male or female, living or dead. Through these rites of passage we are able to contemplate, formulate and reformulate our ambivalent opinions of animals and humans.

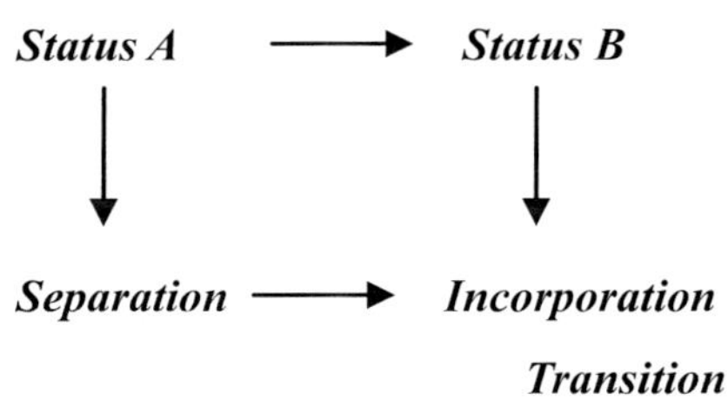

The term ritual denotes those aspects of prescribed formal behavior that do not have any direct technological consequences. The "prescription" or prescribed component in the definition is ordinarily provided by cultural traditions but it may in some cases be a spontaneous invention of an individual. Therefore the majority of "religious and magical" actions are rituals in this sense. Ritual actions are symbolic in that they assert something about the state of affairs, but they are not necessarily purposeful, i.e. the performer of the ritual does not necessarily seek to alter the state of affairs.

According to Beals and Hoijer, "Ritual is a prescribed way of performing religious act, i.e. praying, singing sacred songs, dancing to god, making sacrifices or preparing offerings. A ceremony on the other hand involves a number of inter connected and related rituals."

Ritual expresses the personality, act, relationship, status and the way in which one behaves with others in most parts of the world. According to Durkheim a ritual has four phases namely disciplinary and preparatory, cohesive, revitalizing. For Anthropologists and ecclesiastics, the term ritual always refers to social customs, traditionally sanctioned. But some psychoanalytic writers used the term included for some prescribed and elaborated behavior that has been spontaneously invented by an individual or through compulsion neurotics. For example, Van Gannep analyses rites of passage the following way:

There are two types of rites –

1) Rites that accompany the passage of a person from one social status to another in the course of his or her life.
2) Rites that mark recognized points in the passage of time (New Year, new moon, solstice or equinox) [Mirea Eliade, 1987: 308].

Van Gannep analyzed these rites into subsequent three stages:

a) Rites of separation
b) Marginal or luminal rites
c) Rites of aggregation

According to Gannep the element separation is more important in mortuary or funerary rites, than of aggregation in marriage. The marginal rites, marking the period in which an individual is detached from one status but not yet admitted into the next, are most conspicuous than those initiation ceremonies that involve the participants in a long period of Isolation, cut off from their normal social contact [Mirea Eliade, 1987: 308].

Among Nolias I found these events are equally important.

Birth Ritual

Birth of a child marks an important occasion in every family, in every society. But prior to child birth, the pregnant women of Arakhakuda go through some restrictions. The Arakhakuda society is a mixture of both Telugu and Oriya cultures. But the life cycle of an individual in all cultures are same. While birth is a common occurrence in all communities, the mode of delivery differs from one community to another community depending on several factors including availability of modernized facilities.

During pregnancy period the women are not allowed to go anywhere. There is no restriction of food for the pregnant lady. She can worship the male deities but she is barred from visiting or praying to the female deities.

The delivery of a child is done in the house itself with the help of mid wife or a nurse. Normally delivery in the hospital is safe but, the village has no primary health centre therefore the pregnant women are not taken to any hospital.

In past the people called the midwives or *dhaiis* as "Mantrasani". They were the older fisher women who had experienced life in more profound ways in terms of child birthing and mother care after delivery. One of my informant said that previously in Arakhakuda village only two Mantrasani were working. But one of them called Sabitri Behera had died and other named Bulei Behera was not practicing this profession anymore.

The *mantrasani* had no formal training in conducting delivery. They have learnt the skill through various experiences. They are paid around hundred rupees per delivery. But it solely depends on the economic condition of the mother's family and they are also paid more depending on the financial stability of the household. The *dhaii* uses hot water, cotton clothes and teel oil on the pregnant lady's belly for delivery. After child is born, the *mantrasani* cuts the umbilical cord with the help of "machine blade". The 'nahi' is bound by 'bhendi thread'. But sometimes there have been a lot of complications during the process, doing serious harm to the mother, child or both.

Case Study

Name: Sabitri Behera, Aged: 40, Sex: Female, Village: Arakhakuda (Bhagabat Sahi)

It was in the year 2006, a woman named Parvati Behera (24+) while giving birth to her first child, with the help of *mantrasani* (Sabitri Behera) had developed some complications. The body of the child had twisted inside the belly of the mother along with its umbilical cord. The *mantrasani* had tried a lot to pull the baby out but could not. At last they rushed to the hospital near Panaspada, but unfortunately the patient died on the way to hospital.

But this practice of home delivery has considerably decreased as the fisherwomen have been exposed to modernization and are now become aware of the great risk associated with it. There is one ANM in the Arakhakuda village. Her name is Kadambari "didi". She stays outside the village. But she comes once a month to check on all the pregnant ladies.

Besides that, the ANM has several ASHA members working in the village. These young women are Pratima Behera, Dunia Behera (Anganwadi worker) and Raja Behera etc. These women are given short-term training in conducting delivery. Their educational qualification is generally below class tenth. There is no fixed remuneration for ASHA members. In Arakhakuda village there are ASHA members in each Sahi and sub Sahi.

During the year 2006, one member and in 2010 three members were selected for ASHA.

Year	**Name**	**Sahi**
2006	1) Krusuma Behera	Laxmi Narayan Sahi
2010	1) Gorama Behera	Mangala Sahi
	2) Rajani Behera	Masani Chandi Sahi
	3) Chand a Bala Behera	Bhagabat Sahi

The members are decided by the village committee and suggested to the ANM. Every month the ANM convenes a meeting of the pregnant women in the village. The meeting is called "Matru Mileena Sabha". The meetings are held at Kothoghara. The ANM gives injection to both pregnant and lactating mothers and child. During any emergency and in case of absence of ANM, the ASHA members are helpful. All the pregnant members are given a re-delivery card by ASHA member. The fee charged for this card is Rs.350/- The ASHA members want more money from the concerned family. They told me that they are given only Rs.100 to 200 by the concerned family on taking them to hospital. But in case of any mishap occurred or in cesarean operation cases they bear all the expenses but they are not compensated for their timely help and face loses. Therefore they are not satisfied with the system. The ASHA are chosen because of their inherent dedication to serve others. But some people are landing the job by influencing the committee people.

In one case, a baby was given an injection by ANM Kadambari Panda. But that boy died because of some unknown disease. The illiterate fishermen did not know anything. They started to restrict the ANM and did not allow her to even enter into the village. Presently, in place of Kadambari Panda, the LHB Didi is coming to village. But her visits are very irregular. The LHB has given Folliper and Tetanus shots to pregnant women. She has also given BCG, DPT booster, Hep B vaccinations to the children. Due to absence of ANM, she has given injections and vaccines in the month's first and last Wednesday in two Sahis along with other sub Sahis in Kothoghara or Anganawadi house.

Very few families celebrate the birth of a child in their household. Those families who have a steady financial background celebrate this occasion in a grand way. After delivery, the mother and baby are kept in a separate room and the lady is not allowed to go to kitchen or touch to their deities or any male members and she does not take bath. Both mother and child take bath on the fifth day from birth then the seventh day, the twelfth day and the twenty first day.

On the fifth day they usually invite the *dhaii* (during earlier times it was compulsorily observed but not so much now). She is given some clothes along with sweets. But on the twenty first day they organize a feast and invite their *bansa* people or relatives. On that day the new born baby is given a name by his/her father's sister or father's brother. On that day a special *Jagyan* is performed along with puja to please the deities and keep the young one healthy. This puja is done by their village priest. Both mother and baby are present in the puja. Maternal uncle brings sweets, dresses and gold ornaments for the mother and child. After completion of puja, all the relatives give their blessing to the child by throwing rice on him/her and give gifts for the baby. Then all the family friends and relatives gathered are given a grand feast where everybody enjoy good food. Such a ceremony is believed to purify the mother and now she can socialize with everybody and eats with them but with a few restrictions.

The child depends mainly on breast feeding. The NGO workers and Anganwadi/ASHA members have taught the villagers that breast feeding for the first six months after birth is best for child's health. However, some give outside milk to the baby. Then after six months the child is slowly given other outside foods. Some Nolia families also celebrate the first birthday on completion of a year from the birth date.

Puberty: No ceremony is performed for a male child on stepping into adolescence. But when a girl obtains maturity, it is celebrated in a grand way. The girl is kept secluded in a house or kitchen for seven days. All the essential and usable items are taken out of the room where the girl resides. During that period no male members are allowed to see her. Only female or small girls (aged 4-9) are allowed to visit her. On these days (until six days) she does not take bath, only a paste of oil and turmeric is applied on her body. She is served one meal every day, during daytime by one of the family members of house. Normally the oldest member or youngest member of the family (preferably female) serve the food and stay with her at night. A single plate is given to her to be reused every day and it is washed by her sleeping partner. The girl wears old clothes. She is not given non vegetarian food or any burnt vegetables or spices, only light food without salt.

On the third day her uncle and aunt come and give betel leaves, coconut, clothes, sweets etc. to the girl. But only on the seventh day she purifies herself. On that day early in morning about 3 a.m., she is given seven turmeric pieces to eat. Then she brushes with seven tooth sticks, uses seven cow dung pieces, "*Alindi*" and then she takes bath in the Chilika. She throws away all her useable articles. After that she comes home and takes bath in the tube well then she applies powder on her face and combs her hair properly. Early in the morning she goes to Hari Sahadev Temple along with seven of her friends. Then a feast is given in the temple to ten or fifteen small children of 5-12 years age. On returning from the temple she again takes bath. I found out that on the seventh day she takes bath seven times.

This function is called as "Satatarigadabaiki", which means that the girl will take bath seven times. On that day the girl eats only fruits. In the evening a grand feast is arranged. All friends and relatives are invited. The girl is seated on a "Pidha" by the relatives and they see the "panji" to assess if auspicious time is going on. The girl's uncle's family is specially invited. Seven women take coconut, cake, banana, betel leaf in their *anchal* and keep everything on top of the girl's dress. Then they ask the girl to sit on the pidha and take arati. After that all the invited guests come and give gifts to the girl and have their meal. On that day the girl wears only new dresses. If the girl's had a child marriage, she is sent to the house of her husband after a year.

Case Study-1

Name: Joytsna Behera, Aged-14, Sahi: Majhi Sahi

My informant Joytsna Behera (14+), when she attained puberty, felt quite uncomfortable. She felt that everybody behaved with her differently. Her role in family changed. She had to become more responsible and behave in a conservative way with others. She is the eldest daughter in her family. The family members arranged her maturity attaining ceremony in a grand way as it was the first function in her family. But she told me that they gained Rs.20,000/- in this ceremony. She belongs to *Pokolo* lineage. She said only lineage and marriage alliance relatives are invited. Both vegetarian and non-vegetarian food items are offered to the guests.

Death

The Nolia people believe in spirits. They perform special rituals and sacrifices to satisfy their ancestors. When a person dies, the dead body is taken to the cremation ground, where it is burnt by fire. If the wife dies, the husband goes to the cremation ground and lights the funeral pyre (*mukhagni*). But if the husband dies, the wife is not allowed to go to the cremation ground. The eldest son lights the funeral pyre. If the man has no son, then their close relative lights the funeral pyre. The difference is that in the Odia Nolia family the woman breaks her bangles and stops using vermillion after the death of her husband. In Telugu Nolia family, the woman lives a life of *Suhagan* (married woman) till the eleventh day of the death rituals and on twelfth day she dresses as a widow.

The Nolia people call as *Karbati*, which is up to five days after the death of a person when they do "*Gata Stala*". They offer meat, egg, or fish to the dead person on that day. On the third day the family members take a small mud pot and go to the cremation ground to collect the remains of the dead person (usually some pieces of bones). The people throw these bones at sea in Puri. On the fifth day a ritual is organized. Some offerings are given to dead persons and other ancestors. This is done by "*Aiguru*". The *Aiguru* are Dhanajaya Rao and Appa Rao (two brothers) alongwith their wives who have done all the rituals of dead person. The Nolia people have great faith on them. They come from Puri Nolia Sahi to perform the ritual as they have no *Aiguru* in Arakhakuda village. Up to eleventh day a night lamp is lit in the house in honor of the spirit of the dead person. The lamp is called "*Hia*". In Hindu society people only take vegetarian meal but the Nolia societies have no such restriction. The eleventh day is called "*Padakundu*" and the twelfth day is called "*Panndu*". On twelfth day they give food on twelfth plate.

On twelfth day all the rituals are done by *Brahmin* among Odia Nolia people. But in earlier times all these were done by their "*Aiguru*". But now they invite the *Aiguru* on twelfth day to do rituals for Telugu Nolias. They have no restriction. Along with non-vegetarian foods they also take liquor on the twelfth day and in the offer the same to their ancestors. They believe that their offerings will please the ancestors and keep them happy.

All the relatives and friends are invited to this function, mainly their ritual friends and lineage people. In our society, a *Shradha* is given on every death anniversary. But fisher women do not perform such *Shradha*. They give offerings to the spirit of a dead person once a year on *Makar Sankranti*.

Nowadays some people are burying the dead instead of burning them. This is because of scarcity of wood and lack of money to buy wood. The Nolia collect the remnants of the burnt body at the end of the process and put it in *Gadighara* (where Gods are worshiped) and form a mound shape in the corner of the room called *Ishana*. Then they bring a wooden horse, the symbol of their dead person from the carpenter in a grand procession. The horse is put near the *Ishana* and the people worship these daily.

Family Structure and Kinship relationship

The marriage alliance is different. The Nolia people belong to Nageswar clan. The people marry their son and daughter in the same clan. But the people do not marry their child in the same *Bansa*. In the village I found different flags (lineage), these are:

1) Tirtulu
2) Sidhabalu
3) Kouralu
4) Kandalou
5) Gandugulu

6) Behera ghar
7) Gaura ghar
8) Budi
9) Ankalu
10) Mardulu
11) Ordalu
12) Nagesalu
13) Deurulu

From these entire lineages, Kourulu are the highest lineage. They do not practice same caste marriage and marriages occur between different lineage people.

The Nolia people believe in two types of marriages:

1) Tula Kanya
2) Sula Kanya

In *Tulukanya,* the bride comes to the groom's house and the marriage occurs, whereas in *Sulakanya* the groom goes to the bride's house for marriage.

Among Nolias, marriage to maternal uncle is common. Avuncu local marriages are found. The marriage system is not so rigid. The people can marry whenever they wish and they can also leave their first wife and remarry. There are some cases of polygyny marriage where a man kept two wives with him.

In Arakhakuda village, 55-60 percent of couples are distressed within the confinement of marriage. Every day there are cases in front of the village committee. Often married men take another wife or elope with another woman. This shows that the position of a married woman is very miserable in Nolia society.

As far as family structure goes, normally Nolias live in nuclear family. In earlier times they preferred to live in joint families, go for fishing together, eat jointly, which increased their strength and income. But now the situation has reversed. After marriage the children have separated from their family. Therefore, we found that people now live in very small houses having one or two rooms. Their economic condition has also degraded.

If we look at kin relation, apart from very few people, the majority of people do not maintain a good relationship among themselves. Every day they are busy quarrelling about fishing, property or other petty issues.

The people use different terms for addressing different relations:

Telugu term	English term
Kadalu	Daughter-in-law
Kadaku	Son
Aalata	Mother-in-law
Mama	Father-in-law
Kumtaru	Daughter.
Manralu	Grand daughter
Manwad	Grandson
Madasura	Uncle
Aapta	Aunty

Marriage Pattern

Marriage is a pivotal, universal social institution found in each and every society. According to Jon Beattie, "marriage is a union between a man and woman such that the children born are the legitimate offspring of both the partners."

During ancient times the people practiced child marriage. They married their son and daughter at an early age between 7-10 but both stayed at their respective parental houses. When the girl attained maturity, one year later the mother-in-law along with all materials came and took the girl to her husband's house to be a fully-fledged wife there.

But such a practice is nonexistent nowadays because after growing up, the boy or the girl can decide not to honor such a marriage due to falling in love with another individual or something else.

Case Study –2

Name: Kanti Behera, Age-28, Sahi: Laxminarayan Sahi

Kanti Behera (28+) belongs to Laxmi Narayan Sahi. She had a love affair with Narendra Behera (34+) of Majhi Sahi. But their family did not agree to their marriage. The couple eloped and got married and returned to village after one month. The boy's family accepted the couple and decided to perform their marriage again in front of their society and family.

It is observed among girls that they got married precisely in the age group of 21-25, whereas their male counter parts got married in the age group of 18-30. There are very few male members who got married after 30.

A special type of marriage is found in the village. If a family has more than one sons and the eldest son becomes old enough to marry, then all the brothers are married on the same day. They told me that this practice helps to reduce marriage expenditure. Marriage is a big economic burden to them. A lot of money is spent in serving the guests foods and drinks and it is a very expensive ceremony.

Dowry system is also prevalent among the Nolias. In earlier times the demand from the groom's side was less but now it has increased. In one case the groom's side demanded cash of 1.5 lacs along with all household equipment and ornaments from the bride's family.

In past, Nolia marriages took place within the village between different Sahi's. But found that now-a-days few marriages are taking places with candidates from distant places like Puri, Bhubaneswar, Parikuda, Nayagarh, and Paradip etc.

Before marriage, the groom's side comes to visit the bride with a box and a new sari. The box is filled with all cosmetics. The women from groom side apply turmeric on the bride's face. Then the bride cleans and dresses herself well. The ritual starts with Mantras which is done by the Oriya Brahmin priest. They put vermillion on the forehead of the bride and promise to marry her with their son. This is called as the engagement ceremony and completion of engagement means that they have completed half the marriage already. The engagement function is done just two days or one month before the marriage.

After the priest has decided on the date of marriage and it has arrived, the bridegroom party consisting of men and women reach the temple in a procession. After doing the prescribed puja there, the procession proceeds to a neem tree, near Budhi Maa temple and the groom brings a branch of the tree on his shoulder to the house of the bride. He spreads those pieces of neem tree on the vedi (pandal). Seven married women in a procession accompanied by a drummer go to the Chilika to fetch water in seven pitchers to the house of the bride. With this water, the bride and groom take bath and they come to the pandal wearing new clothes.

The bride wears a white sari, while the groom wears a cotton dhoti. The marriage rituals are performed by the village priest (Brahmin). After the ends of the rituals, the groom ties Mangalasutra (a symbolic necklace signifying marriage) with three/seven knots around the neck of the bride. Then the bride and groom go into the bride's house and play a game, i.e. a golden ring is dipped inside a pot of turmeric water and they have to find it. The bride's side bears all the expenditure.

The bride and groom then come back to groom's house, where they are welcomed by groom's elder brother's wife otherwise known as bhauja. There they live in a room with a relative. But they are not allowed to talk with each other. The bride eats food that's leftover by her husband. All this continues till the eighth day of marriage. On the seventh day, they go to take the blessings of God Hari Sahadev. There the *bhauja* gives them colors to play among themselves and others. The newly married couple takes vegetarian food during this period. The newly wed bride also worships *Ishana* on the seventh day and gives food offerings. Then at night they consummate the marriage.

On the eighth day the couple does not take their meal together. They eat separately. On the ninth day both bride and groom go to the bride's house. The bride stays there and the groom returns home alone. On complction of fifteen days or one month the *Bhauja* comes along with lots of cakes, sweets, fruits etc., to take the newlywed bride to her in-laws home.

Even though child marriage is totally banned now, in Arakhakuda, some cases of child marriage and love marriages are seen in the village.

4

Religious Activities

Concept of Gods and Spirits

From time immemorial humans have significantly evolved both physically and intellectually throughout different civilizations. Hundreds of years have stood witness to man's change from being a caveman and imitating animal to becoming self sufficient, growing and inventing various things and even reaching the moon. But all of this has been possible because various scholars believe that along with their brain power, humans have been aided by the supernatural powers. Any religion rests on a particular set of beliefs and beliefs rest on supernatural entities. According to Wilhelm Schmidt, "Everything develops from simpler and cruder. He thought there is a stage, 'Mana' before animism in which the idea of lucky, the canny and uncanny was the sole constituent of what he called super natural." Andrew Lang said, "Supreme Being of primitive people at any rate in many cases is, no spirit at all, at least in our sense of divine spirit, God is spirit and those who worship him must worship him in spirit and truth."

Supernatural being is mainly classified into two forms – that of non-human origin and human origin. Those of non-human origin are Gods or deities and those of human origin are ghosts and ancestral spirits. Both the forms are represented in anthropomorphic forms. The former category of super natural entities is known as Gods or Goddesses and the later is known as spirits (Oliver 1981, p. 391).

Gods

According to mythology, beliefs, myths, dogmas and legends were the creator of the concept of 'God' not merely as a means of winning their favor but because God represents the subjective pole and is believed to possess the highest meaning and value in the total experience. God is very closely associated with people. The ontological argument by Kant goes to say that god is the sum of all positive attributes and as existence is a positive attribute or there are positive affirmations of existence, therefore god exists. The supernatural beings tend to be removing in several cases. They usually live fairly far away in sky, mountain, air, river, forest which are called as remote. Howell divides gods as creator gods, culture bringers, and departmental deities. A creator god is one who created the world and everything in it. A culture bringer god is one who is responsible for introducing crucial elements of culture. That is, it first gives the idea of state and agriculture. A departmental deity is one, who is in charge of a specific area of activity such as whether to believe in single god or in many gods or polymorphism. So, it is said by philosophers that god is omnipresent, omnipotent and omniscient. His power of omnipotence is reflected in various super natural entities. Faith in these supernatural entities brings various customs and traditions intoa society which later on, is defined as religion (Oliver, 1981: 353-55).

Deities

According to Freud, God is idealized and compared to father. Like the role and place of a father of a family varies with the type of society, the conception of deities too varies exactly the same way.

Spirits

Spirits are less remote than gods and more approachable. According to Maxmuller, after the death of man the body becomes soul. The soul then transfers to spirit which is very important, which may be malevolent and benevolent. Tylor also said dreams give birth to soul and soul is essential for existence of spirit and in later stages of culture becomes that of god. So, the world of spirit is the mental world. Spirit is an immemorial symbol of Mana. Spirits are either deities, who never materialize or are ghosts i.e. souls of the dead. A spirit has a set of values and those values attributed to the spirit are by the group comprising its own value system. Consequently, the group's value system is reinforced by making them inherent in the universe itself rather than a relative matter peculiar to the group. The most common form of worship is intimate conversation with a spirit, which is believed by most of the people (Freud in E.E. Evans Pritchard, 1965: 10-11).

The Nolias are mainly devotees of the goddesses. In ancient times they kept themselves restricted to their culture. But now they are being influenced by Odisha's culture, myths, beliefs and practices. The Nolia village is divided into two Sahis and some sub-Sahis i.e.– Laxmi Narayan Sahi and another is Bhagabat Sahi. In Laxminarayan Sahi, the people are more influenced by Odisha culture and festivals, where as Bhagabat Sahi people are more attached to the Telugu culture. Numbers of flags (*bansas*) are found in the village each having different Ista devata to whom they worship.

The different types of deities of Nolia community are described below:

Masani Chandi – An idol of goddess Chandi has been placed by priest (Pujari*)* Sanatan Behera. Goddess Masani Chandi is present at the outskirts of the village. One night goddess came into his dream and told him to worship her. After that the Devi is being worshipped by all Nolias.

Masani Chandi Puja was known by two flags *(bansa)* – (a) *Gandigula* and (b) *Gandigula.*

In Nolia community, only male persons are allowed inside the temples of female deities. They do not allow their village priest to do the rituals. Masani Chandi is worshiped by their own caste people. On a special Sunday, goddess visited the priest (*pujari*) in his dream and told him to worship her. Then Nolias arranged the worship of Masani Chandi. They put a pot filled with rice on a lotus stick. After that they prepared necklaces of *Arakha flower* and put it on the pot. The *pujari* was not given any remuneration.

The role of the ladies is also important in deity worship. They help the male members in various arrangements. On the day of worship, the males wear different colorful saris. They bath with turmeric paste, put vermillion and dress themselves as females. Male members are also equally purified before doing any arrangement. They are so much devoted to the worship that they feel as if the Masani Chandi's spirit is entrenched in them. They offer goat and cock as offering to the goddess and dig a hole and bury the heads of the offerings. They believe that Maa has taken away the head and bring back the remainder meat. Then a grand feast is arranged for all villagers. The Nolias admire Masani Chandi a lot and believe that worshipping her will ensure good health for them, their children and a safe fishing trip with good catch.

Thakurani Jatra

Gram Devati (Basantee Budimaa) Puja

Budi Maa, who is otherwise called as Thakurani Devi or Gram devati, is placed under a Neem tree and is signified with a stone marked with vermillion. Initially, before roughly 200 years, she was placed under the tree but now the Nolias have transferred her into a temple. Thakurani Devi is their main deity and Nolias admire her a lot. They worship Basantee to get rid of various diseases occurring during the month of Phalguna and Chaitra.

It all started when The *Kalisi* of the village told the villagers that Budimaa's brother Patharas came in dream. Subsequently following his orders, a meeting was arranged and the villagers collected money from each member of every household to perform a Puja. This Puja takes place once in every 3-4 years. It starts on Thursday, with the preparation of a "*panahandi*" in the presence of people from both sahis. On a special Saturday they first prepare a "*Naga Medha*" and then beat the drum and talwar. The Idol of Budimaa is taken from the *gram devati* temple into the village in a grand procession and she visits every house in the village. The Kalisi's wife holds *diya, Jhuna, and pana* on her head and offers them to Maa. The goddess is also called "*Shagadithakurani*". The Nolias prepare a wheel cart and the thakurani (goddess) is placed in the special cart and is taken into the village for a "*parikrama*". An umbrella is made from flowers to provide shade for the Goddess. Every family prepares a special type of *Kichidi* called as "*Mansika Khichdi*" to offer to Maa. Along with this they also offer banana, different types of fruits and beer. The Puja starts at 4 or 5 a.m in the morning. Everyone holds a stick called "Sun Badi". On that day all the Nolias drink a lot. Then they go around with the cart carrying the goddess and beat on the roof of every house in the village.They believe that by doing this, all types of ghosts or evil spirits and diseases like measles, chicken pox, diarrhea etc. will vanish. The cart is handled by the Kalisi. The Nolias do not chant any mantras on that day. Entire village is busy in Puja preparation. Fishing and all other activities are restricted. In the Sahi, they prepare two angles called as "*Sulia pada*". Here, they leave the prasad which was offered by the villagers and sacrifice a goat. All these are later taken away by the *Harijan* people. On Sunday evening the goddess takes rest in the cart at Kalisi's house. After that all the "*parswa devata*" come and join her in the festivities. Then she goes to Sana Maa temple for a visit. Goddess Harichandi, goddess Seven Sister, goddess Hinguli, goddess Ganga Devi, goddess Baidhar seven sisters, Makhat Palama and Nalma are the other goddesses with Basantee Thakurani. They each have their personal Kalisis and rituals. The procession for the goddess is done by all the villagers, male, female and children.

Nolia believe that the deities are two sisters Kali and Gori Basantee and one brother. The Sagadi Devi went to her seven sisters and stayed inside the forest. The girls are also allowed to go with the goddess. Then they bring the terracotta elephant horse and place them inside the temple.

People of a certain lineage like Baseighara in Laxminarayan Sahi and Gandigula in Bhagabat Sahi are allowed to do the worship. All others only participate in the fairs. They allow no evidence of the worship because they believe that whoever tries to take photo of the festival; goddess will kill him/her.

In this puja they sacrifice pig and goat to *Maa*. They celebrate the puja for nine days at home. But in the village, it lasts for fourteen days. A grand fair is arranged in the village. All the families and relatives are happy and busy in doing worship. The Kalisi plays a dominant role in this worship and is given some emoluments by their committee. They paid Rs. 22,000/- to Kalisi in the previous year. At the time of worship Kalisi recites her worship to goddess in Telugu and prays before her to save them from storms and other types of natural hazards.

The Laxminarayan Sahi has Budimaa temple and Bhagabat Sahi has Sana Maa temple. But each Sahi has a different celebration called *fair (jatra)*. First, the Budimaa *Jatra* occurs; in that case the concerned Sahi has made all the expenditures (financially and otherwise) where as Bhagabat Sahi people simply participate. Only after 15-20 days Sana Maa puja occurs, in which the case is reversed. In both cases seven sisters are worshipped.

Bali Hari Chandi/Banteswari

The Nolia people worship Bali Hari Chandi Devi for fishing. On Thursday they burn fish and break coconut. Then the Nolia people go into the sea or Chilika Lake for fishing. At that time, they pray to Maa Banteswari for protection.

When the boat goes to "Simabai", Maa helps them from bad weather and other hazards. In Hari Chandi Sahi, they worship a symbol of Harichandi in a temple. They worship her at the time of Dussehera. Those who have done ***Manasika*** for good catch, to save their life, for good health, offer a special puja and sacrifice goat or cock etc. to Maa Harachandi for granting their *Manasika.*

Story - The people of the area told me the story how goddess Hari Chandi came to be. There was once an old man named Arkat in Andhra Pradesh. He was a very simple man who was staunch devotee of gods and goddesses. One night he saw a goddess in his dream, who told him to take her to Arakhakuda village of Brahmagiri. The oldman took the idol and started towards the village. But on the way to village the Gada king did not allow him to take the idol and asked to give it to him, on that very night goddess came into the king's dream and told 'I cannot stay here, I have to go there'. Next morning immediately the king gave the idol to Arakat and apologized for his deeds. Arkat took the idol and placed it in a temple and called it as Hara Chandi temple.

Simanchal Puja

There is a place Simanchal in Andhra Pradesh. In the month of Baisakha they observe this worship called Simanchal Puja. Only people of lineage Kouimlu, Sidabelu, Sikbelu and Amabelu and Behera belu flags have done the puja.

Nolia went to Simanchal at the time of Chandana fair. Some (four to five) elder persons of Nolia family went there and stayed at Simanchal. There, they fasted and shaved their heads. Then they came back to village and brought a garland from Simanchal. The elderly people enter the village while singing their Telugu songs. The people then put a stick on one of the returnees Nolia's shoulders in which they hang the garland. One of them holds the photo of Simanchal and goes around the village. They called the god as "*Dasul*". The women of their family put water on the elderly persons' feet. In front of the villagers, "*pala and kirtan*" are arranged to encourage them and all go around the entire village. Then the people come and place the god in their Gadighara and arrange a combined feast with all the members of Kourulu, Sidabelu, Sikibelu, Amabelu, Behera belu lineage people. Only these flags people observe this puja.

Ganga Devi

The Ganga Devi is placed at the outskirt of village under a tree. Behera Galu, Goura, and Kesari lineage people worship her. The symbol of goddess is marked by a large stone with a vermillion mark on it and is covered with a black colored cloth. Besides it, they put red and yellow color flags hung by sticks. People from Simanchal also come here and stay for "*Adhia*" by putting up in temporary tent houses.

Ganga Devi is worshiped by both Telugu and Oriya speaking Nolias, primarily in connection with fishing rituals. She protects the people while fishing at sea and blesses them with good catches. In the month of March and April, a festival is also observed. On this day, the Nolias sacrifice goats and chicken to Ganga Maa to get her blessings. At the beginning of worship, nets are stacked in front of her shrine by different families. After the sacrifice of animals, their blood is sprinkled on the nets. Fisher women offer clothes to the deity. The people take flowers, coconut, bananas, wine, vermillion, sandal wood, clarified butter, diya and offer these to the waterbody in the name of Ganga Maa. In any difficult situation or before going for fishing, the people first take the name of Ganga Maa for a safe trip and good catch.

Harisahadev Temple

The deity was worshiped by Loknath pujari. But now his son Nurrottam Pujari worships the god. They are "*Mali*" by caste.

It is a temple of Lord Siva. Every Monday, all the villagers go there to worship the deity. The people believe that the god is an avatar of Sahadev of *Panchupandab*. All other pandabs are there in the nearby the villages as different deities at different temples.

Laxmi Narayan Temple

This temple is located in the Laxmi-Narayan Sahi. Laxmi-Narayan idol is placed in the temple. Priest Narayan Dash has been given the charge of the temple. Every morning he takes bath to purify himself and then arrives at the temple to wash it. He bathes the deity and gives sandal paste and vermillion along with flower and also drapes clean clothes over the god. Then the priest offers fruits or sugar cubes to god. The priest and his wife cook rice (*Anna*) for god. Then in afternoon the priest offers rice (*Anna*) to god. In the night the god is given some liyaas pasad. For these everyday rituals, the priest is given annual emoluments. The temple is situated in the North-east direction.

Fig.1: Priest of Laxminarayan Temple

Bhagabat Temple

The Lord Bhagabat is placed in a temple in Bhagabat Sahi. The priest Simanchal Panda does all the rituals of god. Starting from bathing the god, he also offers prasad to the god thrice every day. He is also given some emoluments. This temple is situated in the north-east direction.

Ishana Puja

The Nolia people called their deity room as *gadighara*. They have placed a mound at the corner of their *pujaghar* which is worshiped as Ishana devata. After the death of a person, they bring the ashes from graveyard and place it inside the *gadighar* which they worship.

Ishana Puja is a family worship. So, it is done by either a male or a female member, whoever is the head of family. All Nolias do not do the worship. Only Karulu, gandigaralu, biseighara, Pokalu, maibelli, Sor Belli, Ogellu, Gouraghara, Kesarighara clan people worship this god.

When a new bride come to their family, they first wash the house with cow dung solution, and worship Ishana bycooking food and offering the same near Ishana in their ancestor's name; vermillion, incense stick and only white flowers are given while worshiping Ishana Devata. Then, the new bride starts her new life. The Ishana God is worshipped in every festival.

Annual Cycle of Festivals

In the definition of religion, it says that religion is also belief in supernatural beings. However, each society or group of people have their own traditional methods for controlling these powers or sub-ordinating them through certain actions of occultism or esoteric practices, rites, and ceremonies or celebrations of accompaniment with offerings, prayers or sacrifices. So it is meant with offerings, prayers or sacrifices. So it is to appease, placate or propitiate in order to enjoy a trouble free life, rituals, procedures etc. through cult or systematized celebrated rituals or manifestations with the passage of time, these are handled down from generation to generation and are entrenched into thickly woven fabric of culture (Tylor, 1874: 425-447).

Rituals and festivals are closely related. Festival is an organized series of special events and performances or any occasion for celebration. Annual cycle of rituals means various ritual activities during various festivals and various puja through out the year. In India festivals do not just offer a temporary reprieve from their daily grind. The day on which a particular festival is celebrated has a special astrological significance and certain observances on these days yield manifold. benefits.

Table-1 : Festivals Observed by Nolia

Month of Observation	Name of Festivals	Worshiping Deities	Purpose of Worship
Baisakha (April-May)	Baseli puja	Horse headed deity	For wellbeing of their community
Jyestha (May-June)	Thakurani Jatra	Gram devati	To free them from all types of diseases and give success during fishing
Ashada (June-July)	Ratha Jatra, Raja	Jagannath, Kalijai, Baliharichandi	To achieve success in fishing and for good health
Srabana (July-August)	Gahma Purnima	Balabhadra	For success in fishing
Bhadraba (August-September)	Ganesh Chaturthi, Bhaga-batbasudevjanmadina	Ganesh, Vishnu	Before doing any new work they worship Ganesh
Aswina (September-October)	Dussehra, Gajalaxmi	Durga Devi, Laxmi Devi	For good catch and success in fishing
Kartika (October-November)	Kartika Purnima	Lord Siva (Sahadev)	For safe and smooth fishing life

Margasira (November-December)	Sudasabrata, Bali Jatra	Laxmi	For more wealth and happiness in the family
Pausa (December-January)	Pausa Puja	Surya Narayan	Un-married girls worship to get a suitable life partner
Magha (January-February)	Makar Sankranti, Saraswati Puja, Maghabisi	Gangamaa,Vishnu, Saraswati, Abhiram Baba	The people believe that by doing Magha Bisi they are free from all disease and also pray for good health for their family members
Phaguna (February-March)	Holi	Sahadev, Garima, Alsati, Erama	They pray for a good catch and to save their life from all kinds of evil spirit
Chaitra (March-April)	Taratarini mela, Chaitra Tuesday, Palla	Brahma,Vishnu, Maheswar, Radha and Krishna	To free all villagers from all types of disease and to have a prosperous life

As the Arakhakuda people belong to fishermen communities, so most of the festivals observed by them are related to fishing. Besides these various Hindu festivals are also observed by them.

Festivals Observed by Nolia

Different Types of Festivals

The festivals observed by them are categorized into two parts, one is festivals celebrated in family/house level and another is at village level.

Family Level

Bhogi is celebrated by the fishermen, when the people dispose all the old things and do house cleaning. On the day of the festival, worship is performed to invite the spirits of the ancestors to take the food prepared by the family, so that they may bless the offsprings and ensure the welfare of all the family members.

Makar Sankranti is the first day of the month of Magha. It falls on 13th or 14th of January. It is the day on which the Sun starts its northern course. It is celebrated in most parts of Odisha.

The Nolia people also celebrate it. Preparation for festival starts much earlier. All the villagers clean their houses. Those who are financially sound; they bring new clothes for their family members. Different types of cake and sweets are cooked in the households. Nolias mainly prefer vegetarian foods is Makar Sankranti.

The speciality of this festival is *'Makar Chaula'*, a variety of offering which is prepared with raw rice, coconut, cheese, honey and milk etc. This *prasad* is offered to the Laxmi Narayan God and Sahadev God by different Sahi people. It is a family level festival. Different families start the worship in time suitable to them. But usually this worship is done early in the morning and people on this auspicious occasion go to Konark Sun Temple to take the blessings of Sun god.

After this day, the movement of Sun started changing. The days become lengthy and warmer. So, the people worship him as a great benefactor. The cooked food (rice) is kept at *gadhighuru* (their goddess room). They buy a goat before one or two months, feed it well and sacrifice it during the festival. While the sacrifice of the goat and chicken take place at the altar of Gangamaa, cooked food is also offered at a special altar. On the first day of the celebration they prepared a pot of new rice cooked with jaggery. This worship is conducted by burning camphor. In addition to the worship of ancestors, another Puja is conducted for Gangamma at the seashore, where all the fishing equipments are kept near the shrine and goats or chicken are sacrificed. Then the blood of sacrificed aniaml is sprinkled on the nets.

Sudasha Brata

This festival is observed by the women in Odisha. It is observed in all communities. It is done on a Thursday, when *Dasami and Suklapaksha* have all combined.

Each Nolia family does the worship with the hope of well being of their family members. On this day they first take bath with a little turmeric, gather different varieties of flowers and make ten cakes (*mandapithas*). All these are offered on a banana leaf along with a thread to Laxmi Devi on a stool (*Pidha*). Then they make ten knots on the thread (brata), tie it in their right arm and utter the Laxmi *mantra*.

They clean their houses with cowdung solution. All the utensils of the houses are washed. Then after purifying themselves, they use rice powder solution to do art (Jhoti) and Laxmi's feet in the front of the house and also in pujaghar. Symbol of Laxmi is placed on a "*Pidha*" or desk and is purified with Gangawater and decorated with "*Jhoti*". The women observe this worship with their own family members and this is done only by married women. Normally Nolia females are not allowed to do worship in their community rituals.

Besides Sudasha Brata, they also do the Hindu's manabasa festivals in which a symbol of Laxmi Devi is worshipped on Thursdays. They pray to goddess for more wealth and prosperity for their household.

Raja Festival

Though Nolias usually follow their traditional rituals, they also observe different Oriya festivals; as they are living among Odias. Raja falls on the month of *Asadha* (June-July) during the rainy season. It is celebrated for three days and is a family level festival. But some families observe it combindly.

First day of the Raja festival is called Pahili Raja. The second day is observed as the main day of Raja (or Raja Sankranti) and the third day is called as Basi Raja. It is a festival for unmarried girls. Girls are prohibited from all kinds of manual work during these days. Some activities that they are not allowed to do are – cut vegetables and earth, comb hair, sweep houses, walk with bare foot etc. However financially weak a household might be, on these three days, the girls are given beautiful new dresses, lipstick, bindi and varieties of bangles to adorn.

They also prepare a swing called as "Raja doli" with the help of their brothers and male friends. In each Sahi, two to three sub-Sahis together hang the swing or *jhula*. They decorate the swing with flower. Gatherings are seen at different swing and the girls have a lot of fun playing and taking turns on the swing. On the first and second day of Raja, they avoid taking meat and fish. Different types of cakes and delicious dishes are prepared in each house. On the third day, they prepare non vegetarian items and offer goat, pig, and cock to Hara Chandi Maa in Hara Chandi Sahi. Relatives of each family come from different villages to visit. Nolia girls also go to their uncle or relative's house during Raja.

The males of the village engage in normal activities during Raja and rest only on the second dayor the main Raja. On other days they go for fishing. During Raja, all the Nolias go to the Kali Jai temple. They worship the Goddess and to get her blessings, the men sacrifice goat, pig and cock at her altar. The Nolias individually offer "Kala Mali, Kala Saree and Kala

Kancha" to Bali Hari Chandi for their success in fishing and good health. A grand fair is also arranged there. All the people go to Hari Chandi temple in between Raja for taking the blessing of goddess.

Magha Bisi

The festival is celebrated in the month of Magha (January-February) in the name of Lord Sun and is also called as "Magha Saptami". It is observed on the seventh day of darker fortnight *(Sukla-pakshya)*.

The Nolias go to the *Abhiram Baba Mattha* in Karmala. There they wake up at 3 o'clock in morning and brush using sticks (no paste or brush) and take bath without using any oil or soap. In food items, they do not take black brinjal and cabbage. After staying there for one day they come back home. Then they go to Konark's Chandrabhaga Sea. Only husband and wife go to Karmala and they do not take children because the place is always crowded. Then on the day of Magha Saptami they take holy dip with millions of other devotees. They believe that bathing in the sea will cure all the diseases of their family members and purify their bodies.

During this month they fast for three days and take light food only at night for a month. They prefer vegetable foods. Then they arrange an *Astaprahari Kirtan* in which everyone is present. On the third day, they give a feast to their friends and relatives. They go round the village, play color and after full moon they take non vegetarian foods.

The people told that those have taken *Dikhya* of *Abhiram Baba* and have visited the Mattha; they can arrange *Astapraharijagyan* in which congregation of all villagers occurs. But those who have not taken *Dikhya* can go to the Chandrabhaga sea for holy dip.

Pausa Puja

In the month of *Pausa* (December-January) the Nolias offer a special type of *puja* to "Surya Narayan". It is done only on Sunday. Only the unmarried Nolia can do the puja. They offer coconut, banana, milk and liya to Surya Narayan god.

They first decide the auspicious Sunday on which the worship will occur, then on that day a girl takes bath early in morning, wears clean clothes and gathers ingredients required for the puja. They take a bell pot filled with water; put turmeric, bermunda grass andraw rice in the water. Then put it on a stool (*pidha* – which is purified with Ganga water). After that they light the incense sticks and diya; put the offerings on a banana leaf and offereverything to their god. This is a family-level festival.

Kartika Purnima

This is otherwise called as Panchuka Purnima. It is celebrated in the month of Kartika (November-December). All the family members of a Nolia household observe this festival. They practice giving up non vegetarian food such as fish, meat and egg during the entire month of *Kartik*. But some Nolias observe this only for the five days which is called as Panchuka. On Kartika Purnima; they float paper boats with *diya* in Chilika. They also sing a song at that time. They believe that if the boat floats in water freely, then their life will also be smooth, their own boat and fishing trips will also be safe. Men, women and children participate in this boat floating event. Most of the Nolia people fast throughout the month and on Kartika Purnima go to the Sahadev temple to get a glimpse of the God and float their boats in the temple periphery. Purnananda Mattha arranges a grand feast and *Kirtan*. Those who have taken *Dikhya* of the *Mattha* perform *Kirtan* inside the mattha periphery. In Sahadev temple, the people also arrange a feast on that day. It is a family level festival but they observe it as a community.

Village Level

Ganesh Chaturthi

Ganesh Chaturrthi is celebrated in the month of Bhadraba. Ganesh, the son of Shiva is regarded and revered as the symbol of intelligence. He can remove all obstacles. Before beginning any every new project, Ganesh is worshiped. In Hindu society, Ganesh puja carries a lot of importance.

As the Nolias have adhered to the Hindu culture, they also worshiped Ganesh. The puja is celebrated at both village and family level. Those families, whose children are students, perform the puja at house. The worship is also performed in schools. All the young boys of the village do the puja inside the Kothaghara.

The village is mainly divided into three Sahis. Each Sahi has a different "*Kothaghara*". In this Kothaghara Ganesh puja is performed. Laxmi Narayan Sahi, Majhi Sahi and Bhagat Sahi have three different pujas.

Baseli Puja: (Gram Devati, Budimaa) (Gadighara)

It is otherwise known as Chaiti Ghoda puja. The festival is celebrated in the beginning of month of Chaitra (March) and ending with Baisakh Purnima (April). In Baseli puja the horse headed deity of the community is propitiated. She is considered to be the titular deity of the community.

It is believed that this festival originated during 10-11th centuries when Hindu and Buddha tantra merged into one. Baseli is one of various deities of tantara culture that evolved during this period. The horse is seated in an earthen platform. She wears a blood red cloth in her full feminine form. In their village, the Gramdevati is worshiped on Saturdays and Tuesdays throughout the year.

The Nolia people on this day worship a Bamboo. They put on it some vermillion, lighten *diya* and *agarbatti*. Then the bamboo is split ceremonially into pieces out of which only twelve are taken for preparation of the frame for the dummy horse. The frame is dyed red with red clay and then covered with a *Pata* saree. Then a painted horse head made out of wood is fixed to the frame. A garland of hibicus flowers is placed on the neck during worship, because female goddess loves red flowers. The dummy horse is worshiped till the eighth day of the dark fortnight after which it is taken out for a dance ceremony. A man enters the cavity and hangs the frame on one of his shoulders and then dances to the rhythm of a drum. *Mahuri* is also played during the dance. Songs are also sung by villagers with a lot of devotion. When the dancer falls into a trance, another person replaces him. "Chaudhua-Chadhuani" or Rauta-Rautani also sing and dance.

The male character dances with a long staff in his hand symbolizing the profession of fishermen's rowing boats. The female character is also played by a male. Both sing songs which last for one whole night. During this dance the dummy horse is ceremonially placed in the centre with people sitting all around it and the performance is held in front of the horse basically in the centre.

When the festival ends, the horse-head is taken out ceremonially from the frame and preserved in the Gadighara. Next year the head is again utilised. One informant named Laxman (29) told that there are three types of Bansa – Gairaghar, Bileigal and Giringa. These three have performed the horse dance (one by one) year after year. The elder person of family has played the key role. Subsequently with advice from their goddess they have performed the puja.

Durga Puja

Durga puja is celebrated in the month of Aswina (September-October) with great pomp and show in Odisha. The goddess sitting on a lion is shown killing the "Buffalo Demon" – Mahishasura accompanied with her two sons, Lord Ganesh and Kartikeya and two daughters goddesses Laxmi and Saraswati. The idol presents a picture of power.

The Arakhakuda people also celebrate the puja for ten days. The two different Sahis have different puja in their "Kothaghara". Majhi Sahi and Laxmi Narayan Sahi are doing the puja together. Bhagbat Sahi with other sub-Sahis are also doing the puja together. All their houses are cleaned and worshipped. If anybody has constructed a new house, they also worship the new house on Dussehra.

They bring the idol from Bentapur (a village) and place it in a decorated Kothaghara. The two different Sahis have different priests. Laxmi Narayan Sahi's priest Narayan Dash does their puja. Simanchal Panda the priest of Bhagbat Sahi does the puja with all rituals and mantras.

The puja starts on Mahalaya, followed by Sasti till Dashami. During Sasti, Saptami, Astami and Navami all the female members and girls take bath in the early morning, wear new clothes, bring different varieties of flowers and fruits and come to worship "Maa Durga". Some male members come and do puja on the seventh day or Saptami of Dussehra, and then they go for fishing. They start fishing only after worshipping the Goddess. They believe that after Durga Puja with goddess's blessings they will have success in fishing. On the day of Dashami the goddess is immersed in the water.

In Laxmi Narayan Sahi the puja (Sanabhai) starts from Saptami whereas in Bhagabat Sahi the puja starts from Sasti. They do not take non vegetarian foods and sacrifice any animal.

Viswakarma Puja - (Chaitra Tuesday)

The lord Viswakarma is the deity of Architecture. He is worshiped in every factory, company and other commercial establishments. A few Nolia families worship him. At first they clean their boat, net, knitting instrument and iron implements. Then the female household members bring fruits and flowers and make arrangements for worship. Prior to all these rituals, both male and female members have taken bath early in the morning in order to be purified. Each family's eldest member does this puja for his family. (On that day they do not go fishing and all the equipments are kept in one place). On a special Tuesday in the month Chaitra, the Nolias restrict their fishing activities and worship their boat, machine, net, etc.

Deepavali

Deepavali is celebrated after Lakshmi puja, in the month of Kartika (October-November). This festival is celebrated throughout Orissa and the Arakhakuda people celebrate it too.

Prior to Diwali, everyone engaged in cleaning their house. On the day of Diwali, they take bath early in the morning and worship and offer their regards to goddess Kali. Then they prepare various food items and cakes. In the evening they decorate their houses with candles and earthen lamps. Bursting fire crackers is a given on this festival. Male Nolia members drink excessively in the evening.

Laxmi Puja

This puja is celebrated on the full moon day of Ashwin or Kumar Purnima and continues for one week. The idol of goddess Laxmi sitting on a Lotus is decorated very beautifully and is kept in a stage. As there are two separate Kothagharas of Laxmi Narayan Sahi and Bhagabat Sahi, the villagers arrange two pandals. On this day, the females take bath, wear new *saris* and dresses. Greetings are exchanged among friends and relatives. The Purohit takes a lot of flowers, diya, agarbatti and fruits for the puja and all the villagers are present in the puja in their respective Sahi.

The married women of the village first perform puja at their house and only after that they take food which consists of fruits, vegetable and rice. In the evening the village is lighted with different types of lights, decoration and people sing various songs in honor of goddess Laxmi.

Dola Purnima

It is another communal festival. Nolias observe it for three days. It is observed in the month of Phalguna (February-March). Their deity 'Sahadev' of Shiva temple comes in a "*Palinqui*". Different types of flowers, sandal paste are put on him and his idol is decorated. Then the priest takes him and goes around the village. All the Nolia people first purify themselves and then as the diety moves from door to door, the female members offer different types of fruits like, coconut, banana, jiggery, apple etc. to the lord. The people are in a very festive mood. The God is taken in a grand procession along with his other "*Parswa devatas*". They call this ceremony as "*Diyobhogokhia*". All traditional rituals are arranged as per their customs to satisfy the deity. *Pala* and *Kirtan* are also arranged for added merriments. After that they observe holi for three days. The temple priest charged Rs.10,000/- for the Sahadev deity's *village parikrama* from villagers.

On first and second day - They take non vegetarian foods and play *Phagu*. All the friends and relatives are invited and served lots of various dishes. They give new clothes and bangles to their married daughters.

On the third day - The people prepare various types of food and eat them. They play with coloured powder and water. Everyone in the village plays among their age group members and the male members indulge in excessive drinking.

On Dola Purnima, they visit the grave yard to offer new clothes, liya, fruits, coconut and money to their ancestors' spirits to satisfy them. They offer cock to Garima, Arama and Alsati only and pray for a good catch, secure life and protection from evil spirits. Along with the goddess they offered cock, goat to Budhimaa and Masani Chandi. Dola Purnima is the most important festival for them.

Nolia Festivals

Satyanarayan Palla

Fourteen Palla: (Chauda Palla)

The Nolia people observe this Palla annually. They call it fourteen Palla which continues for seven days. The two Sahis of Arakhakuda villages (Laxminarayan Sahi and Bhagbat Sahi) have performed two Pallas in a year. Before one month of the commencement of Palla, both Sahis arrange separate meetings in their temple.

First the committee members of Laxmi Narayan Sahi arrange a meeting. At the meeting, they collect money for arranging communal festivals observe throughout the year. They also discuss about the palla and its preparations. The Nolias arrange the Palla in the month of Phalguna on the day of Saptami.

Early morning, the priest Narayan Dash of Laxmi Narayan Sahi worshipped Vishnu and Laxmi at the Laxmi Narayan temple. Then they arranged the Palla singer from outside the village. Throughout the day and night the Palla singer sang sixteen songs. Both male, female, boys and girls were present to see the Palla. Each family offered lot of fruits and flowers to the Lord Satyanarayan for fulfillment of their wishes and wellbeing of their family. On the special occasion, they prepared a special Prasad called "*sirini*". It is prepared from milk, sugar, clarified butter, jiggery, rice powder and black pepper powder. On this occasion after doing some household works, everyone gathered at the temple. They mainly took vegetable and rice. Nobody went for fishing or indulged in any fishing activities.

In Palla, the Palla-singers dance and sing, when two people get tired, they rest and two other people started. It occurs in rotation. In Bhagabat Sahi, this Palla takes place on the day of Sriram Navami, in their Bhagabat temple. Their priest Simanchal Panda comes early in the morning and cleans the Bhagabat temple and the idol. He decorates the idol with new clothes and flowers on Sriram Navami.

Bhagabat Basudev Janamdina/Janamastami

This is otherwise called as Janamastami. The birth date of Lord Krishna is celebrated as Janamastami. This immensely popular festival is observed on eighth day of dark half (Krishna Pakhya) of Bhadrab (August-September) month.

The people of both Sahis observe the festival in their respective temples. Early in the morning, both the priests (Narayan Dash, Simanchal Panda) bath Krishna with camphor and sandal paste at their Sahi's temple. Then they give flowers and new clothes to Krishna, light diya and incense sticks in front of him. On this day they are arranged a Palla. The dramatic enactment of the life Krishna is the special feature of Janamastami. The villagers have their own people who are Palla singers. The puja is done by the Brahmin priest of their village. The Nolia people come to temple early in morning to offer puja and listen to the Palla in the night. A prasad called *Sirini* made out of banana, clarified butter, rice powder, milk and molasses is prepared by the Pujari and offered to all the villagers. They fast for whole day and after taking Prasad, Nolias break their fast. It is a village level festival.

Trinath Mela

In this worship the Nolias worship a photo of Brahma, Vishnu and Maheswar and Ganesh in Kothaghara. It is a village level festival. Nolia people observe twice in every month on the day of ekadasi. The Laxmi Narayan Sahi people observe Ekadasi in their Kothoghara, whereas Bhagabat Sahi people observed another ekadasi of the same month. Also people who have done "mansika" can do the *mela* but only in *Sankranti and Purnima.*

The village priest does the puja. On Trinath mela, early morning, both Sahi people make arrangement for the puja. The priest places the God and sprinkles water on the deity to purify the idol and offers different types of fruits and flowers. Red flowers are not given to the god. Then they arrange *Palla and Kirtan* which continues throughout the day and night.

Rituals

Along with all these festivals, the Nolia people observe some rituals which are specially related to their fishing. Before using a new boat they consult the priest of their Sahi and show their horoscope, whatever is forecasted by the priest after consultation of the horoscope is decided as final. The puja is done on an auspicious day and only by that person of the household whose horoscope is favourable. After purchasing of a new boat, as per their ritual, seven married women of seven families come with seven vessels and fill them with water. Then they take the vessels of water and pour it on the boat, put raw rice on its "manga", mark vermillion and turmeric on it and do *huluhuli* seven times. Then the new boat is operated.

During earlier times, if they did not have sufficient amount of catch then the female members of their village tied a rope on a stone and brought it to village main road. They prayed to their goddess and the sounds of prayer imitated a crying sound. But this practice ended in the year 2000.

Ritual Friendship: (Mestam)

In Nolias, friendship is very predominantly observed as a ritual. There are different types of friendships namely– Makara, Sangata, Phula, Baula etc. and these friendships occur between same age and gender groups. A boy cannot be the ritual friend of a girl.

Boy ⟶ boy (Makara, Sangata)

Girl ⟶ Girl (Phula, Baula)

Makara

Case Study-3

Name: Harihar Behera, Aged: 45, Sex: Male, Sahi: Laxminarayan

Harihar Behera (45) has friendship (makara) with his name sake Harihara. Harihar's son Bipin has done friendship with his father's friend's (makar's) son Atala. After being someone's Makara, they only called them as Makara and not by their given family name. On the day of Makara Sankranti the two friends eat "*Makara chawal*" together in the presence of their parents and exchange new dresses etc. It is not necessary to have only familial friendships; one can be Makara of anybody.

Sangata

The Nolia people make Sangata in a ceremonial procedure. The people who want to make Sangata with their parents go to their Sahi's temple i.e. Laxmi Narayan Sahi people go to Laxmi Narayan temple and Bhagabat Sahi people go to Bhagabat temple.The priest of temple is also present there. They take the permission of priest, and then take coconut, banana, and vermillion with a new cloth, which is exchanged by worship in front of the god among them. Then the people arranged a "palla" and feast for Sangata family members.Telugu Nolia calls it as "Mestam". Phula and Baula are also made in the presence of the temple priest. The only difference is that it is created between girls.

The ritual friendship occurs only between the same age group people, when they maake the ritual friendship they have to follow some restrictions. Whenever Nolias observe any festival, firstthey are supposed to invite their ritual friends. The Nolias also invite them during marriages and death rituals. They do not quarrel with their friend. It is a kind of affectionate relationship through which their family bonding became strong. In Aarakhakuda village about 80 percent people have Makara, Sangata, Baula or Phula.

Magico-religious Functionaries

The Priest - (Pujari)

According to Max Weber the critical feature of priesthood is that specialization of a particular group of person in the continuous operation of a cultic enterprise, predominantly associated with particular norms, places and times of related to specific social group.

The priest is usually considered an expert who has direct access to super natural entities. The priest of Arakhakuda village is a Brahmin. Laxmi Narayan Sahi's priest is Narayan Dash (aged 40+) and the Bhagabat Sahi's priest is Syamanchal Panda (aged 55+). Laxmi Narayan Sahi's priest Balinkiswar Dash had given dowry to Syamanchal Panda to worship the god of Bhagabat Sahi. Now, in place of Laxmi Narayan Sahi, Balinkiswar priest's son is doing worship.

Each year all the Nolias arrange a meeting. Their village council fixes a sum of money which is given to each Sahi's priest by their Sahi. The priests of both Sahis do the worship of their temple with all rituals. In all the festivals of the Odia society oroccasions like pala, ekaisa, marriage, Nolia people invite their respective priests and pay their utmost respect to him. The priest worships Laxmi Narayan god, Bhagabat, Ganesh, Durga, Trinath, Laxmi, Palla puja etc. The people give requisite emoulments to the priest.

The Karisi: (Manari)

The Karisi is a person much revered by the Nolias. He warns the Nolias about their future and forecasts about any future mishaps. They believe that goddesses are transmigrating to him.The rituals specific to Noliasare done by Karisi. In Telugu they call Karisi as "Manari".

Fig.2: Shri Narayan Behera, Manari

They have played the role of Manari for fifteen years. This post is not hereditary. They took Dikhya from Babaji Behera of Majhi Sahi for this purpose. Kalisi is the mediator between their Nolia people and goddess. Goddess came to his dream and told about which puja should be performed by them. If any mishap occured in fishing or any types of disease or any problem affected to village, then the people visited Kalisi. The Kalisi's told Nolia people to obey him. For any worship Kalisi is given emoluments between Rs. 1,000-10,000.

Only male persons are eligible for Kalisi. He is a religious person and deeply devoted to their culture and tradition. If Nolia people face any trouble then they go to Manari. The Manari first cuts "Kothi". Then he puts rice on each "Kothi". After that he holds a stone bounded by a rope with his hand above the Kothi. Manari prays to goddess (Gram Devati) – to help him identify whether the events oroccurances were the doing of the goddess. If the stone moves in a straight direction when Manari shakes it, they believe that the Gram Devati was the reason behind the happenings and she wants some types of sacrifices like goat, cock, pig etc. Whatever goddess wants they offer her. If the stone does not move, it means goddess had nothing to do in it. In that case Manari is helpless and can not do anything. Whenever such cases happen, the 12 Manari is given emoluments starting from Rs. 50 to 100/-.

The Sorcerer (Gunia) -

In Arakhakuda village there are almost more than thirty sorcerers. The people of Bhagabat Sahi have a stronger Telugu based culture than Laxmi Narayan Sahi people and they believe more in sorcery or *Gunia.*

Some of the sorcerers are:

1) Banthura Behera
2) Tala Behera
3) Surendra Behera
4) Sameya Behera
5) Goreya Behera
6) Ashok Behera
7) Bidyadhar Behera (Now in mattha and has changed his surname to Dash)
8) Krishna Behera

9) Kameya Behera
10) Bima Behera
11) Sandha baba
12) Laxma Behera (He passed away)

Bidyadhar Behera is the head of all sorcerers. But now he is not practicing any more. This is not hierachal. The villagers fear and respect the sorcerer. The sorcerer has a *Mantra* called "*Chaulia Mantra*". If anybody has a beautiful girl, the sorcerer does *guni* and the girl starts to feel uneasy andvomits.Then her parents come to the sorcer and offer him Rs. 50 to 100 and their daughter is cured spontaneously. In the Nolia village, one sorcererharmsthemwhile another sorcerer cures them. Therefore, Nolias do not like sorcerers. When an evil spirit enters anybody, they go to the sorcerer's house. They first greet the sorcerer and then ask him what to do and what not to do.

Case Study-4

Name: Jadu Behera, Aged: 40, Sex: Male, Sahi: Harachandi Sahi

A person named Jadu Behera (40) had a son named Bulu who was catching fish in Chilika. There is some dispute related to fish catching. The other party took the help of sorcerer to harm Bulu and the gunia killed Bulu. The sorcerer's name was Banthua Behera. The Nolia people came to know the real fact. Jadu Behera went to the head of the village and told him everything. The villagers punished Banthua Behera by giving him horse urine, eagle urine and various nasty things to drink. This way the villagers formed an indirect control over the sorcerer, so that he could no longer harm the people with his knowledge but help them when required.

How a spirit goes away -

Those who want to do magic; they go to the Sorcerer (Gunia). The sorcerer goes to graveyard and does special puja and the boy or girl (usually unmarried) who is expected to be affected by the sorcerer cuts his/her hand and roams in the village naked. To cancel the sorcery, the relative of affected person goes to another gunia and he prays to goddess and promises to give more blood than the sorcerer who created the spell. Only then the spirit goes away. This used to happen in ancient times but the people started to beat the sorcerer and subsequently gave them "Mathamani" of their deities Syamakali and Jagannath and swore their allegiance not to harm anybody. The village council excused them after giving warnings.

Rituals:

Two types of rituals relating to their fishing are done by the Sorcerer:

1. When Nolias feel that they do not catch sufficient amount of fish they go to the sorcerer's house and tell their problem.The sorcerer takes them to the graveyard and ask them to bring banana. The sorcerer makes an image of man with this banana, hand, foot, nose all body parts are present in the banana. The sorcerer puts vermillion on its forehead, offers liya and some offerings like fruits to the banana man. Then he cuts all the parts of that banana man by blade and tells him to bind thatfish in the net. The people then come back from the graveyard and pray to have a good catch the next day.
2. Sometimes Nolias bring back special magical water given by the sorcerer and sprinkle it on the net while praying for success in fishing.

5

Economy of Fishing Community

Occupation

Primary Occupation:

The Odisha fisheries emerged as one of the most important components of the economy of the state with a coastline of 480 kilometres in length, vast swamp areas, numerous rivers and fresh water lakes. There is huge scope for brackish water, inland and marine fisheries in Odisha.

Freshwater fisheries in Odisha include 2,56,000 hectares of reservoirs, lakes and swamps 1,16,000 hectares of ponds and tanks and 1,55,000 hectares of canals and 1,80,000 hectares of rivers. Brackish or salt water fisheries in Odisha include 8,100 of back water region. The most significant produce of Odisha is prawn. Along with this various other species of fishes are also produced. There are near about 11,00,000 fishermen in the state. Among them the prominent fishing centers are in:

1) Balasore
2) Bhadrak
3) Puri
4) Ganjam
5) Kendrapada
6) Jagatsinghpur

The fishing sector has established a permanent relationship with nature. Fishing is done as a household enterprise undertaken in pursuit of a livelihood leading to a culturally conditioned way of life. Fisher folk have an understanding of coastal aquatic milieu and fishery resources available. The traditional ecological knowledge and skills have been passed from generation to generation.

Primary occupation of the people of the village Arakhakuda is fishing. 64.80 percent of male wage earners (except students) are primarily dependanton fishing activities. Some females (4.94 percent) are also engaged in fishing. 4.66 percent people are engaged in government or private jobs. They need avenues to get into various diverse activities for livelihood purposes.

Fishing is the most common mode of income generation. A division of labour is found in Arakhakuda village. The marine fishermen go for fishing early in the morning i.e. 3 A.M. and come back at 3 P.M. in the afternoon, whereas the Chilika fishermen go for fishing in evening, stay in the boat throughout the night and come back early in morning.

Secondary Occupation

My investigation reveals that traditionally Nolia people were fisherman. But now due to decline in the amount of catches, restrictions on marine fishing, usage of various advanced techniques, now fishermen are also engaged on other occupations. Fishing is banned from (15 May-15 June). During this period they adopt alternative sources of livelihood to sustain their families.

The people do not have any agricultural land. But some people of general caste (10 percent) who live outside the village own some land, so some Nolias work as labourers in the agricultural field. But majorities i.e., 40 percent of Nolias work as labourers in cashew cultivation.

Upon entering Arakhakuda village I saw both sides are surrounded by cashew tree and upon enquiry, learnt that a person named L.G. Narayan had initially bought a cashew field from a Christian organization and later sold it. Of that vast field, the villagers of Arakhakuda bought forty-five acres and the rest was taken by the government.

The present president of Arakhakuda village owns sixteen acres of the cashew field. Arjuna Behera, Bhima Behera and Judistira Behera own eight to ten acres of the field. Mostly women, some children and adult males worked as labourers in the field. They were given payment after cashews were sold. The cashew is stored at a godown near Sunamukhi Giral Chawk. The store solds cashews for Rs.80/- per kg where as in the local market it is sold for Rs.60/- per kg. Parties from outside (Kolkata) also came to purchase it.

One quintal – Rs.6, 000/-

One quintal – Rs.22, 000/- (local market rate)

But now the cashew is sold in tins and the price is fixed per tin. The daily labourers are paid Rs.105/- to Rs.150/- per day. But the rates vary between male and female labourers. Besides, that 20 percent people are doing jobs in schools, post office and local Anganwadi of the area. Along with this, some persons in Arakhakuda village are engaged in NGO activities. Other 30 percent people are (both men and women) engaged in business activities. There are three net shops; nine grocery shops; one medicine shop, three hotels (small), and three pan shops (gumuti). Ten percent people are not doing anything. Rest of the villagers are addicted to drinking and lie on the sides of the road or are seen playing cards during lean period or leisure time. Besides doing fishing activities, the villagers and their family members are engaged in different activities during off season but those who are in the service or business sector are stable throughout the year. The income also varies accordingly, from low to high.

Case Study-5

Name: Khetrabasi Behera, Aged: 40, Sahi: Laxminarayan Sahi

In an interview with a net shopkeeper named Khetrabasi Behera (40+), revealed that he was doing both fishing and business. But he earned more from business, that's why he devoted more time at his shop. He said that he knew the net making method. Earlier he was also doing that. But now the demand is for nylon nets and it is also time saving method. So, he decided not to do fishing any more. He took loan from money lenders by pawning his wife's gold ornaments as deposit. Now he is earning more. He has bought back his wife's ornaments and also built a new house from this income.

The people who are engaged in both primary and secondary occupations like Khetrabasi Behera are financially sound but those who solely depend on fishing are in a miserable condition. Almost all of their income is spent in drinking and for drinking. They are giving excuses like fishing is a very hard task and in order to manage this hard labour they have to drink.

Techno-Economic of Fishing

a) Fishing Craft and Gear

A fishing gear is the tool with which aquatic resources are captured, where as the fishing method is how the gear is used. Fishing methods are continuously changing. Fishermen are inventive and not afraid of trying new ideas. Technological development of fishing gear and methods in the past was aimed to increase production, in the present situation with many over fished stock, limited possibilities to expand fishing on under exploited resources and concerns about the environmental impact of fishing operation, gear development is very much focused on selective fishing and gears with less impact on the environment. [Fishing gears and methods, Victoria, British Columbia, Canada, 14-19 July 1991]

Fishing net is net used for fishing activities. Fishing nets are meshes usually formed by knotting a relatively thin thread. Modern nets are usually made of artificial polyamides like, nylon, although nets of organic polyamides such as wool or silk thread were common until recently and are still used. [Fishing net – Wikipedia - (1 6)]

Fishery

Puri and Ganjam are the coastal districts of Orissa having 26 fishing villages and 14 fish landing centers. About 20,000 fishermen population are dependent on in-land, brackish water and marine fisheries in Ganjam District. Puri has 85 fishing villages with a population of 67,161 who are dependent on fishery as main source of livelihood having 12 landing centers. The total fish catch of both districts is 14053.22 metric tonnes and 25,000 metric tonnes respectively. (Provisional report 2003, 2004; Directorate of Fishery, Puri and Ganjam)

Fishery in Puri and Ganjam can be classified to the nature of operation i.e. capture and culture. Further it can be divided by the type of water resource i.e. fresh water, marine water or brackish water.

Marine Fishing- Marine water fishing is classified into (a) coastal fishing and (b) ocean fishing. Puri has a coastline of 155 kilometers. Fishery activities are undertaken by the fishing villages located along the coastline. Traditionally fishing with catamarans was common but now with the advent of travelers, beach landing crafts and fiber reinforced plastic boat (FRP's) are common.

Coastal Fishing- Coastal fishing can be defined as the fishing operation taken up within 5 kilometers from the coastline. Coastal fishing is taken up by catamarans and country boat. But now motorized boat with In Board Machine engines (IBM's) and Out Board Motor engines (OBM's) are involved in coastal fishing. It is a daily phenomenon. Fishermen go early in morning around 4 A.M. and come back around 3 P.M. in afternoon.

Ocean Fishing- Ocean fishing is beyond 5 kilometers of the coastline. It normally involves travelers, BLC and FRP's for operation. The period normally varies from three to eight days depending on the size of the fishing craft.

Fresh Water Fishing- Fresh water fishing is based on inland water resources and is a main source of fish. The inland water has been exploited for its aquatic resources by the communities to meet their food requirementsand also as a means of livelihood.

Brackish Water Fishing- Puri and Gunjam district are endowed with brackish water coastline of the Chilika Lake. The production of prawn and shrimp is important from economic point of view. The fishing in Chilika Lake in both the districts is regulated highly by the government.

The study is concerned with Puri district. Data are collected on various traditional fishing implement, craft and economic activities of Nolia people of Arakhakuda.

Traditional Fishery Methods used by Nolia

In 1996-97 there were 310 numbers of different fisheries found in Chilika area or brackish water fishing.

They are:

Jano-109

Shrimp-71

Bahani-33

Dian-88

Utthapani-9

From them about 60 percent by bahani (net fishing), 25 percent by trap (shrimp fishing) and 15 percent by Jana (encolosuring by bamboo screen) methods were used by earlier fishermen. [Source: A research report of CDA by Samal C. Kishore Meher Shibalal]

Now the Jano and Dhaudi Baja have been replaced by Khondawhich is popularly called Disco Nets, and the Bahani method is replaced by gill-cum-drag netting which is commonly used by Nolia for capturing fish in Chilika. [Source: Chilika Lagoon, Ghosh K, Asish Pattnaik, K Ajit]

Table-2: Fishery Method

Name	Method	Period
Bahani	Net fishing	Throughout year.
Jano	Enclosure in shallow region by split bamboo and net	Leased August-February
Dian	Upland near Jano areas (for non-fishermen people) 100-200 yards from the shore	June-July
Utthapani	Near shore; in shallow water both by fisheries and non fisheries	June-July
Shrimpor prawn khatties	For capturing prawns, total 70 were operative	March-August

Jana (fixed cruives) - It is an extensive bamboo enclosure in the shallow water near Chilika, cut from the main Lake, where fish swim in for shelter. Each Jana is over mile long and hundred meters wide. It is normally used in the month of September to November. During this period plenty of fishes are captured. Fishes like Kabala, Khainga, Menjea, Khuranti, Jagili and Bekti, Borogo, and Sahal and Shrimp are caught with this Jana.

The north-west side channel between inner Chilika and outer Chilika fills with rain water in the rainy season. Exchange of water between the two parts of Chilika occurs. Fish and shrimp enter into this channel.

In the month of Kartika (October-November) some areas of the channel are closed by tattabada (Bamboo screen) from both sides. Fish and shrimp are caught from the enclosure by two ways viz: Jana and Dian. Tatta (Jana) has one opening. In this opening fish enters and swims into the box. But in south-east parts of Chilika, the Janas are placed on the shore.

Dian - When fishes remain in enclosure; it moves and strikestata; then fishes jump and fall on the nets on the other side of the enclosure and are called dian (Jumping).

Utthapani - When the first monsoon appears in June, the rain water flows from sea shore to Chilika lake, along with this a lot of fishes also rush in against the flow of water and go into small ponds. Sometimes this rain water gets checked with certain ridges and usually small fishes like Kantia and other small varieties get trapped there.

Line and Hook Method - In 1990 the fishermen decided to ban hook and line fishing. The primary reason was that most often sharks got attracted towards the hook, got entangled and injured and their blood frightened other fishes away from the shore. The people operate line and hook in the "Muhana". Now a new Muhanahas also opened there. This ban will ultimately cause low prawn catching. The Nolias say that they should not attract the shark with baited hook as this will cause depletion in the fish population.

Fishing Trap- Nolia people use different types of fishing trap with different types of nets.

Baza is fishing traps (jala) with small holes. It is kept in row in shallow water (50-100 numbers are kept). Baza is used for catching of shrimp collection created during January to March.

Dhaudi (Kundara) - It is similar in form to Baza. It is made of Bamboo. Its opening is called Singhamucham.

Tatta - Small tattas are known as naharas.

Khandas (Kundaras) - This is also meant for capturing shrimp.

Fishing Implements

Fishing is an activity, which requires necessary apparatus mostly a net and a boat. In earlier times nets are knitted by Nolia people. But now advanced nets are used with very fine thread, which is not possible for them to knit. It also needs less repairing compared to the previous net. Two parts of well finished nets are available. Nolias buy and join it with their implement. They buy the net from their village shop. Boats are also hired and built by specialized carpenter with a lot of mechanization.Net making was the job of both men and women. But now only men are doing this job. Net making requires two things Phai and Tail.

Phai–Phai is a bamboo used to make net. It is usually splitto the length of 4-5 inches and breadth of 3-5 inches according to the size of meshes required in different parts of the net. The operator, holding the Phai in his left hand, goes on increasing the meshes with the help of tail (another piece of bamboo) holding in theright hand, in such a way that a knot is tied every time. Four knots are made on four corners of each mesh. Each side of mesh is known as 'foot'. The size of the net also gradually increases with the mesh. And the size of mesh gradually decreases at the holder end.

Half of each horizontal mesh rowis known as pata and two successive meshes complete one single row of square meshes fair knots at each corner. The numbers at meshes on the upper and lower rows are not always the same. It increases or decreases according to the desired form of thenet.

Tail - It is a bamboo split at both ends keeping the middle portion intact. This knitting is done by needle. This type of net is small in size and was used during earlier times in their private ponds or for inland fishing.

Net Repairing

Net making and repairing are done by an ushi (now called Sheudingi), knife and bamboo patta. A net is repaired once in every two years. Small repairing is done by Nolias themselves. If the damage is large, they either buy a new net or take it to the machine for repairing. Both males and females can do this job.

Gillnets (Vala – Jalo)

Gillnets are found in almost all the coastal belts of Odisha. But there is lot of difference in the size of meshes found in northern and southern parts of coastal areas.

A gillnet is a net the lower end of which is weighted by sinkers while the upper end is floated. Larger fishes, while struggling to free themselves become entangled in the net and get caught in the meshes, which is why gilling is very combined with entangling. The meshes have a particular size to catch the fish. It is operated in two ways, drifting on the surface, connected with a rope to a fishing boat or set on the bottom of the sea. The gillnets are also known as driftnet.

The gillnets used by Nolia people are Jaga Vala (bottom driftnet), Kilumala (surface driftnet), Katlata (surface drift net) etc.

Jagavala - It is used as a bottom driftnet and is used to catch prawns, Kokili, pomfret etc. The net is operational from March to August upto ten kilometers at the coast with a large teppa Catamarans. It is normally fixed in early mornings and after they take it out.

Operation - The net is lowered towards grounds by adding additional weights to the lower parts of net and then drifted over the ground tied to a teppa. Three people are required to handle it. 10 to 12 nets are joined to form a unit. The mesh size is 55 mm to 65 mm. Now though, its use has decreased, recently they have started using Jaga Jalo.

Kilumala - Kilumala is a surface driftnet. It is used to catch fishes like prawns, small fishes, Khoinga, Kabala etc. The net is operated throughout the year except in bad climate i.e., during the rainy season (July-August). This net is fixed more nearer to sea than Jagavala. The distance is not more than six kilometers from the shore. Two fishermen are required for its operation when its size is about four pieces and four members are required for the larger size net. Its mesh size is 40 to 60 mm. Its lifespan is two to three years.

Katlala - It is the only gill net used by Nolias which is made of cotton. The net has wooden floats and lead sinkers. Two fishermen are required for its operation. It is used from October to March. Its meshes are of different sizes; only one piece of net is usually used for catching fishes. Its mesh size varies from 12-40 mm. Its lifespan is also 2 to 3 years. Nets of smaller size are operated from three kilometers of distance from the shore. Whereas nets of larger mesh size are operated to a distance of five kilometers from the shore. During peak season, when more fishes are available, the net is operated less than two kilometers from the shore. Fishing starts early in the morning and continues throughout the day. Fishes like anchories and sardines are caught in this net.

The cotton thread provides protection to fishes because sometimes when large amounts of fishes are caught they might get damaged by getting entangled in the nylon thread.

Encircling Nets

These surrounding nets reach from the top to the bottom of the water. These are encircling nets. Boat seines have long wings on both sides as well as long hauling lines, which are attached to the wings. They have a strong center to collect the fish caught, sometimes with a net bag attached. They are operated by two Catamarans. Beach seine consists of a bag in which two wings are attached. They are laid out in a semicircle facing the shore and then pulled towards it. The encircling nets are mostly used in northern coastal belt. But in the southern region especially in Puri and Ganjam, the Nolia use beach siene and boatsiene to catch the shallow fishes close to the shore.

Iragali (Beach Siene)

This Irgali net is operated by two Catamarans from early morning to afternoon. This is set in a distance of 3 to 4 kilometers from the sea shore.

This net is made of cotton. It consists of two wings and a bag. The wings are 25 metres long and the bags have a length of 10 metres and a depth of 2 metres. The mesh size is 110 mm, 50 mm in mouth of the belly and 15 mm in the cod end. There is a preservative used from a plant called Acacia. They also use powder of tamarind seeds for its preservation. Through this net, fishes like, ribbon fish, silver bellies, shrimp, jew fishes are caught.

Operation – Two Catamarans are used in the fishing ground. Both of them stretch the net on the teppa, move away from each other. When the net is fully released the Catamarans turns at right angle and moves on a parallel course, usually with the cement. As they move close to each other and haul the lines and wings together, the fishes enter in the bag.

Bada Jalo - It is otherwise called Bada Jalo. The beach net is operated from October to April. This net catches fishes like anchovies, sardines and silver bellies.

Operation - This net is loaded on a bar boat. The net has a bag, which is released at the time of fishing. The boat moves in a semicircle and then the net is pulled by ten to twelve persons on each side. Two to three people remain in the water to guide the net into the beach. Before reaching the shore, the bag is detached from the net. Around forty people are required for its operation. The mesh size is 62 to 75 mm near the wings and 20-25 mm near the Kachhi. Now-a-days this large net is renewed with some modified features and technology is called as Sukum Net.

Hand Lines and Long Lines

The Nolia told that earlier the use of the hand lines and long lines were widspread. But now they are used only for specific reasons.

Kata - The Kata is operated by a single person at the mouth of the estuary (or Muhana). This is used in the early morning or in the evening. The main fishes caught here are perches. The gear consists of 250 metre long nylon lines of one mm diameter each. A piece of wood is attached to the line, in which lead is attached and is wrapped in a white cloth so that it looks like a fish. Two hooks are attached to the wood and are also wrapped in cloth; one hook is large and other hook is small. During catching of fish, the wood floats on the water with the lead and hooks below it.

Burdu - It is operated from a Catamaran. It consists of two nylon lines of lengths between 150 metres to 180 metres and diameter of 1 or

2 mm, lead and stones are also attached to it; hook is also attached. The hooks are baited with small fish and put into the water. The hooks are pulled at certain intervals. Fishes like Kantia, Dog fish, Perches etc. are caught through this medium.

Suti- It is made of nylon. Its usage is now decreasing. This is operated throughout the year. It is operated three kilometers from the sea shore. Two fishermen are required for its operation. One end of the gear is connected to the teppa while the other end is fixed to a buoy. The lines are shot and hauled by hand.

a) Various instruments were used by Nolia people in ancient times. But due to shortage of bamboo and repeated failures during fishing, different types of modern nets along with various modern instruments were invented.

   In earlier times, people used to soak cotton in "Kanji" water for two days. Then they rubbed the cotton on their legs and made nets from this.These people spoke Telugu and were very daring in nature. All the nets made were used for marine fishing. These nets were large and large quantities of fishes were caught. But as time passed, the villagers came in contact with Nolias of Kujang and started to live in their village among them. The government banned marine fishing. The opening of "Muhana" posed as a great problem for them. Marine fishing became quite difficult and the catch size decreased substantially.

Gradually, with changing times came different types of nets with advanced technologies (mostly with varying mesh sizes and thread). This was because the present generation people found it difficult to operate the huge nets used by their ancestors. The net operation process remained same but names of nets changed and people started using them only during inland fishing. Very few nets were used for marine fishing.

The gill net and the fishing lines are seasonal and the rest of the nets described below are operated throughout the year. The people in recent times are using their famous nets i.e. Chingudi Jala and Benti Jala for inland fishing, and Ring net for marine fishing. The Nolia people classify their nets into two types based on the area required of fishing:

1) Inland Net – This type of net is used for fishing in Chilika.

2) Marine Net – This type of net is used for fishing at Sea.

Inland Net	**Marine Net**
Chingudi Jala	Sala Jala
Benti Jala	Ring Jala
Khepa Jala	Chapada Jala
Jaga Jala (or Jagavala sea net)	Disco Jala
Crab Jala	Kokili Jala
Nanala Jala	Sukum Jala
JanalaJ ala	
Ghai Jala	
Bhekti Jala	
Chara Jala	

These two categories of nets are also based on the sizes of fishes caught. The inland net is zero meshed size net as mainly small fishes are caught on. The marine net is large sized to facilitate large fishes catches.

Different Types of Net

Chingudi Net (Jala) - This net is of 5 types;

a) Box Net	c) Kadi Net	e) Sona nadiki
b) Benti Net	d) Bada nadiki	f) Mantle Net

a) Box Net (Jala) - This net is made from white coloured plastic threads and is surrounded by green sticks. Its thread size is 0-0.5 mm. Thread size is an indication of the sizes of fish to be caught.

The net which is also called 'Puda Jala' is fitted in a box form by using sticks to spread each corner. The cost of one Puda is Rs. 500 and 10-20 Pudas are required to make one net. So the cost comes to nearly 10,000 rupees.

Operation - The net is secured at one particular corner of chilika using sticks during evening. Then it is floated on water and the people go back home only to return the next morning and secure their catch. This net is used mainly in rainy season.

b) Benti Net (Jala) - It is a size zero white colored plastic net with bamboo polls attached in between the threads to give strength to the net. The length of the net is 100 meters.

Operation **-** The net is spread straight. Normally two to three people are required to hold the "benta" (pole) although the actual number of people required always depends on the size of a net. Nolia people use a boat (teppa) to go to a particular place of the fishing area in Chilika. They spread the net there and wait for two to three hours and then pull it out and collect the fishes caught.

The Chingudi nets are mainly operated in ponds and for in land fishing. Very small fishes like chara, shrimp, polora and various other species are caught through this net.

c) Bada Nadiki and Sana Nadiki - These Chingudi nets have white colour thread and number one mesh size. They are used in inland fishing.

Operation **-** Only two individuals are required for its operation. First they bury a bamboo in waist deep water and then they attach a net to it. Small fishes like prawns, crab, tiger prawns, morala, kunu etc are caught in this net.

d) Mental Net (Jala) - In this net, the colour of thread used is white and of very fine quality with 8 number mesh size. This net is meant for catching small fishes and is used in inland fishing.

e) Khadi Net (Jala) - It is also a Chingudi net which is knitted with thin blue or white colour thread. The mesh size maintained here is 0, 0.5 and 1. The size of the hole created is large.

Operation – Only two people are required for the operation of Khadi jala. This net is used on full moon nights or during high tides. The Nolias take their Kattamarans and go to their fishing place. This net has 5-6 pouches (muna) and is also called bag net. The people throw the net into the tide with the help of "*Khadi*". The force of the tide compels fishes to enter the nets. Then the people pull the "Khadi" to bring the net near them. Only small fishes and prawn are caught in this net and it is used for inland fishing.

Khepa Net (Jala) - It is also known as wheel net. The net is knitted from white or blue plastic threads of 1-0/2-0 size and the cost of making this net is Rs. 1000.

Operation **-** It is controlled by one hand. The Nolia uses this net for their regular day to day fishing activities. When they see fish, immediately throw net and once it becomes heavy indicating that fishes have been caught, they drag the net with the help of the tail or "kacchi" of the net. This net is only used in inland fishing and various sizes of fishes are caught in this net.

Sala Net (Jala)

The net is very large and made of blue or white plastic (nylon) thread. The mesh sizes used are 2, 3, 4 and 5. The Nolias measured the net as "300-400 hata" in their traditional measurement (which is actually 600 meters). In their local term the Sala Jala is known as Alimnet and "Bada Phanda" net. It has two parts "talapere and uparapere". Previously, it was knitted at home but now it is machine-made. The talapere of the net has two parts (kani) – baharakada and Talakada. It costs around 1-1.5 lakhs in making. The high price renders it impossible for all Nolia families to afford Sala Net. Fishes of different varieties, species and sizes like Sala, Ilishi, Bhekti, Rohu etc., are caught by the net. This net is used only in rainy and summer seasons both for marine and inland fishing.

Operation **-** Thirty people are required for the operation of this net. It is not fixed at any particular place in the water. Thirty people, together in a teppa go into the water and collectively spread the net length-wise in the sea. Then they come back to the shore and pull the rope of the net to bring in the catch.

Ring Net - (Sea jala)

The Ring net is a big net made of nylon white or blue thread, used in winter seasons having a characteristic "*bada-phanda*". It is used mainly for marine fishing. In one catch more than 10 quintals of fishes are caught. The thread size used in this net is 3/4 size. This net is otherwise known as sea net.

Operation - Fifteen or twenty individuals are required for the operation of a sea net. The people go by teppa to sea. When they see a fish, they spread the net in a round or ring shape surrounding the fish completely and then pull up the net using the ropes attached to the net. They catch big fishes in this net.

Chapada Net–This net is huge in size having a length of 50-60 feet. It is on record that Nolias have caught fishes weighing 50-55 kilograms by this net. The net is white colored having thread and mesh size of 2-0. Fishes like Kokili, Kala, Lenga and, Bhekti etc., are caught by this net. The

Nolias buy three parts of the net from the market and join it lengthwise at home. For this net 1 kg thread and 1 kg *solo* is required. One kg of nylon thread costs Rs.500/-, so the total cost of net comes to Rs.20,000. The *solo* are fixed on the upper part of net and in the lower part of net, bamboo poles are attached.

Operation – It requires a minimum of three people for smooth operation of the net. The Nolias use Chapada Jala at sea only. The people spread the net while going into the sea on teppaso that its *solo* are inside the water. Two sides are held by two people; one person holds the net lengthwise in the middle and marks the net. When fishes enter into net the solo gets pushed into the water and upon seeing this, the people pull the net from two sides to secure the catch. The number of people required and its operation varies according to the size of the net.

Jaga Net (jala) - This type of net is mainly used for catching small fishes. It has no sticks. Its net size is 0 to 0.5 mm. The net is of white or violet colour nylon thread. This is used for inland fishing.

Operation - First the Nolias mark the place where they locate large numbers of fishes inside the water for a substantial catch size. Then they throw the net into the water length wise and pull the catch back to the shore.

Crab Net - This net is used only for catching crabs. Nolia people use this net in the winter season. It is square in shape and bound by bamboo on all corners. The net is green in colour. Triangular stones are attached on four corners of the net and a spherical shape is created in a series for catching crabs.

Operation - Only two individuals are required for its operation on a particular place (waist deep water). The Nolias fix this net at night. Early next morning they go and take it out. Sometimes one person is sufficient for its handling.

Janala Net - It is of two types - Janala bandha and Janalathela Jala.

a) *Janala Bandha Jala* - This net is made of pressure thread and is white in colour. It is a large net of length 15 hand span and width 4 hand span. It is thrown into 10-15 feet deep water inside Chilika.

b) *Janala Thela Jala*- It is a small thread sized net, trianglular in form and one person can carry it with himself for catching fish. The net is 3 hand span in length and 2 hand span in width.

Disco Net - (Khonda Jala) - The net is made of blue nylon thread matching the color of the sea water to confuse fishes and catch them. This net is very costly. 5 ril nets are joined to make one disco net. The cost of 1 ril net is between Rs. 2,000 to 2,500/-. The net also needs repairing in every two years. The size of threads on this net is 2–0 or 1–0. In Disco net, three parts are joined to form a large net. Its one part is used as Kilumala net.

Operation **-** When Nolias go into the sea for two to three months at a stretch, they take this net for fishing. They totally spread the net inside water after seeing the fish. They can know where the fishes are by dipping a stick in water. When the stick starts shaking, it is a cue for them and they pull outthe net by holding two sides of the rope.

Fishes of all types are caught in this net. It is also called as Chapada Jala. Due to some changes in its features, it is called as Disco Jala.

Phasi Net/Kokili Net- This net is used in January and February. It is used for marine fishing. The net is made of white nylon thread of size 2–0. This net is operated at a distance of 3 to 4 kms from sea shore. It is used for catching Kokili and Kala, that is why it is called Kokili Jala. Two to three people are required for its operation. The total cost of the net is approx. Rs. 10,000 –Rs. 15,000.

Charana Net - This net is for catching small fish like Kabala. It is operated in a round fashion. For its operation two people required, one is in teppa and other holds the net and spreads the net. It is an inland fishing net.

Sukum Net - The length of this net is 100 metres. It is a marine fishing net. It requires ten to twenty people for its operation. The thread size is number 8 and its colour is blue or white.

Operation **-** The people first see and track the fish in the sea. Some of them are on the teppa while the others are near the shore. Then the people spread the net in a round shape and the last tail of the net is held by the people waiting near the shore. All types of large and small fishes are caught in this net.

Ghai Net - This net is used for inland fishing. The thread number of the net is 6 and it is blue and white colour. Length of the net is 100 metres. More than 10 people are required for its operation. It is same as Sukum net. But the only difference is that the former one is a marine fishing net while the latter one is an inland fishing net. The net is like volleyball net and large sized fishes are caught in this net.

Bhekti Net - It is also a large sized white colour net. The thread number is 8. They told that it is "three and four anda". This net is used for inland fishing and seven to eight people are required for its operation. The mode of operation is normal; when they see a fish they spread the net. Large fishes like bhekti, khoinga and kabala are caught in this net.

The information was collected from a net shopkeeper, Laxmi Narayan Sahi, which was given below.

He told that the net threads are of different colors.

1. Green - 2 -3 thread (1 bundle rate is Rs.15/-)
2. Blue - 100 gm required (1 bundle is Rs.20/-)

   Rope is yellow in colour. For every net 1 kilo rope is required. Its price is Rs.140 to Rs.100.
3. White thread - 1 – 6 (1 bundle – Rs.15/-)

   The threads are of different companies like Ruftuf, Netfine and harwar.

   These materials are required for each net and are same for every net depending upon its colour.

   For Jaga net- 10 kilo net requiredfor large sized Jaga net.

   5 kilo net is required for small sized Jaga net.

   1 kilo cost – Rs.580/-

   The thread is of blue colour- (fishing line)

   Net is of violet colour.

   1 kilo thread - Rs.400/-.

   For Jaga Jala it requires 50 gm – 75 gm thread.

   For catching big fish *orongo* required.

   For one net, it requires 400-500 solo (small sized solo).

   Big solo rate is cheaper.

   Small solo rate is higher.

   Guli – 7-8 kilo (1 kilo costs Rs.140/-).

It is the cost of total net. A net is half finished. Nolia people buy this net and with their instruments; joint the net at home and use it for fishing.

Table-3: List of giving details of Materials required for Net.

Name of Net	Materials required for 1 kg. Net (given in Odia term)	Price of Net per 1 kg.
1. Bol Jalo	Bamboo Kadi Badu	Jala 1 kg. - Rs.100/-; total price of Net per 1 kg. - Rs.500/-
2. Khadi Jalo	Badu, China (1 kg. - 300 Rs.) thread, Kadu	Net 1 kg. - Rs.300; total cost of Net per 1 kg. Rs.15000/-
3. Benti Jalo	Stone, Badu, Kata, Kadi	Cost per 1 kg. Rs.10,000/-
4. Khepa Jalo	Stick, goli, Doro	Net cost Rs.1000/-
5. Sala Jalo	Guli, thread, kata, badu	1 kg. net - Rs.500/-; total cost net – Rs.15000/-
6. Ring Jalo	Ring, Badu, Kata	1 kg. net Rs.2 lakh
7. Chapada	Guli, Kata, Dabi	Rs.15,000/-
8. Jaga Jalo	Stone, Badu, Kata	Rs.15,000/- (Recent rate)
9. Katlala (Kokili)	Kata, Suta, badu	1 kg. Rs.15,000/- (Recent rate)
10. Crab jalo	Badu, Stone	1 kg. thread – Rs.500/-; total cost Rs.1000/-
11. Janala Jalo	Kadi, Badu	1 kg. thread Rs.600/-; total net Rs.1500/-
12. Disco Jalo	Dabi, Guli, Kata, Badu	1 kg. Net- Rs.600/-; total cost per 1 kg. - Rs.2000/-
13. Charana Jalo	Badu, Kata, Doro, Goli	1 kg. Net- Rs.700/-; total net per kg. Rs.1200/-
14. Sukum Jalo	Badu, Kata, Goli, Doro	Rate Rs.20000/-
15. Ghai Jalo	Doro, thread, Guli, Badu, tin	1 kg. Rs.10000/-
16. Bhekti Jalo	Kadi, Badu, thread, Guli, Doro, tin	1 kg. net Rs.2000/-

(The rate may vary from market to market)

(The data have been collected from a village shop keeper)

Boat

Odisha has a 529 kilometre long coastline extending from Subarnarekha river in the north to Sunapur in the south. Marine fishing has shown a steady increase due to the use of modern mechanized boats and nylon nets. But still the traditional fishing crafts and gearsplay a major role in the fishing communities.

The southern coastline of Odisha is narrow. Earlier the people mainly used Catamarans or Teppa. Now-a-days their use is quite reduced. Other boats that are shared and used by the Nolia people of my concerned village are – bar boat (Padhua) and Nava.

Teppa (Catamarans)

The length of Catamarans varies from 4 to 8.5 meters. It is made of 4 to 5 logs. The two sections of logged Teppas are boat Catamarans and need three to four men to be managed where as a smaller teppa can be operated only by two men.

Teppa is used throughout the year. It is non-motorised and its operation is limited to a coastal belt from 15 upto 20 fathoms. But now people do not use teppa for deep sea fishing. They use it while fishing in Lake Channels.

Teppa -

Materials required	Albyzzia Stipulata
Length	6 metre to 8.5 metre
Dimension	8.3 m x 1.5 m x 0.54 m
Construction	Two halves. Each half comprising of two boys with a wash strake. Both halves are lashed together with a cross beam for additional stiffness.
Fishing season	Throughout the year, except bad climate.
Cost	Rs.5000/-
Annual maintenance	Rs.200/- Rs.400/-
Its life	4 to 5 years.

3 – Big Catamaran

Wood	Erythrina indica / Alby zzia stipulate
Length	4.2 metre to 5 metre
Dimension	4.2 m x 0.76 m x 0.42 m
Construction	Three bogs lashed and pegged, outer layer 250 mm wide, centre bog 200 mm wide but deeper.
Mart	4 m 30 mm diameter bamboo
Fishing area	8 km from sea shore
Fishing season	Throughout the year
Cost	Rs.3000/-

Annual maintenance	Rs.250/- - Rs.350/-
Life	3 years.

4 – Bog Catamaran

Wood	Erythrina Indica / Alby zia stipulate
Length	4.5 metre to 5.5 metre
Construction	Four bogs are lashed and pegged. Inner logs are 140 mm wide, outer logs are 230 mm wide.
Fishing area	Up to 8 kms from the seashore
Mart	4.5m x 35 mm diameter bamboo
Fishing season	Throughout the year, whenever surf is negotiable
Cost	Rs.1500/-
Life	3 years.

Padhua:

The bar boat is locally called as Padhua and is made from the trunk of the mango tree (Magniferaindica) without any frame. In ancient times the people used padhua not only for fishing but for carrying men. The padhua carries 8 to 10 quintals of fish. In earlier times, the builders who built boats were illiterate and the art of boat making was in their blood. But now Nolia people buy boat from Puri.

Wood	Magniferaindica
LoA range Length	7 metres to 8.3 metres
Dimension	7.40 m x 2.2 x 1.14 m
Construction	Planks stitched to each other by coir ropes with straw caulking.

Nava

It is also a plank boat. This boat is operated usually at night. This boat was brought from Andhra Pradesh and is operated at the open beaches from October to February.

Length is	8.5 metre - 10 metre
Mart	5.5 metres

The Nolias told that in past when they were migrated from Andhra Pradesh, they used these types of boats. Those were mainly for marine fishing. But now they used Teppa with an outboard engine.

Maintenance

The maintenance of a boat is an expensive affair. But Nolia people told that maintainance of a boat is a necessity and each year the expense is Rs. 25000–Rs. 30000 (in case of a big boat) and Rs. 10000- Rs. 12000 (in case of a small boat). The Nolias give a fibre coating to the boat which is costly. Besides that Nolias give a type of coal coating to their boat every fifteen days. Otherwise different types of insects found in the Chilika water damage the wood of the boat.

The people usually prefer mango and sal wood for making the boat as the wood of these trees are very strong. But now they also use "Chakunda" and Khusuni planks for making boats. The boat is made by the carpenter and is plentily available in the Puri market.

Now-a-days they use fibre boats. The boats are made of a special type fibre which cost Rs.1.5 lakh to Rs.2 lakh. Boat engine also costs Rs.50000/-. These engine boats are mainly for marine fishing. The Nolias buy the engine boat with Rs. 22,500 as subsidiary from the government through their PFC. For running the boat, diesel is required, which they get at a lower price in every month. A motor boat requires approximately 22 litre of diesel to run.

The Nolias classify their boat as–

a) Marine fishing boat

b) Inland fishing boat

Now-a-days the people are using mechanized fibre boat, which is expensive.

Inland Boat Costs

Bhuter fibre costs	Rs.80000 – Rs. 1 Lakh
New Big boat costs	Rs.95000 – Rs. 1 Lakh
Length	10 mt.
Width	42' - 45"
Small size boat	9 mt.
Width	25' -30" / 32"

Contd...

Costs	Rs.60000 – Rs.75000
Marine fibre boat length	9 m – 10.6 m
Upper portion length	1 m – 4 ft.
Costs	Rs.2 – 4 lakhs

The fibre boat can carry upto 20 individuals, having 5-10 quintal fish carrying capacity. It is operated both in the sea and Lake.

Chilika Boat

The front portion of the boat is called manga; middle portion is paita and backside is called pachhamanga. Now the people are using three types of boats, these are:

a. Ambapata Donga – It is made of mango plum. It is less costly. The price rate varies with Rs.8000 – 10000 ranges. Its size is 32 ft. - 35 ft. Length – 32 – 35 inches, width – 2-2$^1/_2$ inch. It can carry 4 to 5 quintal fish. The boat's capacity is carrying two-five individuals.

b. Salua Pata Boat – It is a costly boat. The price varies between Rs.35000- 40000; Fifty to Sixty individuals can go in this boat for fishing. But now it is Rs. 1$^1/_2$ lakh with modified features. Its length is 35-38 inches. It can carry all types of fishes and nets.

c. Alupatana - It is also another boat used for inland fishing. The boat is small in size carrying a price tag of Rs.5000-6000/-.

These are the different types of boats seen in Chilika lake.

Table-4: Gears used in Marine Fishing

Name of the Block	Landing Centre	Gears used		
		Type	Qty	Nos
PuriSadar	Penthakota	Tramel Net	50000	2500
		Gill Net	125000	12500
		Long Line	15000	1500
	Sapakothi	Gill Net	18960	1896
		Shore Seiner	600	4
Bramhagiri	Harachandi	Gill Net	37970	3797
		Shore Seiner	450	3
		Cast Net	90	45

Contd...

Krushnaprasad	Arakhakuda	Gill Net	129000	129000
		Shore Seiner	600	4
		Cast Net	890	445
	Kiri sahi	Gill Net	29980	2998
		Shore Seiner	300	2
		Cast Net	210	105
	S R Lanka	Gill Net	18980	1878
		Shore Seiner	300	2
		Cast Net	190	95

Arakhakuda's surrounding villages use more or less the same types of gears. But the quantity of fish caught in Arakhakuda village is more in comparison to other villages.

A comparative analysis is always essential to know the status of our target village. The total number of crafts used in Arakhakuda village is 153. Number of crafts used by Penthakota village people is highest in comparison to other villages. Due to this the production is also high. Recently, a Jetty has been constructed in the Arakhakuda village but connecting road is yet to be developed, so people are not getting the benefitted by the Jetty.

Navigational Ethno-Science

Navigation and fishing methods are dependant on each other. Fisherman's perception or their worldview of thc winds, current, tides and detection of different varieties of fish species are described below.

Wind - Wind plays an important role in the life of a fisherman. The people segregate the wind as per the four directions. These are East (Faigali), West (Darigali), North (Turpgali), South (Parotogali), N–west (Molagali), N–east (Turppagali), S–east (Salcumpaigali), S–west (Wadagali). These terms are Telugu terms which were used by the earlier fisherman. But recently few of these terms are used and some people use the Oriya terms.

Faigali and Darigali blow from October till February. Paigali blows during day and in the evening aiding the return of the fishermen from sea whereas Darigali blows at night and in the morning which helps the fishermen to go out into the sea. Molagali blows in December. Turppaigali blows from November to January.

Current- The Nolia people classified the currents as – Turupudi (North), Tendoli (South), Karakutodi (East) and Newarodi (West). The people told me that from October to January (Turupuodi) Northern current helps them to have good catch while fishing. Tendoli follows the turupuodi and flows from March to September. The other two currents are prevalent throughout other seasons. The fishermen told me that if there is no current, they are rendered incapable to catch fish.

Prediction of Cyclone

The Nolia people can predict the coming of a cyclone. These are the following signs they look out for –

1. Dark clouds in either N-East or N-West direction.
2. The nets become infested by Jelly fish one to two days before a cyclone.
3. A soft wind blows in the direction opposite to that of the path of the impending cyclone.
4. The cyclone can be predicted from the waves breaking on the beach, the shape and the size of the waves also act as indicators.

Tides – The only importance of a tide is that while the fishermen are launching their boats on the water, a tide either helps them or hinders the launch. Low tides are called padi and high tides are called Neeri. The Nolias also have adequate knowledge of the effects of full moon or new moon ontides.

Fish Detection Methods

While fishing in the deep sea in teppa, the Nolias hold a wooden stick whose broad end is placed in water and narrow end is held close to the ear. By listening to the sounds in the water, the fishermen can say what types of fishes, if any, are present below the surface.

If the sound is–

1. *Sheeee* .... high to low then, it indicates prawns are moving and if the net is pulled out, a large numbers of fishes are caught.
2. quack ... quack .... this sound signifies that tarpon and catfish are below the water surface.
3. For the detection of pelagic fish, the methods are dark patches on sea surface and often accompanied by the sound of breaking of the water surface. The people told me that the sound resembles rain falling

on the sea surface. The pelagic fishes come to surface whenever a strong wind blows because they live in deep sea. Along with pelagic fishes, other fishes like turpon, hilsa, black pomfret are brought by the southwest wind and strong Northern winds bring tiger prawns, ribbon fish and jewfish.

4. If a flock (15-30) of a particular bird named Kalipeta is sitting on the water surface, it means a large numbers of fishes are there. The people again use the sticks to listen to the sound underwater, and immediately throw their nets.
5. Stars are guiding factors for them while navigating in the sea during night time.

The Telugu fishermen are very conservative and they have perfect and clear cut knowledge of winds, navigation and other aspects of sea fishing.

Economy of Fishing

Tietz (1985: 80) distinguishes five functions in the division of the traditional fishing economy:

i) Production i.e. catching fish
ii) Processing
iii) Marketing
iv) Finance and credit
v) Manufacture of the means of production e.g. boat building, net making (Salagrama, 2006 p. 43-50).

Producers

Nolia people of Puri district (Arakhakuda village) are involved in both marine and fresh water fishing. Fishing is undertaken by men whereas the women's role is confined to post harvest and shore based activities. The people operate–

(i) wooden catamarans (teppas),
(ii) wooden boats with engines,
(iii) FRP catamarans and
(iv) bhutbhuti.

Some of them are used while fishing in Chilika and others are used in marine fishing. Except teppas, all the boats have a distinction between owners and fishing crew.

a) Fishing Crew

Fishing crew comprise of those fishermen who are very poor. Those who work in the teppas are considered to be the poorest among different categories of fishing crew, and those working in mechanized boats and trawlers are considered to be in better conditions. The Nolia people normally go for fishing at 3 A.M. in the morning and come back in the afternoon. In very rare cases they stay on boat for two or three days. In particular seasons (from October-December) they go for fishing for two to three days.

In the village where this study has been conducted, most of the people have their own net and fibreteppa. But a few people have FRP catamarans and boat with engines.The fishing people are called Jalaries and the fishing crews are called Bahania and those who help in loading and unloading are called orderloo.

b) Beach - Seine Owners

In earlier times nets were spread along the coastline and were generally owned by collectives or fisheries; who also contributed for their operation. But now these nets are not operated. Each Nolia has his Chingudi Jala of all varieties to catch prawns and different varieties of fishes. Jaga Jala, Benti Jala, Khepa Jala, CharanaJala, Crab Jala; etc. are called as Chingudi net. The marine fishing nets are very costly. Some rich people possess it. Some fishermen have no boat or nets. They are only skilledin catching fish. These people hire boats and nets from other people (mainly from non fishing community) and do not pay rent in terms of money.

Crab Fishers - Many varieties of Crabs, particularly mud and spotted crabs are found in the Chilika lake. Nolias have a Kankada Jala. Operation of this jala/net is very simple, even children can operate it. This net is fixed in muddy shallow water and crabs of different sizes are caught. Crabs are sold at a cheaper rate. A small crab costs Rs.8 and a big crab costs Rs.10. Fisher women prefer to sale these crabs in nearby markets to get double the price. The fishermen pay the rent for the boat and net in terms of fish. The catch is divided equally according to the boat, net and labour used.

The Jalaries hire the orderloo for their fishing activity and the catch is shared as below:

One – for teppa

One - for Jala

One - for engine

One – for Bahania (Orderloo).

The Orderloo is responsible for any damage that occurs to the boat during fishing activity. In different types of gill nets, the share division system differs. In Katalala the catch is divided into three equal shares out of which two shares go to crew members and one is for the boat and net. In Kulimala fishing the operational unit consists of four pieces, the catch is divided into eight shares out of which five go to two crew members and three shares are for the boat and net. All these systems started in very early times and are continuing till today. This is a form of balanced cooperative fishing.

Case Study-6

Name: Sahadev Behera, Aged: 38, Sahi: Masanichandi

This is a case study of two peoples– Sahadev Behera and Loknath Behera. They both do not possess boats. Sahadev hired a boat from a boat owner and invited Loknath to go for fishing. Their catch was shared among Loknath Behera, Sahadev Behera and the boat owner in 1:1:1 proportion.

Boat Owners

Boat owners of motorized boats are different from crew members. A boat owner never goes for fishing especially in the mechanized sector. But in some cases boats are owned by non fishing caste groups, who are more concerned about returns on their investment than about equity and sustainability. Twenty percent of the people own fibre teppa boats, 200 people have motor boats, 150 households possess fibre teppas. The Jalaries are quite rich and lead peaceful lives.

Some of them are:

1) Bijay Behera
2) Bulamani Behera
3) Indramani Behera
4) Narashima Behera

Orderloo sleada poor and pathetic life, some of them are:

1) Hari Behera
2) Era Behera
3) Ramsan Behera

In Arakhakuda village, about fifty percent people are using traditional crafts, forty percent are using motorized traditional crafts and only seven percent people are using mechanized gears.

Table-5: Monthly Income of the Owner of a Motorized Boat (in Rs.)

Sector	Summer (March-June)	Rainy (July-September)	Winter (October-February)	Annual
Northern	3967	2425	2341	34473
Central	3334	2118	2197	30320
Southern	2755	6259	3159	45246
Outer Channel	2897	3007	1843	29236

Table-6: Monthly Income of the Owner of a Non-motorized Boat (in Rs.)

Sector	Summer	Rainy	Winter	Annual
Northern	3507	1903	2097	29481
Central	3513	2956	2269	33955
Southern	2546	5000	3130	40231
Outer Channel	3669	4323	2782	39879

Table-7: Monthly Income of a Boat Crew Member (in Rs.)

Sector	Summer	Rainy	Winter	Annual
Northern	996	747	856	10506
Central	991	949	831	10964
Southern	817	1005	811	10336
Outer Channel	1069	847	777	10702

There is not much difference between motorized and non motorized boat owners of different sectors. In the above mentioned four sectors, the crew income is nearly the same. In Arakhakuda landing center there are seventy-two motorised crafts and ninety country crafts (as per data collected in 2009).

Shrimp Seed Collectors (Janala Collection and Shrimp Agent)

Shrimp seed collecting is an important part of the fishing routine of Nolia people. Men, women and children of all age groups are engaged in shrimp seed collection. They collect different varieties of seed, but only bigger shrimp seeds are taken by the collectors and others are discarded. This is a profitable business and an easy way to obtain money. The shrimp seeds are taken away by the middleman and used for shrimp gheris.

But shrimp gheris caused a lot of damage to Chilika and its environment. A numbers of seeds died. Therefore the government banned shrimp seed collection in 2011. This caused a lot of dissatisfaction among Nolias as they could get easy money through this process. So they started collecting Janala from February 2012 again.

The Janala collection occurs in the month of Phalguna (February-March) and Baisakha (April-May). In these months, water leaves the shore during daytime (bhatta) and comes back during tides (Juaro). The area turns muddy with little patches of water everywhere. The Nolias use masoorie net for catching Janala. While sorting the seeds, only those Janala seeds in demand are collected and the others are thrown away. The Janala are taken by shrimp agents from Jadupur, Ganjam, Puri (Parikud) area. The Nolias bargain while selling Janala and sell only to those agents who offer high price. Their daily catches are 250-300 fry per day. The space for collection is one acre. The middlemen between the exporting firms and the real shrimp farmers are called Chingudi agents. Like the role of commission agent is important in case of capture fishing, similarly in culture fishing, shrimp agent plays a vital role.

Processing of Fish

Processing of fish is an important work done only by females. Due to the absence of cold storage facilities, fishes are exported mainly in their dried form to different places like Cuttack, Bhubaneswar, Kalupada, Balugaon, Howrah etc. Dry fish supply is quite profitable livelihood source in Arakhakuda village. In this practice surplus fishes and prawns are sun-dried to preserve them for future consumption. As the process lacks scientific techniques and is unhygenic, there is post-harvest loss, product quality is poor and returns are affected. People dry fish on their *Chandi*, an unsanitary cemented place outside their home. Small fishes like prawns, chaulia, phulura, patharamundi are dried.

Due to the advent of the government and extension of technological support to fisher women under "Support to Training for Empowerment of Women Programmes" (STEP), the fisher women were motivated to form SHG groups. Each SHG group buys fishes with some money and engages in dry fish business. In addition to training, common infrastructure projects like godown, drying machine and water source have developed over time.

A dry fish seller, Bulei Dei was the first woman who was motivated enough to form an organisation named – Ma Mangala Nariseba Samiti. Later on, the Fisheries Commissioner, Satyabrata Sahoo, inaugurated the organisation in 2003 and named it as **Gajalaxmi Primary Marine Fishery Women Cooperative Society.**

The organization initially had 65 members which later increased to 130 and then some of them got divided into a different SHG group. The Samiti has a house where the drying machine bought by the founder (Secretary) Bulei Dei is kept. The machine was brought from Tamil Nadu with loan from Puri Fishery Department and UNDP.

Total Machine Cost	2, 50,000
House	65,000
Machine Platform	35,000

There are about twelve SHG groups in the village presently. But only Gajalaxmi SHG is operative and the other groups are only for marketing dry fish.With the help of ORMAS and Fishery Department the products prepared by the SHGs like dry fish, fish pickles, fish cutlets have occupied a good market. Now they are being supplied to nearby towns like Puri, Gopalpur, Berhampur, Balasore etc. In Cuttack's famous *Bali Jatra*, they have been given some space by ORMAS for selling their products.

A special training on preparation process for different products is also given to the SHG members by Fishery Department and Bulei Dei. Bulei Dei has become quite experienced over time to teach and guide in such trainings.

Methods of Making Dry Fish

The fishes dried in the rainy season are salted. But in other seasons dried fishes are kept unsalted. The mechanical process of drying large fishes is different. First the group members buy fishes from the village fishermen. Then they wash the fishes and cut them into two halves. After that, again they wash the fishes. The fishes are dipped in salt. For 1 kg fish, 250 grams of salt is required and 4 kilos of fish need 1 kg salt. Then the fishes are kept in draws for 24 hours. Next, the fishes are dipped in sodium benzalite water. After sometime the water is drained and the fishes are inserted into a solar machine for two hours. The machine has fans which are switched on to dry the fishes.

Fig. 3: Machine for Processing Dry Fish

For Prawns

The prawns are first washed and then put into the machine without adding salt. The prawns are prepared during the day and in the eveningthey are ready for selling.

For Small Fishes

First these fishes are cleaned with water. Then the fishes are dipped in salt water. For about half an hour they keep the fishes dipped. Then the women insert the fishes in the machine for drying. The people told me that after drying the fish, it loses its moisture content and its quantity decreases.

When 1 kg prawn is dried it becomes	200 gm
Like that when 1 kg Kabala and Khainga is dried it becomes	400 gm

But the rate increases in ratio to weight. The prices of fresh fishes are less compared to dry fishes due to value addition.

This recent technique is quite helpful to Nolia women and minimizes the labour required for fish drying unlike earlier times. But the process is a group process which requires a lot of cooperation. Besides women, a number of men are also involved in drying fish. But a lot of them still use the natural process of drying. They go to Nuaga, Jankia, and Kunus for dry fish selling.

Case Sudy-7

Name: Laxmidhar Behera, Aged: 42, Sahi: Laxminarayan

A dry-fish seller (Laxmidhar Behera–42) reported that he dries all the fishes he has collected on his own. Three-fourth of one day is required for drying. A group of 15-20 individuals get together and collectively take nearly five to ten tons of dry fish to Humma Haat for selling. To carry the dry fishes, they hire a small vehicle which charges Rs.1500/- which they all bear equally. Besides that, the owner of Humma market also charges some money from them. Humma Hat is eighty kilometers away from Arakhakuda. The market stays open throughout the night. After earning some profits from selling their products, the people return to their village. Bijay Behera (age - 38+) of Arakhakuda village is also a dry fish seller in Humma market.

Weight and Measures -

The weighing systems of Nolias are different:

1 Dhada is 5 kilograms

1 Bisa is 2.5 kilograms

The people sell their dry fish by using these measurement units.

Table-8: Prices of Different Types of Dry Fish

Fishes Name (local)		Their price in market (fresh fish) – 2½ kg fish	Price in market (dry fish) – 1 kg
Chilika fish	Khainga	150/-	500/-
	Kabala	100 – 150/-	400/-
	Soroda	80/-	350/-
	Menjia	70/-	300/-
	Khuranti	60 – 70/-	300/-
	Balangi	50/-	200/-
Sea fish	Kokili	150/-	300/-
	Saala	150/-	500/-
	Khainga	150/-	500/-
	Bhekti	200/-	600/-
	Kanagarada	20/-	60/-
	Kabakukuli	20/-	60/-
	Patharamundi	20/-	60/-
	Paniakhia	20/-	50/-
Chilika / Sea	Chauli	70-80/-	200-300/-

Prawns are considered the best dried fishes and Khainga and Chauli are most demanded among the dried fishes.

Table-9: Zoological Name of Fishes

Sl. No.	Zoological Name of Fishes	Their Local Name
1	Callichrouspabda (Ham)	Pabada
2	Ailia Coila (Ham)	Baunsa – patia
3	Amphipnouscauchia (Ham)	Kochia
4	Mystus Cavasices (Ham)	Kantia
5	Silonia Silondia	Jalanga
6	Hilsa ilisha (Ham)	Ilishi
7	Thynnichthyes Sardkhol (Sykes)	Bareengo

Local Name of Fish	Zoological Name
Khainga	Mugil cephalus
Kabala	Mugil cephalus
Bhekta	Latescalcifera
Sahala	Dleutheronematetradactylum
Borago	Psendosciaenocointer
Bolangi	Chataessusnarus
Khuranti	Aragyropsspiniper

Methods of Preparing Fish Pickles

Prawns are brought, peeled, cleaned and mixed in a paste of turmeric and salt. For 1 kg prawns, 10 grams of turmeric and 40 grams of saltare required. Fishes are kept in the mixture for 2 hours. Then 100 grams of green chilli, 100 grams of garlic, 100 grams of ginger are half grinded and added. Some of these are also left in cut pieces for use at a later stage. Then the fishes are fried. After that Methi (10 gms), Black pepper (10 gms), mustard (10 gms), Vinegar (700 gms), curry leaves (20 gms), mustard oil (300 gms) and chilli powder are added to the fishes. Then the cut pieces of spices previously kept aside are fried in the oil along with the fishes and boiled for 15 minutes. Then the mixtures are kept for cooling. This is the receipe for one type of pickle. Other types are also prepared and packeted for selling purposes.

From 1 kg fish – the pickle produced is 100 gms (costing Rs.40/-)

Fish cutlet - First the fishes are cut and mixed with turmeric and salt. Then they are boiled and their skin is removed. Boiled potatoes are added to the fishes. Then a *tadka* (fry) of mustard, ginger, garlic is given. Then flour or besan is added with an egg. Everything is mashed and shaped into fingers and deep fried in oil.

Fish powder - The prawns are dried for three to four days after being fried in oil. For one kg prawn four coconuts are added along with green chilli, small pieces of ginger and garlic, mustard (which have been given tadka earlier) and everything is grinded into fine particles. After that it is packed. One kg fish powder costs Rs.300-400/-.

But it is a strenuous job, only on special demand they prepare fish powder and fish cutlet.

Traders – [Head-Load Traders (women) or Fish Vendors]

A large number of women in Arakhakuda village are head load traders.They take about 15-20 kg of fishes on a bamboo basket and sell it from door to door. Normally the women take prawns, crabs and dry fish for selling. Majority of women sell fish outside their area of residence. Some of them sell fish in surrounding markets. The local traders are Laxmi Behera (38), Suna Behera (40), Kamali Behera (35), Gandu Behera (41) and Ira Behera (45). They buy fishes at seventy rupees and sell it at Rs 100/-. This rate varies according to the type of fish. Their income varies between Rs.60-90/- per day.

Fig. 4: Fresh fish vendors

The local ladies fish vendors are very specialized in their occupation. Their source of income is to sell fishes. It is a tedious and strenous job. They purchase fishes from their village at a minimal price and sell it at a higher price. But because of lack of vehicular transportation facilities, sometimes they have to walk four to five kms by foot for selling fishes to the nearby villages like Keoutikuti, Sahadevpur, Koupada, Sitaipada, Gopinathpur, Brahmagiri etc. Some women are also involved in loading and unloading of fishes. A few men are involved in selling fish, a few cycle sellers are seen in the village.

In earlier times fisher women went into sea along with their husbands for fishing or to work as labourers. But now the changing technique of nets forced them to stay at home. They could not handle sitting idle. That is why a few of them helped with loading and unloading and a majority (80%) of them got involved in selling, drying and collection of fish.

Case Study-8

Name: Gandu Behera, Aged: 41, Sahi: Bhagabat

One informant Gandu Behera, who is a fresh fish seller told that she along with her other friends formed a group. The group comprises of seventy-eighty individuals. They all buy fishes from the Bahania (fisherman) who comes with fishes early in the morning. Some women's husbands are also fishermen. So they do not buy fish but take their husband's catch. Then they go to Puri by Devi bus. This bus goes to Puri three-four times in a day. At Puri, they have their specific Sahis where they sell fishes regularly. Then about 3-4 o'clock in afternoon they gather at a common place. They all come back to their village by the same bus. While coming back home, they buy some usable items with the earned money. Sometimes, they also quarrel with each other for money.

Fish Types and Market

Normally the fishes are classified as Chilika fish and Sea fish. It may be further classified into bigger fishes and small fishes. Fishes of different varieties are found near Chilika Lake. The peak season for fishing is from October to February. The most important fishes are prawns, kokili, perches, khoinga, bhekti, hilsa, pomfnet, carangids etc. The average annual production of fresh water fishes of Puri district is 15,971 metric tonnes.

Table-10: Species found in Different Seasons

Sl. No.	Months (in Oriya)	Months (in English)	Species (Local name)
1	Baisakha-Jyesta	April- May May-June	Kantia, all types of small fresh fishes.
2	Asadha-Sravana	June-July July-August	Khainga, Bekti, Sahala, Brogo, Kamda, Singada, Prones of all species.
3	Bhadraba-Aswina	August-September September-October	Hilsa, Jagla, Dangla, Khuranti
4	Kartika-Margsira	October-November November-December	Prones of all species, Jalanga, Kochia, Different types of crabs, Bhekti.

Contd...

5	Pausa-Magha	December-January January-February	Panu, Kantalia, Kanti, Seba, Pabda, Chigudi, Kabala, Rangua of all varieties
6	Phalguna-Chaitra	February-March March-April	Bolangi, Kundala, Chara.

These species are available in different seasons with varying prices. The rise of price for big and small marine fishes were 0.89%, 0.68% respectively in Odisha during 1984 to 1992. The prices are highest in Balasore and then in Puri (1.17 indices per month). It is because the major portion of the marine catches exported and fresh water fishes are consumed locally.

[Source: An economic Analysis of marine fish marketing in Odisha by Dr. Naik Dibakar]

Table-11: Fish Types

Lake	Sea
Khainga	Kanagarta
Dengula	Kokili
Rangua	Sanala
Khuranti	Golera
Sala	Gadhasa
Jagiri	Bhekta
Gana	Singada
Phulara	Patua
Chaulia	Oranga
Ora	Rangua

The sizes of fishes vary and are termed as large fish and small fish. The size of Khoinga and Sala varies from 2 feet to 3 feet where as Ora, Chaulia are small fishes with a size of 1 to 5 inches.

Fish Production in Odisha

Table-12: Fisheries Statistics (in MT)

Year	Fresh Water	Brackish Water	Total Inland	Marine	Total
2000-01	125114	13442	138556	121086	259642
2001-02	147400	20660	168060	113893	281953
2002-03	154237	19964	174201	115009	289210
2003-04	165594	24477	190071	116880	306951
2004-05	170091	23776	193867	121929	315796
2005-06	179740	23495	203235	122214	325449
2006-07	191632	22951	214583	128141	342724
2007-08	195747	22969	218716	130767	349483
2009-10	215802	25508	241310	129332	370642

Table-13: Year-wise Resource-wise Fresh Production from Brackish Water Sector (in MT)

Year	Culture Shrimp	Estutaries	Chilika	Total
2000-01	6430	2029	4983	13442
2001-02	7204	1467	11989	20660
2002-03	7171	1899	10894	19964
2003-04	8112	2312	14053	24477
2004-05	7875	2641	13260	23776
2005-06	8930	2880	12225	23495
2006-07	9654	3341	9956	22951
2007-08	10187	2735	10047	22969
2008-09	11659	3971	10702	26332
2009-10	10979	2514	11955	25508

This table shows year wise fish production from brackish water sector. There is an increasing trend in the fish production which slows down during the mid years. But there is an increase in fresh fish production.

Table-14: Fish Production from Chilika Lake (in MT)

Year	Fish	Shrimp / Prawn	Crab	Total
2000-01	3817.81	1071.38	93.60	4982.79
2001-02	9530.03	2347.78	111.07	11988.88
2002-03	8265.16	2478.28	149.81	10893.79
2003-04	10286.34	3611.37	155.51	14053.22
2004-05	8097.77	5000.71	161.89	13260.37
2005-06	7774.81	4296.02	154.08	12224.91
2006-07	6463.92	3368.97	122.94	9955.83
2007-08	6610.23	3298.08	139.12	10047.43
2008-09	6534.85	3929.68	237.50	10702.03
2009-10	7892.98	3851.49	210.89	11955.36

This table shows the production of fish, shrimp and crabs from Chilika. This year-wise quantity shows quite a sizeable fluctuation in production. But shrimp production has increased every year.

Table-15: District-wise Year-wise Marine Fish Production (in MT)

Year	Balasore	Bhadrak	Jajpur	K. para	Puri	Ganjam	Total Year-wise
2000-01	34915	9350	33899	13206	22939	6777	121086
2001-02	30341	9206	28196	13594	25168	7378	113883
2002-03	32009	10405	28527	9483	26164	8421	115009
2003-04	30061	10001	29344	10795	27503	9176	116880
2004-05	32400	10853	29985	10923	27911	9857	121929
2005-06	33787	10856	31008	7971	28557	10334	122213
2006-07	34938	11854	33179	7787	30283	10100	128141
2007-08	35163	11973	33026	7289	32243	11073	130766
2008-09	35916	12310	34388	7364	34325	11185	135488
2009-10	35998	12811	33012	4798	31431	11282	129332

The above table shows a comparative fish-production statistics. Balasore and Jajpur districts show an increase in production. Ganjam district also shows increased production.But puri district shows a decreased tendency of year wise marine fish production; the reason for this cited as ban on marine fishing.

Arakhakuda

Marine fisheries activities of Puri District with special focus on Arakhakuda (G.P.) village-

Table-16: Marine Fishery Activities

1	Length of coastline	155 km
2	No. of coastal blocks	6
3	No. of marine extension units	4
4	No. of fish loading centers	12
5	No. of fishermen villages	86
6	No. of fishermen families	12476
7	Total fishermen population	78317
8	No. of active fishermen	24598
9	No. of marine fishing cooperatives	23
10	Average annual fish landing	31000 MT

Table-17: Fish Production of Arakhakuda in comparison to Puri district-

Year	Fish Production (Puri)	Fish Production (Arakhakuda)
2009-10	31430.90	1710.82
2010-11	31880.15	1060.52
2011-12	31000.00	1200.56

The table provides production numbers of Arakhakuda in comparison to puri district. Even though only three years data has been provided, a noticeable change is visible and it can be clearly seen that the contribution of Arakhakuda village makes for a major part in the district's economy.

For overall development of a product, its popularity is as essential as its adequate production. Proper marketing and establishing the product in all localites is very important. Market is a selective group of people who are most receptive to a particular product.

Arakhakuda villagers sell fishes in local markets of Puri, Balugaon, Bhubaneswar, Pipli, Konark, and Astarang. Besides that fishes are also exported to Kolkata, Mumbai, Delhi, Japan, China etc. The recent opening of a cold storage near the village has helped the fishermen to store fishes for a longer period and obtain a good market price while selling.

List of Important Market for Fishery

Sr. No.	Local market	Regional market	Outside country market
1.	Villages along the coastline	Kolkata	Japan
2.	Balugaon	Chennai	USA
3.	Puri	Tatanagar	China
4.	Aastarang	Mumbai	
5.	Brahmagiri	Bhubaneswar	
6.	Pipli		
7.	Kakatpur		
8.	Konark		

Important Landing Centres in Puri

1. Pentakota
2. Sapakothi
3. Chandrabhaga
4. Ramachanchi
5. Nuagarh
6. Kaliakona
7. Sahana
8. Tolia
9. Harachandi
10. Arakhakuda
11. Khirishahi
12. Sciandi Ramlanka

Of the above given landing centres, Nuagarh (Astrang and Balugaon) on Chillika have proper Jetty built for anchoring water crafts. In recent times with the help of Government the CDA has built a Jetty in the Arakhakuda village for fishing and to attract tourists. The government is also providing fuel for boats. The people bring receipts from petrol pump andare reimbursed by the FEO.

Commission Agent

A study on fishing is incomplete without looking at works of the commission agent. The catch amount of fishes and shrimp are not uniform throughout the year. There is a drastic fall in fish catch in March and April. Nolias have a negative quality of engaging in heavy drinking and they often spend their entire income on alcohol. This forces them to go to money-lenders or *mohajan* in lean months. Their monthly and annual expenditure is a reflection of their causes for poverty and indebtedness.

Fishing is essentially the only source of income for these Nolias. So whenever a financial crisis arises, they turn to borrowing. First they try to take loan from their relatives at aminimal interest rate which is usually 7 percent per month. They payback their loan amount from their daily earnings. For example, if they take a loan of Rs.5000 for fishing, after completion of fishing they add Rs.1000 more to the initial amount and give Rs.6000 to the loaner. The time period for repayment is between fifteen days to a month. But it is flexible as the loaners are their relatives. Therefore they prefer this kind of loan.

Sometimes they also take loan from other people. One such middleman who gives out loans is Laxmi Narayan Behera, he takes twenty paisa interest per Rs.100. Another person's name is Bhima Behera. These middlemen also belong to Arakhakuda and are more attached with the Nolias that is why the Nolias are more exploited by them than by outsiders. But the Mahajan rates are different. In a case of Siva Behera, he takes a loan of Rs.50,000-100,000 in fishing season. He also takes boat, net and Bahania along with him. The Bahania takes Rs.7000-8000 as security deposit. From the total catch they make together, one share is for the boat, another is for the net and one is for bahania. They make a contract with the bahania for the season. If he leaves that boat or contract he has to return the security deposit. Then the Mahajan comes and takes away trays of the fishes at a minimal price. One tray contains fifty kgs of fishes. If the Mahajan wants, then he gives Rs.400/- for the fish after three or four months. The fishermen depend on the money-lenders for purchase of fishing elements, maintenance of livelihood in lean seasons and for personal expenditure. The name of some middle men are given below-

(1) Jhuna Behera

(2) Sahadev Behera

(3) Jagannath Behera

(Usually these people have sound economic and social background).

They charge 10 percent interest rate - i.e., for Rs.1000/- the interest is Rs.100. But those who want to avail loan more than Rs.40000 to 50,000, borrow the money from nearby village mahajans who are richer and well connected people. Some of them (1) Braja Jena (2) Sam Prusti (3) Bhima Mahajan are from Brahamgiri, Jenapur, Jadupur, Gobakunda and Gokhara village respectively. People borrow lakhs of rupees from them. They do not take any interest in form of cash, but interest is charged in the form of goods. These people take away fifty percent of the fishermen's catches.

The commission agents have boat which is known as "Commission Boat". They do not charge any interest for the money taken as advance by the fishermen. They either take fifty percent of the catch or people are bound to give their catch at a price usually ten-twenty percent below the market price prevailing in local market with more weighing goods than the standard weights set. As the commission agent acts as a middle man for the fish merchants of Bhubaneswar, Kolkata, Delhi and other places, due to his reach, he gets a lot of prestige in the village. Due to this system the people are not attached with Primary Fisherman Cooperative Societies (PFCS). The commission agents are known persons or relatives that is why the Nolias are also more attached to them.

Fishing Cooperatives

The government (fishfed) has given the license to people for fishing. To help their economic upliftment, cooperatives were formed in the village. The cooperatives were formed by traditional fishing people and named "Arakhakuda Prathamika Matsyajibi Society". The Central Cooperative Society (Balugaon) obtained lease of fishery sairats from the government and sub-leased to the Primary Cooperative Societies. This helped the poor fishermen to come out of the web of middle men and earn a fair price for their catch.

In 1995-96, the society had Gangadhar Behera as president and Kailash Behera as secretary. There are three fifty members in the society. Each has given Rs.52/- as entry fees per head. So the fishing people have been given license or insurance. Incase of any mishap to them or their net and boat, they are given compensation (Rs.50,000 or 1 lakh). The lease policy is for capture source or culture source. In each year the two Sahi (Laxminarayan and Bhagabat) has separately deposited Rs. 55,000 and

Rs. 30,000 in Balugaon Bank. Some people accompany the president for the deposit of money.

In this lease policy each person has given a particular area for their boat and a total of 4500 acres have been in leased for fishing. But now this organisation exists for name-sake, only to get the lease. They have not even given any lease amount to the government since five years due to ban on the Janala collection. Non-fishing people have also entered into the village with the help of middlemen. There is squabble among their leaders and the organization is unoperational now.

In Arakhakuda village there are two others marine PFCS. These are Maa Mangala and Maa Durga. Both the societies have a president and a secretary. The entry fee is Rs.10 only along with Rs.50/- given in the beginning. At first only thirty-fourty people were its members. But after the dysfunctional APMS, some people of that society came and became members of this marine PFCS. At present, there are 104 members. The people take loan from fishery department of Puri. After showing loan papers and permission, the people are given license for marine fishing. They are allotted particular places near tonda for their boat and net. If they have taken loan of Rs. 50,000 for buying a net or boat, then 50% i.e., Rs. 25,000 is given as subsidiary. Rest amount has to be immediately repayed by the people or by the *bahnia*.

Shrimp culture is also another important factor for the Nolia people because of which their social and economic life has totally changed. Now-a-days this field is totally controlled by non-fishing caste people. These people are allotted some patches for shrimp culture by government in Brahmagiri of Puri district. Due to this, there are some major changes like–

1) Reduced use of capture fishing equipment,
2) Large scale enroachment,
3) Decreased salinity of Lake water and
4) Increase in middlemen in their villages.

Marine PFC

There are two types of PFCs in Nolia society. One is Maa Mangala Marine Society and other is Maa Durga Marine Society. Maa Mangala Marine Society was formed in the year 1996 and Maa Durga was formed in 1997. At present the president and secretary of Maa Durga Society are Jateswar Behera and Judistira Behera.

All the members give Rs.600/- each per year. Then government gives Rs.1200/- to each people. This benefit is only given to BPL families. Non BPL families do not get this benefit. From 104 members, only twenty members get benefit from the government. The president told me that this is a large village and 225 people are included in BPL list. But due to improper government counting, only a few people are getting benefitted. Majority of people are deprived of the facility. This is the reason of their migration to Chennai, Delhi, and Kolkata. Few people went to Goa to work in a marine scheme for ten months. The people are not getting the member's deposit and are not interested in the membership of marine society. For license of one year the people have to pay Rs.70/- but for machine boat an amount of Rs. 100/- is chargable.

In March 2012, the officials of ICZMP formed four SHGs in Arakhakuda village. These groups consist of fifteen members belonging to different Sahis of Arakhakuda. These are as follows:

(1) Ganga Devi

(2) Baidhara

(3) Musanichandi

(4) Maa Durga

These SHGs are for male members.

(1) Name: Ganga Devi
President: Jagannat Behera
Secretary: Sanjeev Behera
Meeting: Once in a month
Place: Shelter House
Member fees: Rs.100/-
Member: Fifteen

This SHG is doing dry fish business.

(2) Name: Baidhara
President: Laxmidhar Behera
Secretary: Narashima Behera
Meeting place: Shelter house once in a month
Member fees: Rs.100/-
Member: Fifteen

This has been formed for building cow shelter houses. Loan was given and the shelter house for cows is under construction.

(3) Name: Masani Chandi
President: Dusana Behera
Secretary: Birendra Behera
Place: Shelter house
Member: Fifteen

This SHG people are engaged in poultry and dockary.

(4) Name: Maa Durga
President: Abhiram Behera
Secretary: Sukanta Behera
Place: Shelter House
Member fees: Rs.50/-

These people are engaged in selling fresh fish.

The APO of fishery has given training to these people at shelter houses. People from near by villages and Arakhakuda, are gathered at this common place. The training is given for three months. The training is on how to dry fishes using machine and how to market them, how to do fresh fish business, poultry and cow business. It is a five year scheme. A cheque of Rs. one lakh is given from Panaspada Bank to each group. A shelter house for cow, a machine for drying fish and storage house for fresh fish are under construction in Arakhakuda village. If the people do it successfully and earn profit, then only government will extend their license. The government again gives another cheque for Rs. Ten lakh for expansion of business.

These are the factors which focus on their economy. But besides their primary economy (fishing), some people of their village are also engaged in secondary occupations along with fishing.

6

Political Organisation

Political organization means political institution, political parties, advocacy of group, interest group etc. Political organisations are engaged in political activities aimed at achieving clearly-defined political goals, which improve political system and benefit the interests of their members.

Political organization refers to those aspects of a social organization specifically concerned with the management of a society's public policy "...refers to the way power is distributed and embedded in society...." (326) "the way power is used to coordinate and regulate behavior so that order is maintained" (326) the means through which a society maintains social order and reduces social disorder, the term political organization does not mean or imply government, not all political organizations make use of a government; although some do. (Wolford, 324-359)

Leadership Pattern

Leadership has played an important role in human society. The historians have glorified heroes in battle and valued the importance of their deeds for the future generations. The roles of politicians, statesmen and emperors in the development of empires, territories and nations have received considerable attention in the empirical history. In modern society too, there is a great emphasis on leadership and men with such qualities are always sought after.

According to Machia Velli, there is nothing more difficult to take in hand, more perilous to conduct or more uncertain in its success, than to take, to lead in the introduction of a new order of thing. (B M Bass, *1983)*

Anthropologically speaking a leader is a person of charismatic ability who as a hereditary principal of society holds the position of headman usually accompanied by common people as his followers. Leadership is an important aspect of political system. It is measured by the ability of taking decision, the leader being regarded as the person who either takes decision himself or herself in adecision making forum. Thus leadership occurs in a multiplicity of contexts of social actions and is not always part of a political system. Political leadership or the existence of a leadership role, which plays a part in the political system, also takes a variety of forms. Analysis of the definition and functions of a political leader is a part of the analysis of the total system of political roles of the group.

Rural conflict is a highly involved and complicated affair. A host of other factors, old ties; localism and parochialism intermingle and intertwin to produce a complex picture to which the degeneration of Indian as a man during more than a century of foreign rule, the narrowness of approach, the greed and jealousy, blind self interest and all simillar evil traits make a profound contribution. *(Desai, 1961, 409)*

Due to all these factors a leader is required in the society in order to settle disputes and conflicts and lead the society in a correct way.The leadership pattern is explained in two waysi.e traditional and modern leader.

Traditional Leader and Their Function

Family level - Nolia families hail from ancestors who were patriarchal in nature. This trait has been passed down for generations. The Father has sole authority to control and head the family. All family members obey him. After the death of the father, any property is inherited by his sons. Normally after the marriage of a son, the family breaks down. In a joint family where the brothers stay jointly, the eldest brother becomes head of family; he is the decision maker. As they have extremely poor financial background andposess nothing except boat and net, these are their only properties.

Case Study-8

Name: Kapil Behera, Aged: 45, Sahi: Laxminarayan Sahi

Kapil Behera and Jaga Behera were brothers, Jaga being the elder brother. Jaga married a girl from Andhra Pradesh and his wife didn't want to stay in the village. So they settled in Puri. Kapil along with his wife and children continued staying in their father's house. They possessed no property or land except the parental house. After five years, Jaga came and demanded share from their father's property. There was some dispute between two brothers which led to division of family and property.

The family level leader is hereditary in nature.

Lineage Level

Lineage consists of a numbers of families together. The eldest members among them are the lineage leaders. This is not hereditary. The lineage leader possesses several criteria. He is calm; and a person who has capacity to solve the problems of families. In case of marriage, different types of festivals and worship, all the lineage people of a family are invited and gathered at a common place and enjoy. In case of mortuary rites the presence of lineage leaders and members are essential. Rituals can not be done without them. The lineage leader solves:

a. Problem or dispute at family level.
b. In any problem or dispute in family property, the leader arranges a meeting and tries to solve this.
c. The lineage people can not marry within their lineage. If any such cases or intermarriage occurs in the families, these are solved by lineage leader personally. But if they face difficulties, the case comes to the village committee.

Village level- Traditionally the village leader is called as Pradhan. The Pradhan is more powerful than the modern leader. They are the sole authority; whatever they say and think is right. The post of Pradhan is hereditary. After the father, his eldest son inherits the position and in case of absence of eldest son, the youngest son also inherits it. In some cases people elect the Pradhan by other criteria such as,

1. He must be above forty years of age,
2. He must belong to financially sound family,
3. He must have the capacity to handle difficult situations,
4. He must be helpful in nature.

The villagers admire the Pradhan. He gives money to crew members. Nobody is allowed to marry in the village before the Pradhan's son. If two marriages occur simultaneously, first Pradhan's son's procession goes out, then other procession are allowed. Those whose son's or daughters' marriages are solemnised, they give eight and nine cakes (pittha) to Pradhan's house, only then their marriages are allowed.

During the year 1990 there was a custom called Pradhan Pratha. People used to call the village headman as "Pradhan" and the person next to him as "Upa-Pradhan". In 1982 a person named Masani Behera was the Pradhan who presided for eighteen years. At that time the up-Pradhan was Narayan Bisoi and Secretary was Gajendra Behera.

The villagers have been divided into two Sahis, the Telugu Sahi and the Odia Sahi. Each Sahi has two Pradhans for their political council. For every two hundred individuals each Sahi has nominated one Pradhan. Earlier, there was a system called "Dui athara Jalia" system. It meant that eighteen individuals of each Sahi and one Pradhan constituted a village committee. Both Laxminarayan and Bhagabat Sahi have different committees. But the committee is of *Jalias* or people who own net and boat. Those who don't own net and boat are called *Bahania*. They are not allowed to become members of the village committee. The Bahania's son is *bahania*; only thing is that he is given food not money.

Masani Behera was very powerful during his time because he was the only one Pradhan who ruled both Sahis for several years. The place where village meeting occurs is called Kothoghara or Palamandap. At that time when Masani ruled, the Kothoghara was made of mud and had no roof but now it has been cemented and has an asbestos roof.

During every festival, the sacrifice to their religious deity is first performed by the Pradhan. The altar is made from the coconut scalp that comes from the Pradhan's house. The soil from Pradhan's house is used by villagers for making altar. People take water from Pradhan's house called "Baduapani" which is used in rituals by the unmarried girl or boy, before getting ready for marriage. In case of birth, death or marriage, the Pradhan is the first person to be invited. People offer him "dasahata" dhoti and Brahmapur Pata as an honour when he attends any ceremony. No body can walk in front of the Pradhan with an umbrella or while wearing shoes. If Pradhan is going on a road then people stop there and bow down. This is the kind of respect that the illiterate and simple Nolias give to their leader.

In case of Thakurani Jatra, the Pradhan is first to decide everything and give money to Kalisi for the festival. There is always coordination between two Pradhans. In case of any intervillage dispute the two Pradhans along with some selected members go and try to solve the case. The other caste folks like Gouda or Kandara do not give the same respect and prestige which is given by Nolia people.

But all these customs did not last for long. The former president Narayan Behera in 1996-98 tried a lot to establish different regulations in the committee in order to maintain peace and security, where everybody got equal status and justice. During Pradhanpratha the punishment was not so strict. People were even allowed to practice polygamy but now this is a serious crime andmany cases of polygamy are found in the village.

Traditional Political Organisation

Village Level:

The village is a uniclan village i.e (all the people posses the same gotra, Nageswara). But there are different lineages with have leaders. The village also has a particular committee called village committee. The selection of the leader depends on the economic condition and this post is not hereditary in nature.

The village is divided into different Sahis and sub-sahis. Two of them are large Sahis named Laxminarayan Sahi and Bhagabat Sahi. They have different presidents or secretaries. Their headman is called Sabhapati (President) and the Secretary is called Upsabhapati.

Structure of Their Hierarchy in Village Committee

President

↑

Vice-president

↑

Cashier

↑

Assistant treasurer

↑

Secretary

The name of president of the two Sahi-

Bhagabat Sahi	Laxmi Narayan Sahi
Gangadhar Behera (2011)	Narayan Behera (2011)
Simanchal Behera (2010)	Maguni Behera (changed within 3 months) (2010)
Rabindra Behera (2009)	Judhistira Behera (2009)
Gangadhar Behera (2008)	Pabitra Behera (2008)

(2011year)	BhagabatSahi	Laxmi Narayan Sahi
President	Gangadhar Behera	Narayan Behera
Vice President	Simanchal Behera	Kalicharan Behera
Cashier	Krushna Ch. Behera	Judistira Behera
Asst. Treasurer (Secretary)	Konda Behera	Dabru Behera

The term of the president is normally one year but they have no time limit. Whenever Nolias wish to have a new president, they change the current president. The village committee comprises of 25 members of whom 5 are core members and other 20 are heads of some selected families. Each Sahi holds different village meetings at different places. But in some complicated cases like divorce, remarriage or murder, a meeting of both village committees along with some other headmen of families takes place. Other sub Sahis like Majhi Sahi, Harachandi and Masani Chandi are attached with Laxminarayan Sahi and Bhagabat Sahi. Their problems are also solved by the respected village committee.

Normally the election of president is held once a year. But this year (the year when this data was collected) due to a number of disturbances the people have changed their president within the first three months of his presidential tenure. This year's election process has been a hugewaste of time which and has created political instability in their village.

The committee members belong to the age group of 30-62 years. Normally those who are of advanced age having more life experiences than others are elected as the president. The middle aged people remain as members of the committee. In the absence of the president, secretary has the sole authority in all matters.

Fig. 5: Kothoghar

The meeting occurs in the Kothoghara of each Sahi. There is no fixed time to hold a meeting. In a general meeting people elect their president and the president elects other core members. Together, they elect other committee members. Some people are not interested to become committee members due to lack of time. In that case, if the person is an efficient one, the president tries to convince him to be a part of their committee. The committee members are replaced in phases. In case of allegation against any of the committee member, the president removes him immediately.

Functions- The village meetings are held before any festivals like Thakurani Jatra, Dusschra, Ganesh Puja, Ramnavami and Phagu Saptami pala. A person who belongs to harijan caste is given some money called "chatia" to beat the 'ghanta' and goes round the village informing the villagers about the meeting.

In each Sahi the committee sells some parts of Chilika to their village members and earns money. This is deposited with the president, which they use at the time of their Sahi's festivals. Especially prior to Ram Navami, Bhagabat Sahi's committee held a meeting to decide how to do pala and what the future expenditures will be for the year. Likewise in Laxmi Narayan Sahipala occurs in Phagu Saptami and prior to this all committee members sit and decide the expenditure for the entire year. The village (Sahi) committee also gives allowances from its funds to the priest. The priests of Laxmi Narayan temple and Bhagabat temple are paid for the whole year in advance.

All the problems of Nolias, their everyday troubles, problems relating to fishing, marriages, dowry, remarriage, wife-beating, inter-caste marriage, black magic, property disputes, quarrel for dry fish or selling of fish etc. are solved by the village committee.

The Nolia females are economically self-sufficient. The families totally depend on females and yet the dominance of male members still exists. The females are not allowed to participate in village meeting. The male head of every family participates in case of any disturbances among females. Now-a-days some of the female cases are solved by SHGs. In villages near Arakhakuda, females are gradually participating in the village meetings. The selection of ASHA members are done by the committee. The Anganwadi workers, cooks and supportive teachers also get some preference from committee.

Role of a Leader

When a case comes to the village committee, the members of committee listen to both parties attentively and finally give the decision. In case of inter-family dispute, the president first tries to act as mediator between the two families to solve the problem smoothly. In case he does not succeed then the case goes to village level meeting.

All the villagers have a special respect for the committee members and when the presidents are no longer in power people still show some respect to them. But when some cases are not solved by the committees, those cases are taken to the police station in Brahmagiri.

Mode of Punishment - Punishments are of different types, oath and ordeal are also present in their society.The amount of punishment varies. They consider theft as the most offensive crime.

For eveteasing the fine is between Rs.1000/- to Rs.2000/-.

The president Judistira Behera told -

- If some body has stolenteppa, then the culprit was fined Rs.500/-.
- If some bodyhas stolen the pillar (*khunta)* of boat then he was fined Rs.5000/-.

The difference in the amount occurred because the stolen teppa is recovered from the guilty person. The khunta, by which the boat moves to sea is expensive and if it is stolen, heavy loses are incurred to compensate which heavy fines are imposed.

In one case study, some women and girls of the village started jumping around naked. The people suspected black magic and complained to the committee. The president and committee decided to call all the Gunias and asked about this but they told the president having no idea about the incident. In that case all the committee members dragged them and locked them in Kothoghara and beat them thoroughly. After that, they agreed to accept that everything was done by them to frighten the villagers, so that the people would respect and give them money. The committee told the relatives of Gunias to give a fine of Rs.10,000/- per head and freed them. The sorcerers were also told to cancel their magic. In some cases the Gunia are also forced to take oath in the name of Lord Jagannath's Prasad and Thakuranibudi. The people also carried out ordeals to identify the real culprit. Gunias were given physical torture like a pinch of fire on their tongue to tell the truth.

Usually the committee continuously asks a person to tell the truth when he is accused of any crime. If he does not confess through oaths, he is subjected to tormenting ordeals. This is the only way to catch the real culprit.

These types of social control hint at the regulation of human behaviour. It may be regarded as referring to the aggregate of values and norms by means of which tension and conflict between individuals and groups are mitigated in order to maintain the solidarity of some more inclusive groups and also to the arrangement through which these values and norms are communicated and instilled.

The president told that in case of misappropriation of funds by any committee members, he is bound and charged to return the missing sum and is ousted from their society. For Nolias, ousted from society means he is not allowed to fish or use his net, boat etc. The person who sold liquor in the village deposited a fine of Rs.5000/- and the committee shaved his head and made him walk barefoot round the village.

Modern Political System

Panchayat Raj System:

Panchayat raj is a system of governance in which Grampanchayats are the basic units of administration. It has three levels: Gram (village), Janpad (block), Zilla (district). Mahatma Gandhi advocated Panchayat rajas the foundation of India's political system, a decentralized form of government where each village is responsible for its own affairs.The term for such a vision was Gram Swaraj. (Village self governance) (Mitra, 2001)

However the local governance rules of the colononial government did not make panchayats the agency for local development. After independence, following the guidelines of the union government under the Balwantrai Mehta Committee report, the Odisha government adopted a three tier Panchayati Raj system in the state. The Panchayati Raj laws were revised again and made more effective after the73rd Constitutional Amendment. The Panchayati Raj system in the state has undergone systematic changes in the post-colonial period and the recent changes following 73rd Amendment and PESA Act is treated as a landmark revision. (Pradhan, Biswadayal, 2011)

Panchayats in Pre-independence Period: Like other states, Odisha has a long tradition of panchayat system, which is informal and there is no evidence to substantiate this since there are no written records. Generally, small disputes as well as everyday problems were solved through the village panchayat system. Except for major crimes like murder etc., where they took the help of police but other petty crimes were solved through the village panchayat. During the colonial period Britishers tried to initiate formal division to take control over the local administration for their own benefit but there was no local administration in the rural areas. In order to control and collect revenues from rural areas they appointed local Zamidars or local elites as agents.

So their objective was to keep people away from power and self governance. But, their main aim was the protection of imperial interests and hence they paid more attention to urban administration rather than rural (Joshi and Narwani, 2002). They were concentrated near trading centers; their interest in the beginning was limited to the creation of local bodies of nominated members in the major cities and towns.

Panchayats in Post-independence Period: Odisha became a separate state in 1936. There arised a need to empower the grassroots people. After independence Orissa Panchayat Act, 1948 was enacted. This shows how Odisha had already tried to empower its panchayats even before the formal Panchayati Raj system came into existence. During that time some programmes formed by the centre to empower the rural people like Community Development Programme (CDP, 1952), National

Extension Service (NES, 1953) came up but these two programmes failed to achieve the goal. An attempt was taken to abolish the Zamidari system and provide power to local-self-government in the state and make its services more accessible to the ordinary people (Bailey, 1959). The Balwantrai Mehta Committe, 1956 was appointed by the centre to review these programmes. This resulted in the creation of a three-tier system of Panchayati Raj Institutions to organize and manage the rural development activities. The Orissa Anchal Sasan Act, 1954 was repealed after the introduction of three-tier Panchayati Raj system on the lines of Balwantrai Mehta Committee Report in 1959. Since the gram panchayat had already been constituted at the village level in 1948, Orissa Panchayat Samiti and the Zilla Parishad Act, 1959 was passed. The framework of the new institutional arrangement comprised Village Panchayats at the village level, Panchayat Samiti at the middle and Zilla Parishad at the apex level. After this Odisha accepted three tiers Panchayati Raj system in 1960-61. A new act called the Orissa Gram Panchayat Act, 1964 was passed in 1965 relating to the gram panchayats in the state and empowered the state government to establish and constitutethe grama, the gramasasan (village government) (Pradhan, 2011).

The main aim of the Panchayati Raj has been democratic decentralization, rural self-government and rural development. Socio-economic development of rural India has been a major goal. Panchayat Raj has been designated to encourage the people of rural areas to meet their needs locally.In modern political system the pranchayat raj is in action. There is a 50 percent reservation for women in panchyat elections.

This system is now found in each and every villagein Odisha. In Arakhakuda village the former Sarpanch was a man namedBalabhadra Naik whereas now the Sarpanch is a lady called Mohini Behera. The majority of people are followers of either one of the two parties – BJD and Congress. Constantly, there is discord between the party members and it often leads to murder or injury of a person. Arakhakuda is a politically sensitive village.

In Odisha, BJD is the ruling party. The former Sarpanch of Arakhakuda village was a BJD party member (Bhalabhadra Naik) who ruled on his own terms. Even though his contributions to the village are major he always favored his party people.

The list of BPL holders, beneficiaries of IAY, Mokhudia are finalized by the Sarpanch and given to the block. In all these schemes, the Sarpanch

Naik always preferred to include BJD supporters. This resulted in anti-BJD feeling among the villagers. The Sarpanch did not belong to Arakhakuda village. So this year again the election for the post of Sarpanch took place. There was a contest between BJD and Congress Party. Some independent candidates also participated in the election. Bulei Behera's symbol was an open book where as Mohini Behera's symbol was a fish. Both of them campaigned for themselves. Mohini Behera won by a majority of votes.

In an interview with Mohini Behera, she narrated that her success goes to her husband Harihar Behera and sons. Even though she is not very educated, she understands the problems of her village people. She wants– (a) to dig ponds, (b) include more people in BPL list and (c) provide toilets for village people.

The inter-village disputes are resolved by village committee. But when it is not solved or any inter-ethinic group conflict arises then it is solved by the Sarpanch.

Case Study - 9

Name: Sahadev Behera, Aged: 38, Sahi: Masanichandi

A person named Sahadev Behera married a woman named Aramani Behera last year. But shortly after his marriage, Sahadev Behera eloped away with another woman. After fifteen days he came back home. The village committee summoned Sahadev and conveyed to him that his second wife was a prostitute. Therefore he should divorce her and accept his first wife. He did not agree to their proposal. So the village committee fined him Rs.50,000. Sometimes the fine amount exceeds upto Rs. one lakh. The fine that was collected from Sahadev was given back to his first wife along with all the items included in the dowry that she had brought during her marriage, so that she could lead a smooth life without the support of her husband and remarry in future.

Case Study - 11

Name: Narayan Behera, Aged: 49, Sahi: Majhi Sahi

Shrimp seed collection is a good source of income for the people. The shrimp mafias are present to collect shrimp seed for their business.

Collection of Janala is banned by the government in Arakhakuda village. In 2012, the present president Narayan Behera (52+) helped

Nolias in lifting the ban on Janala collection by requesting some MLAs. The people of Arakhakuda were very happy and started collecting shrimp seeds. But the former president Maguni Behera (54+) opposed this lifting of ban as he found that school children skipped school to engage in shrimp seed collection. In another ill-effect of shrimp seed collection, many other species of fishes either disappeared or decreased. Due to Maguni Behera's opposition, some people chopped off his right hand. Even though he has recovered from the injuries he sustained and approached the village committee for justice, the case is pending.

Case Study - 12

Name: Gadia Behera, Aged: 42, Sahi: Harachandi Sahi

This case deals with a theft incident which happened about three years back. One day a person named Gadia Behera stole the catch of fishes which the Nolias had brought back and kept in their teppa. At first he could not be pinpointed but his subsequent theft of the net of Raghunath Behera helped to identify him. The village committee cross-questioned a child who was initially caught and came to know about their leader. The committee excused the child, but punished the leader, Gadia Behera. He was ordered to pay a penalty of Rs.5000/- and return the net. The person, who had purchased the stolen items and sold it, was also fined with a penalty of Rs.2000/-.

A person unable to pay the penalty amount is given physical punishment. He is given a pot containing hundred litres of water to carry on his head. They write "choro" on his back and take him bare-bodied on a procession through the village.

Case Study - 13

Name: Sankar Behera, Aged: 32, Sahi: Harachandi Sahi

The case is of Harachandi Sahi of Arakhakuda village. Sankar Behera (32) was the eldest son of Loknathand Laxmi Behera. Loknath Behera had two sons and two nieces. Both of his sons left their wives and home, fled to puri and stayed with other women. The parents of these men wanted to accept this situation and drive away the first wives of their sons Parama/ Uma Behera (wife of Sankar Behera) and Narashima Behera (wife of Shiv Behera).

The first wives demanded justice and the case is now pending under village committee. Harachandi Sahi has a separate village committee. In case of complicated cases, the Harachandi Sahi committee takes advice from Laxminarayan and Bhagabat Sahi village committees.

Case Study - 14

Name: Duryadhana Behera, Aged: 38, Sahi: Bhagabat

Dryadhana Behera (38+) is a fisherman who kept his net in his backyard. Dhanu Behera (37+) has stolen his net while being in a drunken state and sold it in the market. Dryadhana Behera he went to committee for justice when he found that his net was missing. He narrated the entire incident infront of the village committee. Then the committee asked various questions to guess the real culprit.

The committee fined Rs.400/- as punishment to Dhanu. In theft cases they also send the people to jail.

Case Study - 15

Name: Arjuna Behera, Aged: 43, Sex: Male, Sahi: Laxminarayan

In the 1980s, there was inter-Sahi dispute in the Arakhakuda village. Before that, both Sahi combinely celebrated all the festivals. During Thakurani jatra, when "Nagamedha" of Thakurani went through the village, suddenly a disturbance happened and the two Sahi people started throwing stones at each other and the matter escalated. The village committee was helpless. So gentlemen from nearby maujas of Bhagbanpur, Sana Patna, Manikpatna, Jenapur were invited and the case was solved.

Case Study - 16

Name: Mohini Behera, Aged: 50, Sahi: Laxminarayan

Mohini Behera (50) was contested for panchayat election. Her husband name Harihar Behera (57), two sons and two daughters supported her. She contested the election for the first time in the year 2012 from Congress party. I found that majority people of Arakhakuda village supported the Congress candidate. Even though her educational background was poor and there were three other candidates, Mohini Behera won by a majority of 150 votes. Mohini Behera got support from her family as well as from villagers Laxmidhar Behera, Judistira Behera, and Duryadhan Behera. The former Sarpanch of BJD party was not concerned about the development of their village and they wanted a development oriented person.

When I interviewed her and asked what she wanted to do for her village, she told that she wanted to dig a pond as the village lacked toilets. She also wanted to provide BPL card to the needy people, and keep the environment and village clean.

Case Study - 17

Name: Jaga Behera, Aged: 32, Sahi: Harachandi

Jaga Behera (32) is a fisherman who goes for fishing in Chilika. Raghu Behera (36) of same village did not want Jaga to become more prosperous than him. To render Jaga incapable of fishing, he struck Jaga on his head. Jaga complained to village committee and Raghu was found guilty. He was imposed a fine of Rs.500/- for his misdeed.

The fine amount varies for different crimes and is fixed by the village committee members. With the changing times the amount has also changed. The present amounts of fine levied for each crime is given below:

(1) If someone strikes a person on his head he has to pay a fine of Rs.1200/-,

(2) If someone beats somebody with a stick then he has to pay a fine of Rs.600/- and

(3) If one has used slang language then he has to pay Rs.100/- to Rs.200/-.

When somebody was unable to pay the fine, he was boycotted by the community and barred from fishing.

Case Study - 18

Name: Jayanti Behera, Aged: 20, Sahi: Majhi Sahi

Jayanti Behera (20+) of Harichandi Sahi married Gyan Behera (25+) of Majhi Sahi, Arakhakuda village. It was an arranged marriage and both of them were happy but after a year of marriage Gyan had an affair with a woman from another village and eloped with her. Jayanti was very sad and came to village committee for justice. The committee fined an amount between Rs.50,000/- to Rs.1 lakh to her husband. Gyan was forced to divorce Jayanti and return all dowry money and both went their separate ways.

Case Study - 19

Name: Dantu Behera, Age: 45, Sahi: Bhagabat Sahi

Generally every man/group is allotted a particular area/phase in the sea for fishing activities. But dispute arises when one catches more fish than the other.

It is a case study of two people Dantu Behera and Dev Behera. As per practice they both went into the sea for fishing but Dantu observed that Dev had more catch than him. Dantu tried to find out the cause for his failure in fishing. He thought that due to some mantra-jantra, he was not able to catch more fish. Out of anger Dantu killed Dev.

FIR was lodged against Dantu. Village committee intervened to solve the issue amicably and charged an exorbitant fine of Rs.80,000/- but Dantu did not respond. The case remains unsolved as the police have no further information to solve the case.

Case Study-20

Name: Erandi Behera, Aged: 30, Sahi: Bhagabat Sahi

She is the mother of the victim (Chabi). Chabi was married to a person named Kailash Behera. On the fourth night of her marriage, the husband eloped away with his girlfriend. Then the victim went to committee and started crying. Committee called both the parties and charged 1.5 lakh rupees fine from boy's side. This amount was taken by the committee, and another marriage was arranged for Chhabi and she was given the rest of the money. But the second husband Promad Behera also eloped with a handicapped lady after six years of having a daughter with Chhabi. Again the case went to committee. The committee told Promad to live with one wife. Promad went back to Chhabi (his first wife and daughter) and gave compensation of Rs.50,000/- to the handicapped girl.

In every case the judgement of village committee is different. The committee members are matured enough to handle all problems. That is why the Nolias obey the committee and have great faith on the committee.

7

Women Empowerment

Empowerment is the process of obtaining basic opportunities for marginalized people, either directly or through the help of stable organizations or groups of people who are well informed about various opportunities. It also includes actively thwarting attempts to deny those opportunities. Empowerment also includes encouraging, and developing the skills for self-sufficiency, with a focus on eliminating the future need for charity or welfare in the individuals of the group. This process can be difficult to start and implement effectively.

Women empowerment is the process which enables women to fully access personal or collective power, authority, influence, and to employ that strength when engaging with other people, institutions or society. In other words, "Empowerment is not giving people power; people already have plenty of power in the wealth of their knowledge and motivation to do their jobs magnificently. Empowerment may be defined as letting the latent power out." It encourages people to gain skills and knowledge that will allow them to overcome obstacles in their life or work environment and in due course help them develop their inner self and position in the society.

It does not mean ignoring males but the truth is both genders desperately need to be equally empowered. Empowerment occurs through improvement of conditions, standards, events, and global perspective of life. (Choudhury, N., 2009)

Empowerment is the one of key factors in determining the level of achievement of development in the status and position of women in the society. India specially focuses on empowering women and girls, because we believe that they hold the key to long lasting social changes in any community. Therefore there is always a united approach to empower women socially, economically and politically.

Women bear most of the responsibilities for meeting basic needs of their family and yet they are systematically denied resources, information and freedom of action which they might need at any point of time to fulfill these responsibilities properly.

Studies have shown that when women are supported and empowered, the society benefits overall. Their families are healthier, more children go to school, agricultural productivity improves and incomes increase. In short, communities become more resilient. This study focuses on fisher women of the Arakhakuda village.

In fishing society women play a critical role. According to Marine fishers' Census 2005, 756,931 fisher folks are involved in fishing and allied activities, of them 365,463 are women. About 152,692 women are engaged in marketing of fish against 54,670 men. (*Sharma, Chandrika: 2010)*

Odisha is a state in which most of the fisherwomen are engaged in catching and vending fish. They observe Telugu tradition in their day to day social life, but over the period of time and as a result of cross culture they have learnt to speak Odia while keeping their Telugu tradition intact. Now there is a mixed culture. *(Patnaik, 2011)*

Women in Social Life

The woman is the fulcrum on which the home hangs. Her role at home is something only she can do. The classical women's movement of the 19th and 20th century was a movement by women. They sought fundamental changes in gender relations by improving women's condition for economic, social, political and cultural perspectives both in comparison with their traditional situation and in relation to men.

In past women were mostly illiterate (about 90%). But now the situation has changed. The female literacy rate is much higher than males. During this study, I came across a lady named Malati Behera (35), wife of Judhistira Behera who is engaged as Anganwadi worker. She is quite active and sincere. But unfortunately her husband is jobless. He is also a graduate. Malati is managing both her home and job front. She told "it is quite strenous on her part to support her family as well as doing job". She is the first educated bride of Arakhakuda village. Another lady Naini Behera (37) wife of Kailash Behera is also an Anganwadi worker. I found a healthy number of women who are working in Anganwadi centre.

Among school going children, female students are less in number. But this year nine girls have passed out from Arakhakuda UGUP School. Many girls are going to college. In my study I found a girl named Rupa Behera (16 year), mother – Aruna Behera, Father – Sahadev Behera who is studying plus II science in Panaspada College. She told me that her inspiration was her teacher and the desire to improve the bad condition of women in her village.

Table-18: Contribution of Women in Different Activities

Sl. No.	Activities	Contribution of Women in %
1	Cooking	96.00%
2	Child care and education	85.00%
3	Family health	85.00%
4	Sanitation	80.00%
5	Finance including repayment of loan.	52.00%
6	Business	40.00%

The above table shows in percentage, the contribution of women towards various activities. The percentage has been taken on an average basis. From the table we can notice that women have almost equal contribution in every sphere of life.

The Nolias have a patriarchal family. In the past they used to live in joint families. But their difficulties made them realize that after their marriage to another person, they had a better life if they stayed in a nuclear family. One informant of the village shared her feelings with me and explained why it is difficult for them to stay together. As they are financially very weak, having many mouths to feed is not their cup of tea. So she stays withher husband and children because of which she can give quality education to her children and easily manage the financial needs of her house.

If we take a look at the case of marriage or birth rituals, the situation faced by women is quite negative. The dowry system and child marriage have harmed the women. About 31 percent of the respondents were married before the age of ten. Only 36 percent women were married at eighteen years. About 33 percent of them were adults at the time of their marriage.

The delivery of a baby takes place in the house or at the hospital depending on the situation. The ASHA members play an important part during delivery along with the midwives and nurses. The Arakhakuda village does not have a hospital. In case of any emergency one has to go to Panasapada hospital.

Besides that the women also participate in various religious functions, festivals and rituals. The role of women is prominent while celebrating all types of rituals. Rituals specifically related to fishing, boat making are arranged by women but done by men. Each ritual has sacrifices. Whatever male animal sacrifices like (goat, cock, pig) are given to their goddess, the offerings are taken both by male and female members. But in some tribal societies these offerings are taken only by male members. The people observe festivals like Dola Purnima, Makar Sakaranti, Durga Puja, and Chaiti Ghoda puja. In all these festivals we found a dominant role of men. Females of Arakhakuda are allowed in the temples of goddess but with restrictions. But the unmarried girls are not allowed to participate in rituals relating to fishing.

In case of marriage and divorce there is no hard and fast rule for settlement of marriage. It is very flexible. Whenever they wish, they can divorce their spouse and remarry. The position of a widow in their village is very precarious. The women do *Ishana* puja in their house, which is placed in their "Pujaghar". A festival called Bhogi is done by women where offerings are given to the ancestors. Women have empowered themselves in every sphere. Their roles in activities are changing.

In Arakhakuda village the total numbers of males are 2291 and total numbers of females are 2284.

Table-19: Showing Activities Cart of Women of Different Age Groups

Age group	Activities
15 – 25	Going to school /college, doing household works
25 – 35	Selling fishes, rearing cocks, ducks, goats and doing other post harvest activities, Anganwadi worker
35 – 45	Selling fishes, drying fishes, members of SHG or ASHA
Above 45	Repairing nets and drying fishes in an open space.

The above table shows that there is a division of labour among Nolia women according to their age groups, the women do diverse activities.

Women in Economic Life-

The division of labour among fishing community is quite visible. When men go out for fishing, women take care of other activities. Women are involved in all post harvest activities such as loading handling, sorting, grading, drying and marketing. The entire fisher household comprises of boats, nets and some net making instruments. All people have nets but only 30-40 percent people have their own boats. Others have catamarans and rented boats.

From two hundred women respondents, hundred are regular fish vendors. Others are occasionally engaged in fish vending. In fishing season, 56 percent fisher women spend 8-10 hours per day in fishery activities besides attending to the regular household activities. But during the lean season the people work only for 5 to 6 hours a day. Apart from that adult members and girls are also involved in fishing. The girls also support their mothers by helping them in household activities.

The division of labour shows that men go out for fishing while the women are engaged in distribution. Majority of women are engaged in dry fish business. Only some percentages of women are involved in fresh fish marketing. But villages around Arakhakuda and near Gopalpur are more involved in fresh fish marketing (seventy percent).

Whenever a catch arrives, on the shore, the best fishes in the lot go to the money lenders. The remaining fishes are taken for door to door selling by women and for this purpose, the women walk nearly 11-12 kilometers. The fish that remain after the door to door selling is over are taken for drying to again help in their disposal. Now-a-days, the amount of catch has substantially reduced. Therefore, some women are buying fresh fish and taking it directly for drying as dry fish marketing gives better returns. In Arakhakuda village, I found that women who have no kins, and are economically in a very detrimental state, are involved in fish vending.

The women also work as labourers in cashew-fields generally for three months in a year. Some village women also collect shrimp seeds which are taken by the shrimp agent. But they are paid minimal amount. In the recent years the marine fish economy has gained importance because of substantial foreign exchange earned through export of prawn and other fishes. But the women are not aware of this situation. They are still accepting frugal pay because they need to make ends meet. Nearly 40 to 45 percent women are involved in business. Some families, who have sound economic condition, are engaged in both fishing and non fishing activities. In those families women are engaged in business like managing bettle shops (eight women), grocery shop (fourteen women) vegetable shop (three women) etc.

Case Study - 21

Name: Urulu Behera, Aged: 29, Sahi: Bhagabat Sahi

During this study, an informant Urulu Behera (29+) told me that she manages a grocery shop. Her husband is a fisherman. When he goes for fishing for the whole day, she managed the shop. After coming back in the evening, her husband takes charge of the shop. In early morning Urulu finishes all works and sends her son to school. Then she opens the shop at about nine o'clock in morning. She closed the shop only for one hour in afternoon. Her daily income from the shop is Rs.80-100. She manages the shop more efficiently than her husband.

In past when women went for fishing, they carried country liquor with them. But now the custom is totally changed. The people of Arakhakuda have built their temporary shelter near Chadchadi and Dhalabali for fishing. These are in between Chilika and the sea. The women make country liquor in the temporary settlement area. People from their main settlement village go there for liquor and the charge is Rs. 10 per glass.

Table-20: Division of Labour in Fishing

Sl. No.	Fishing Activities	Sex-wise Division	Remarks
1	Fishing	Men	Taboo for women
2	During the first catch	Men	Taboo for women
3	Sorting of Fish	Women and Children	–
4	Repairing of Net	Women and Men	–
5	Making of Dry fish	Women and Children	–

Contd...

6	Catching the Janala	Men, Women and Children	–
7	All rituals of fishing	Only Men	–
8	Trading of fishes	Mainly women, sometimes men	Taboo for women.

The table shows a clear cut division in labour in fishing caste communities. Some fishing activities are done by males where as processing, marketing, janala collecting etc. are done by females. Mainly male persons of age group of twenty to thirty-five go for fishing. But older men do not go for fishing as it mainly depends on the physical condition of people. Women of different age groups are involved in all types of activities.

Women in Politics

The principle of gender equality is enshrined in the Indian constitution in its preamble, fundamental rights, duties and directive principles. The constitution not only grants equality to women but also empowers the state to adopt measures of positive discrimination in favour of women. The 73rd and 74th Amendments (1993) to the constitution of India have provided for reserevation of seats in local bodies of panchayat and municipalities for women, laying a strong foundation for their participation in decision making at local level. *(Dawan, Subodh 2010)*

The fisher women have shrugged off their traditional role of fish vendors and come a long way. They are now involved in politics. The story of Bulei Behera is noteworthy.

Case Study - 22

Name: Bulei Behera, Aged: 58, Sex: Female, Sahi: Bhagabat Sahi

The story is 25 years old. A lady named Bulei Behera (58+) had lost her husband in a severe attack of disease. She had four sons and three daughters. She had nothing to do. She then started to sell dry fish on her head. She worked hard to support her family. With the help of UAA she started a Mahila Samiti in 2003 i.e., Primary Marine Fishery Women Cooperative. After that numbers of Self Help Groups (SHG) were formed under her guidance and government support. Now she is the Vice Chairperson of Krushnaprasad Block. She devoted herself totally for welfare of people and the village. She helped a lot for women empowerment, cleanliness of village, good health and education. She is a strong personality and dominating lady. In 2012 she also participated in Panchyat election from BJD party. But she lost by 150 votes.

This is a true success story of a woman, who empowered herself and became an example for the Nolia society. Most of males are jealous of her.

Arakhakuda village has a village council, in which selected family headmen are members. Women are not allowed in the village meeting. Now most of the cases of women are solved by SHG groups.

Another lady Mohini Behera also contested in panchayat election and won the election. But in this success only her husband and son were excited.

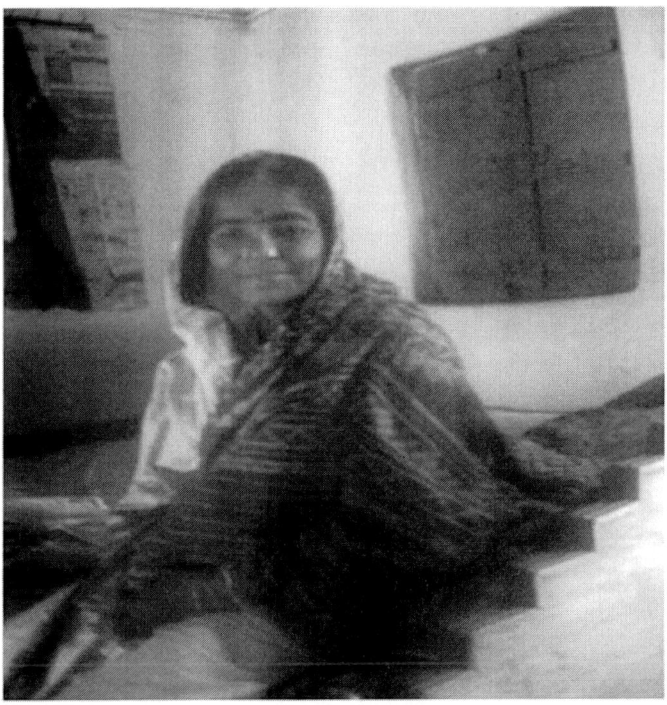

Fig. 6: Mohini Devi

They were the brain behind her sucess. Still the lady by interacting with various outsiders and dealing with complicated situation may know the real power to utilise it and enhance her position in future.

Self Help Group (SHG)

Despite a decline in poverty over the years, wide inter-state disparities continue to prevail in the poverty ratio in India. Bihar, Odisha, Tamil Nadu and West Bengal had more than 50 percent of their population below the poverty line in 1983. While Tamil Nadu and West Bengal have showed reduced poverty, Bihar and Odisha continued to be the poorest states with 43 percent and 47 percent of population below poverty line compared to 27.1 percent Indian average. The micro finance programme started in 1992 but after super cyclone in 1999, Odisha economy was severely affected and a large numbers of NGOs have now also taken interest in our economy. Most of the SHG credits are linked with banks.

Social inclusion and participation in political process are impacted by SHGs. There is improvement in school enrolment, attendance, drainage facilities, toilet facilities and electricity access. Along with financial support and poverty alleviation the political process picks up momentum with the SHGs being federated and also establishes links with local self governing bodies.

Govt of Odisha launched a Self Help Mission titled 'Mission Shakti" in the entire state on International Women Day i.e. 08 March 2001. The Mission envisages strengthening of existing Self Help Groups and promoting new groups for poor women.

The objectives of the Mission are:

i. To facilitate creation of conducive environment through Self Help Act.

ii. To expand the self help movement in Orissa

iii. To build cluster associations at Block Level, Federation of Clusters at district level and network of a federation at the state level.

iv. To provide institutional capacity building support to strengthen SHG movement, and create a built-in monitoring system.

Goal of the Mission

The goal of the mission is to help develop any micro-finance federation that is already being managed, controlled and is owned by a client, during the Mission period i.e., from 2001 to 2005. They also aim to enlist the number of SHG clusters/ federations in their respective districts and grade them into categories as per the criteria fixed by the Mission, to create a benchmark of the SHGs, clusters/federation for future impact assessment, to create a resource team in each district, to develop capacity building measures/materials, to develop conduciveenvironment in the districts as to involve 80 percent women in the SHG movement by the year 2005 and to establish sustainable social intermediation between Govt. / Non Govt. Organisation and SHG members.

Approach

Mission requires a collaborative approach of different players and organisation for appropriate policy decisions, implementation, monitoring, evaluation, rating of SHGs, cluster/federation and documentation etc. The structure envisioned will be advisory in natureand would be guiding the functions of the team at different levels of SHG mobilisations. In order to implement the programme a high level steering committee is headed by the Chief Minister of Odisha and High Level Executives of the government. At the district and block level it is under the Chairmanship of District Collector and BDO respectively. Its mission is to strengthen the existing SHG and promote new groups of poor women. In this the role of NABARD is important. Not only government sector but NABARD assisted a number of NGOs for formation of SHG.

No. of NGOs involved	SHG targeted	SHG saving linked	SHG credit linked
83	8022	5438	3082

Different types of NGOs have been working for coastal districts comprising Balasore, Bhadrak, and Puri and Ganjam. But NGOs working in Arakhakuda village are very few in number. Particularly for women, SHGs are less than ten. Only one NGO UAA came and helped Budei Dei to form first Mahila Samiti which also inspired to form a SHG. After that a numbers of SHG formed with the help of bank officials.

List of Self Help Groups (SHGs)

The first Nari Seba Samiti which is called as Maa Mangala Nari Sseba Samiti or Mahila Samiti was formed under leadership of Bulei Dei by UAA organisation. Later on it was renamed as "Gajalaxmi Primary Marine Fishery Women Cooperative Society" by Fishery Department in 2003. In initial days it had 65 members, later it started increasing. Then it was divided into SHG groups. Those who were below BPL were taken and formed SHG.

1. Name of Group – Gajalaxmi SHG
   Village – Arakhakuda
   Sahi – Bhagabat Sahi
   Savings quantum – Rs.50/-
   Secretary – Bijuli Behera
   President – Dunia Behera (earlier – Budei Behera)
   Bank A/c – Panspada Neelanchala Gramya Bank

   Total Savings in Rs.1,50,000/-

This is the working and active SHG of Arakhakuda. The SHG has acquired first Position among all SHGs. It is a marketing SHG. It inspired to form number of SHGs in Arakhakuda.

2. Name of Group – Maa Mangala
   Sahi – Laxmi Narayan Sahi, Arakhakuda (L) Sahi
   No. of members – Fifteen
   Savings quantum – Rs.50/-
   Total Savings in Rs. – 85,000/-
   President – Brushna Chandra Behera
   Bank A/c (Now non-operational) – Panspada Neelanchala Gramya bank

3. Name of Group – Maa Santoshi
   Village – Arakhakuda
   Sahi – BhagabatSahi
   No. of members – Sixteen (Started recently from July 2012)
   Savings quantum – Rs.50/-
   Total Savings in Rs. – 25,000/-
   Bank A/c – Panspada Neelanchala Gramya Bank
   Secretary – Bijuli Behera
   President – Raghu Behera

	Bank A/c (Now non-operational)	–	Laxman Behera
4.	Name of Group	–	Masani Chandi
	Sahi	–	Laxminarayan Sahi
	No. of members	–	Fifteen
	Savings quantum	–	Rs.50/-
	Total Savings in Rs.	–	22,000/-
	Bank A/c	–	Panspada Gramya Bank
	Secretary	–	Monarama Behera
	President	–	Parbati Behera
	Bank A/c (Now non-operational)	–	Laxman Behera
5.	Name of Group	–	Maa Tarini
	Sahi	–	Bhagabat Sahi
	President	–	Maini Behera
	Secretary	–	Eruni Behera
	No. of members	–	Thirteen
6.	Name of Group	–	Maa Ganga Devi Group
	Sahi	–	Laxminarayan Sahi
	No. of members	–	Twelve
	President	–	Sabitri Behera
	Secretary	–	Ema Behera
	Savings quantum	–	Rs.40/-

All are working but Masani Chandi's work is slow and Maa Ganga Devi Group has now closed. The numbers of membership vary in each group. Their main aim is to prepared dry fish. Earlier the people borrowed money from money lenders, at an interest of 5-10 percent per month. The groups are engaged in dry fish activity in Buleidei's Nari Seba Society house.

The Gajalaxmi SHG took loan of Rs.50,000/- for buying some fishes for drying. Then whatever profit they earned was deposited in bank. All the members of SHG's deposit their collection in bank. After six months, only by seeing their collection, bank gives them loan at a very low interest.

Each month (starting or ending) they organise a meeting in which all members are present and discuss their issues.

In Bhagabat Sahi Maa Tarini and Gajalaxmi SHG's are marketing units. Others SHG's are productive units. Besides drying fishes, they also take loan for duck farming, goatery, poultry etc. Some members of the groups have started small shops in their locality. All the members of SHG's are illiterate.

7.	Name of Group	–	Maa Harachandi
	Sahi	–	Harachandi Sahi, Arakhakuda
	No. of members	–	Sixteen
	Savings quantum	–	Rs.50/-
	President	–	Radha Behera
	Secretary	–	Laxmi Behera
	Bank A/c	–	Panspada Gramya Bank

This SHG is now interested in doing goat herding along with dry fish business in their Sahi.

8.	Name of Group	–	Laxmi Narayan Swayam Sahayak Gosti (2007)
	Sahi	–	Laxminarayan Sahi and Bhagabat Sahi
	Place	–	Kothoghara
	No. of members	–	Fourteen
	Savings quantum	–	Rs.45/-
	President	–	Sunamani Behera
	Secretary	–	Chandrakala Behera
	Now their fees has increased to	–	Rs.50/- in 2011.
	Savings A/c	–	Rs.89,480/-
	Bank	–	Panspada Neelanchala Gramya Bank

This SHG is not working now. They said their earned money is safe with their Secretary. After six month their savings are deposited in banks, and then only bank gives them loan. The SHG gave loan to Jayanti Behera Rs.4,500/- for prawn business. One of their members Kamala Behera (38+)

is working for two groups. She was given Rs.2200 for dry fish business. But she did not inform anyone and worked for another SHG. So all the SHG members forced her to leave this SHG and she was fined to return the principal and interest money.

9.	Name of Group	–	Arakhakuda Laxmi Narayan
	Sahi	–	Laxminarayan Sahi
	Place	–	Kothoghara or in barandah of houses
	No. of members	–	Fourteen
	Savings quantum	–	Rs.35/- (At first they deposit Rs.50/-)
	President	–	Malati Behera
	Secretary	–	Reba Behera
	Bank	–	Gramya Bank
10.	Name of Group	–	Maa Budima SHG
	Sahi	–	Laxminarayan Sahi
	Place	–	Shelter house
	No. of members	–	Thirteen

During my field trip, a training programme was going on. It was a SHG's training programme. In 2012 February month, a training programme was given by Premplan (NGO – Berhampur Mandiapali). There were fifty women in four groups. Training programme was given in Kothoghara. Two SHG's for Harachandi and other two for Bhagabat Sahi were formed. They have given training on how to put signature and made aware of the different functions of SHGs.

Erini Behera, president is an ex-ward member. She does not compromise with corruption. So she did not get another chance to become ward member. Erini Behera belongs to Harachandi Sahi and has worked a lot for her sahi people. Others SHGs gave their name and earned profit from that. The SHGs are engaged in both dry and fresh fish business. They buy fish at Rs.200/- and sell it for Rs.250/-. They also learn how to do goat herding and poultry.

The newly formed SHG are given below,

1.	Name	–	Bali Harichandi group
	Sahi	–	Bhagabat Sahi

	Members	–	Fourteen
	President	–	Bamala Behera
	Secretary	–	Padma Behera
	Place	–	Cyclone shelter house.
2.	Name	–	Basudev group
	Sahi	–	Bhagabat Sahi
	Members	–	Eleven
	President	–	Bani Behera
	Secretary	–	Subhashree Behera
	Place	–	Cyclone Shelter House.
3.	Name	–	Maa Tarini
	Sahi	–	Harachandi Sahi
	Place	–	In the Harachandi temple
	President	–	Kausilya Behera
	Secretary	–	Chaabi Behera
	Members	–	Fourteen
	Savings quantum	–	Rs.200/- (formed before two months)
4.	Name	–	Sana Maa
	Sahi	–	Harachandi Sahi
	Place	–	In the Harachandi temple
	President	–	Akama Behera
	Secretary	–	Sumumani Behera
	Members	–	Fourteen
	Savings quantum	–	Rs.100/-
5.	Name	–	Maa Durga
	President	–	Laxmi Behera
	Secretary	–	Draupadi Behera
	Memers	–	Fourteen
	Savings quantum	–	Rs.100/-

The meeting place is common and meetings occured combinedly with different groups. These groups are presently active. Both the president and secretary are illiterate but now they are trying to understand their SHG's activities. All the SHG members organize a meeting once every month or every fortnight. There are fifteen members in each SHG. All members collect Rs. 50/- per head in each month. In the meeting, they discuss daily business and problems.

The main functions of the SHGs are to clean their village street, clean water outlets and tubewells. If there is any problem in the house of their group members, they solve it without going to the village committee.

All the SHGs have more or less the same functions. All members help each other and maintain co-operation. The members of the SHG take loan at the time of their need e.g. marriage, disease, or any loss in fishing, from the corpous that has been built from their deposits. They pay back the loan amount in instalments or at a lumpsum with interest. In case any individual member does not pay back at agreed time penal interest that is higher than the normal interest is charged on them.

Presently only seven SHGs are in working condition. One of my informants told me that in Arakhakuda village it is difficult to know the exact number of SHGs and keep track of who is a member where. Still it helps the women to have a distinct identity.

8

Impact of Developmental Assessment of Plans, Programmes and Policies

A. Types of Development Programmes by Government

All the development programmeshave been implemented in the block. The Arakhakuda village comes under Krushnaprasad block. The block is 5 kilometers away from the the village. The Chairman is the Chief Executive Head of the block office. The Vice-Chairman attends the executive work in absence of the Chairman. But the BDO is the executive head in the block office. He stays in Puri and regularly comes here to attend office work.

The programmes in India are:

1) SGSY – Swarnajayanti Gram Swarozagara Yojana - (NRLM)
2) IAY – Indira Awas Yojna
3) Mo Kudia Yojna
4) PMGSY – Pradhan Mantri Gram Sadak Yojna
5) a) OAP – Old Age Pension
   b) WP – Widow Pension
   c) NOAP – National Old Age Pension
6) BPL Card – Below Poverty Line Card
7) Antodaya Yojna
8) Arnapurna Yojna
9) Rural Water Supply Scheme (RWSS)
10) NFBS – National Family Benefit Scheme
11) ICDS – Integrated Child Development Scheme
12) Balika Samrudhi Yojana (BSY)
13) T T Immunization

14) Education – MDM

15) Health

(Upadhayay and Pandey, 2003)

These different programmes are implemented by selection of beneficiaries. This is an important task. These are the different stages by which beneficiaries are selected.

BLOCK Preparation of the list of beneficiary Pallisabha with Sarpanch and ward member (each house hold)

For the selection of beneficiary, a village meeting is arranged at Gram Panchayat office. This is conducted by Sarpanch and ward members to assist her/him. This meeting is attended by each head of household under the Gram Panchayat. The Palli Sabha is held on a particular date of the month. Palli Sabha is held every month. In that the villagers told about their problems. For solution of their problems some steps are taken through various development and welfare programmes. In pallisabha village level workers are also present. The needy people are given preference. Beneficiary is selected unanimously in pallisabha. In the selection of Sarpanch, ward member and some influential persons of the village take part.

The programmes implemented in the Arakhakuda village of Orissa are-

- SGSY – Swarnajayanti Gram Swarozagara Yojana
- Madhu Babu Pension Yojna (MBPY)
- Old Age Pension / Widow Pension / National Old Age Pension
- PMGSY
- GGY – Gopalbandhu Gramya Yojna
- IGNOAP - Indira Gandhi National Old Age Pension
- Swajal Dhara
- MGNREGS - Mahatma Gandhi National Rural Employment Guarantee Scheme
- Mattha Pokhari
- Arnapurna Yojna
- Antodaya Yojana
- Indira Awas Yojana

- BPL Card
- Integrated Child Development Scheme (ICDS)
- Education
- Health

1. Swarnajayanti Gram Swarozagara Yojana (SGSY)

The Swarnajayanti Gram Swarozagara Yojana is a centrally sponsored programme which is jointly funded by the Government of India and the State Government of each state in the ratio of 75:25. The programme is smoothly implemented through concerned District Rural Development Agency (DRDA) at the district level and through concerned Panchayat Samities at Block level. It was first started on 1st of January 1999.

SGSY aims at establishing a large number of micro enterprises in rural areas, in order to increase the potential of poor rural inhabitants. Those who are called as Beneficiaries or Swarozgaries may be families or SHGs. Efforts are made to involve women members in each SHG. The beneficiaries are financially below poverty line.

Under this scheme atleast 50 percent of the benefits are reserved for SC and ST, 40 percent are for women and 3 percent is reserved for differently abled people. In Arakhakuda village, the number of beneficiaries under the scheme is low. Individual beneficiary gets a subsidy at uniform rate of 30 percent of the project cost, upto Rs.7, 500/-. However, SC/ST is given subsidy at a further subsidised rate of 50 percent of the scheme cost, upto Rs.1.25 lakh. SGSY emphasises on well designed training courses. It also promotes marketing of goods produced by SGSY Swarozgaries.The individual beneficiaries are mainly defaulters. Once they get money they do not pay back. This is the reason bank approves loans only to SHGs and not to any individual applying for the same.

The Gajalaxmi SHG group is given only a revolving fund of Rs.15,000. Under this scheme there is a grading system i.e., I-II grading. For any project, the group has to run successfully for a minimum of 6 months then only loan is sanctioned. If the loan amount is Rs.2.5 lakhs then the subsidy provided is Rs.1.25 lakh.

But nowadays in place of SGSY a new programme National Rural Livelihood Mission (NRLM) is being implemented in which loan is being given without any subsidy and rate of interest is also low.

Table-21: List of Beneficiaries during 2002-2003 under SGSY

S. No.	Name	Amount recieved in Rupees	Percentage of Subsidy	Repayment of amount in Rupees	Purpose
1	Dabru Behera	40000	30%	27000	Net / boat
2	Sahadev Behera	40000	30%	Did Not repay	Net / boat
3	Era Behera	40000	30%	23000	Shop
4	Padwa Behera	40000	30%	23000	Shop
5	Manas Behera	40000	30%	Did Not repay	Net / boat
6	Tarini Behera	40000	30%	22000	Net / boat
7	Lochan Bowda	40000	30%	22000	Shop

Case Study - 23

Name: Manas Behera, Aged: 38, Village: Arakhakuda (Majhi Sahi)

Manas is a beneficiary under the SGSY scheme. After sanction of his application in Palli Sabha, it was sent to the concerned block through the VLW. After verification it went to BDO and finally Manas got the loan from the cashier of the block. After getting the loan money, he opened a grocery shop. But he could not profit from his business and subsequently was unable to pay the loan availed under the scheme. So he paid certain amount of his loan. In the village, I found more than ten grocery shops. Often times Manas was found busy in playing cards or fishing. Hence, he did not earn so much profit from his grocery shop.

Madhu Babu Pension Yojna (MBPY)

2. Old Age Pension / Widow Pension / National Old Age Pension

Both OAP and Widow Pension have been introduced by State government. NOAP was introduced by the Government of India effective from 15 August 1995 for providing relief to senior citizens existing below the poverty line. The Government of India provides Rs.75/- per month and State government provides rupees twenty five per month to each beneficiary under NOAP scheme.

Eligibility Criteria:

For NOAP, a person's age needs to be 65 years and above.

For OAP, a persons age needs to be 60 years and above.

For availing widow pension, a woman's age must be more than 18 years. Widow pension is only for females.The pension is given to a person whose income does not exceed Rs.300/- per month. Leprosy patients with visible signs of deformity and destitute widows irrespective of age whose annual income does not exceed Rs.3200 are eligible for availing this scheme. Under MBPY, facilities provided have seven categories. People get hugely benefit from the old age pension scheme (OAP/WP).

Table-22: List of the number of people who are getting pension

Age	Rupees to be reveived	No. of people eligible for pension
70 Years	Rs.300/-	123
80 Years	Rs.500/-	2
90 Years	Rs.600/-	–
Disabled	Rs.300/-	13

PMGSY

The rural connectivity programme has been declared as a separate programme called Pradhan Mantri Gram Sadak Yojaja on 15th August 2000 under PMGSY. Additional central assistance is provided as 100 percent grant by the Government of India to the States.

Objectives - The main objective of this programme is to improve the social and economic standards of rural areas. Roads for rural areas are constructed for facilitating connectivity of poor people with the outside world and for their economic and commercial development, and improving their education, health and lifestyle.

Facilities under the programme - The length of the rural roads are improving and increasing from the last five decades. A well communicated pacca road is built into the village from Brahmagiri-Satpada main road. The expenditure under the programme during 2001-02 was Rs.240.02 crores.

The inter-connecting road in the village is under construction. For Majhi Sahi a concrete road has been constructed for which a fund of Rs.1 lakh was given under TFC.

Gopabandhu Gramya Yojna (GGY)

The road from Panchayat Office to Main Road is under a State Government sponsored programme. Also, under GGY scheme, an amount of Rs 50,000 is given to UGUP school complex for its renovation.

Gram Panchayat–Panchayat Samiti (GPPS) - Under this scheme Rs.3 lakh has been given for construction of roads from Arakhakuda main village to Harichandi Sahi.

Indira Gandhi National Old Age Pension (IGNOAP)

This category is subdivided into different subheading-

Category	Amountto be received in Rupees	No. of Pensioners
Disabled	Rs.300/-	5
Person > 80 Years	Rs.500/-	2
Widow pension	–	–
OAP	Rs.300/-	60

Those people who are not getting benefitted from MBPY; they are given the opportunity to avail benefits from IGNOAP.

Swajal Dhara

Under this scheme,a pump house has been created near Jenapurmauja and a number of boring water taps have been provided to the villagers by the government. Recently, Rs.15,000 was given for boring a new tubewell.

Mahatma Gandhi National Rural Employment Guarantee Scheme (MGNREGS)

Under this scheme, the people covered in NREGS (who belong to BPL category) have been provided a job card by GRS (Gram Rozgar Sevak). Each person has an account in the nearby bank i.e. Panspada Bank, people are given hundred days employment through the job card and amount given to them is directly deposited in their bank account. If work is not provided to them then they are given the amount through account. BPL categories people are covered under this scheme.

Mattha Pokhari (Pond)- A sum of Rs. 4.5 lakh was given under the scheme. The people who had job cards are provided work. Nearly hundred people were engaged in this project. A pond was dug in the village. But due to party politics, the work of matha pokhori remains incomplete. The people decided to hire other labourers for the Pond. The village labourers, who have job cards, are not expertised in this work. But some other party opposed and told only job card labourer could do this work. The internal dispute increased and due to lack of knowledge the labourers did not dig the pond completely and finally the work remained unfinished.

Another work i.e. renovation of Harichandi Sahi Naikula Pokhari (pond) was completed. Matha Pokhari is an individual scheme, under this scheme there are two beneficiaries-

1) Laxmidhar Behera (42+) Job Card Rs.50,000/-
2) Sanjay Behera (35+) Job Card Rs.50,000/-

There are total 675 job card holders including Manikpatna revenue area.

Bharat Nirman Rajiv Gandhi Seva Kendra was built for office purpose near panchayat office. For this construction Rs 10 lakhs were given and people having Job Cards were engaged in this programme.

Arnapurna Yojna

The worse outcome of poverty is lack'of food. To ensure food security among the poor, the government has implemented this programme.

Aim – Distribution of food grains through public distribution system at a lower price for BPL card holder who is more than 65 years old.

Eligibility:

1) A person should be a BPL card holder
2) Person's age should be more than 65 years.

Facilities - The BPL people are given 35 kgs of rice at price of Rs. 2/-per kg.

Case Study - 23

Name: Gandu Behera, Aged: 39, Village: Arakhakuda (Bhagabat Sahi)

During the interview with Gandu Behera, I found that in the year 1999 she got ten kgs of rice free of cost from the Arakhakuda Gram Panchayat Office and was given a card. By showing this card, she got rice for her own livelihood. She has no source of income. Her husband died early this year. She used to earn some money by selling fresh fishes. But that income was insufficient for her. Due to old age, her body could not permit her to continue her occupation. Due to this pension scheme she is getting food every day. Now the amount of rice per individual is increased as compared to 1999.

Antodaya Yojana

It is a state government sponsored programme. Its aim is to distribute rice to poorest families who have BPL card. Through this programmethirty five kg of rice at a rate of Rs.2/- is given to the beneficiaries per month. In Arakhakkuda, ten people are Antodaya Card holders.

Indira Awas Yojana

This was launched in May 1995 to provide free houses to families below the poverty line. From 1989 to 1996, this scheme was operated as a component of Jawahar Rozgar Yojana (JRY), 10 percent fund was earmarked for IAY. But from April 1996, this scheme was made a separate scheme. IAY and PMGAY became one scheme i.e. Rural Housing (housing for everyone).

Facilities - The unit cost under this programme varies from time to time because of material cost in house building.

Table-23: List of Beneficiaries and Amounts given for House Bulding

Programme	Year	Name of beneficiary	Amount given in Rs.	Purpose
IAY	2001-02	Laxmidhar Behera	22000	House building
IAY	2003-04	Bijay Behera	22000	--- do ---
IAY	2004-05	Ramachandra Behera	22000	--- do ---
IAY	2006-07	Manali Behera	25000	--- do ---
IAY	2009-10	Jayanti Behera	35000	--- do ---
IAY	2010-11	Era Behera	45000	--- do ---
IAY	2011-12	Harihar Behera	45000	--- do ---

An applicant should be below poverty line. In first term he/she gets Rs.5000, then Rs.20,000 and again Rs.20,000. The payment given is sanctioned in three phases. Some influential persons inside the village with good connection with the political leaders may get money easily in two to three phases but others get money in five to six phases because of their poverty.

Table-24: Beneficiaries under the Programme of IAY

Name of Programme	Year	Name of Beneficiary	Amount given in Rs.	Purpose
IAY	2011-12	Raghu Behera	45000	House building
		Harihar Behera	45000	--- do ---
		Kanda Behera	45000	--- do ---
		Judhistira Behera	45000	--- do ---
		Bisoi Behera	45000	--- do ---
		Prafulla Behera	45000	--- do ---
		Minati Behera	45000	--- do ---
		Prabhati Behera	45000	--- do ---
		Rupa Behera	45000	--- do ---

Case Study - 24

Name: Harihar Behera, Aged: 42 years, Village: Arakhakuda (Laxmi Narayan Sahi)

Harihar Behera is a beneficiary under IAY scheme. He got the intended amount in 2010 for building a house. He got Rs. 45,000 in three installments and he collected the money from the cashier of block office. But in the process she faced difficulties many times. He had to visit the block office for money many times. The communication to the block office was not direct. The staffs of block office were absent. He was told that most of the staff came from Puri so they came for 1-2 days in a week. So he got the money after a lot of delay. Besides that he complained that those who are actually poor or possess BPL cards do not have IAY. Influential people who are above the poverty line have illegally enrolled themselves under IAY by bribing the village Sarpanch.

Case Study -25

Name: Maguni Behera, Aged: 38, Village: Arakhakuda (Magala Sahi)

Maguni Behera is a beneficialy of IAY. His parents live with him. Under the scheme his family was given with Rs.45,000 to construct a pucca house. However, he had to invest another Rs 40,000 to construct a two bed room house. He hired labourers and built a well finished house. The house consists of one room and one drawing room. He is happy to have benefitted from IAY scheme.

BPL Card

BPL cards are provided to those families who belong to below poverty line. The scheme has started since 1992.

Eligibility:

(1) People whose annual income is less than Rs.15000 and

(2) People who have less than 2 acres of land.

Facilities under BPL

BPL card holders are given thirty-five kgs of subsidized rice, two litres of kerosene, one kg sugar and five kgs of wheat.

In Arakhakuda, the dealers who provide the provisions are Rabindra kumar Behera and Rabi Narayan Behera. There are 225 BPL families in Arakhakuda village. This census is updated every five years. This year the people have demanded more families to be included in the BPL list. The people get rice at Rs.2 per kg, kerosene at Rs.11.50 per litre, sugar at Rs.17 per kg and wheat at Rs.12 per kg.

Integrated Child Development Scheme (ICDS)

The Integrated Child Development Scheme was launched in 1975 as a comprehensive scheme to promote incorporated development of a child. The services of ICDS are provided by Anganwadi – a focal point for deliverance of services at the community level.

Name of some selected person who are included in the BPL list.

List of BPL Card Holders of Arakhakuda Village

Name of Programme	Year	Name of Beneficiary	Eligibility
BPL Card	1997-2002 Census	Saraswati Behera	Whose monthly income is less than Rs.300/-
		Gajendra Behera	
		Sitaram Behera	
		Narayan Behera	
		Gajia Nayak	
		Braja Nayak	
		Raghunath Behera	
		Sahadev Behera	
		Sukhadev Behera	

The specific objectives of ICDS are:

- Improve the nutritional and health status of children in the age group 0-6 years.
- Provide environmental condition needed for physical, social and psychological development of children.
- Reduce the incidents of low birth weight and severe malnutrition among children.
- Reduce the school drop out rate by providing stimulation of 3-6 years olds.
- Enhance the capacities of the mother to provide proper child care.
- Achieve effective coordination at the policy and implementation level of government departments to promote child development.

The ICDS projects are being implemented in the state through 281 ICDS centers

The target group under the programme consists of children in the age group of 0-6 years and expectant and nursing mothers in the age groups of 15-45 years belonging to families below poverty line. The scheme provides a package of services covering supplementary nutrition, immunization, pre-school education, health check-up, referral services, and nutrition and health education for women.

Under Special Nutrition programme (SNP) nutritive food is supplied to children between age group of 0-6 years and nourishing and expectant mothers in ICDS block with detachment from CARE, WFP and the state government. The ICDS provides through Anganwadi centres.

Under this programme, children below 6 years are given vaccines for prevention of contagious diseases like T.B., diptheria, whooping caugh, tetanus, polio, measles, Hepatitis-B and booster doses etc. This is done by ANM and ASHA members. The programme is organized by Anganwadi workers. The National Pulse Polio Programme was implemented throughout the state with a view to make the state polio free by immunizing infants and children of age 0-5 years. The pregnant women are also given iron tablets and tetanus injections by ANM.

Anganwadi - The Anganwadi acts as a developing centre. Arakhakuda village due to its large size is divided under different Anganwadi centres. These are:

Table-25: List of Anganwadi Center

Name of Anganwadi Centre	Strength		Teacher	Sahi
	No. of child	Population		
Arakhakuda - A	62	940	(W) Rollilaxmi Behera (H) Laxmi Behera	Laxmi Narayan
Arakhakuda - B	89	–	Malati Behera	Bhagabat + Harichandi
Arakhakuda - C	30	500	Nalini Behera	Majhisahi
Mangala Sahi	52	600	Jayanti Behera	Mangala
Masanichandi	40	800	Malati Behera	Masani Chandi

All the Anganwadi workers help in cooking mid-day meals. The monthly salary of the workers and helpers are Rs.3500 and Rs.1750 respectively. The qualification of the Anganawadi workers is below matric.

All the Sahis have their individual Anganwadi center. But in Laxmi Narayan Sahi they use Kothoghara as their Anganwadi center. The child takes admission in the Anganwadi center after completion of three years. But after completion of 6 years the children are sent to school. Earlier the workers used to go from door to door delivering foods and medicines for pregnant women. This made their work life very hectic. But now the ASHA workers have shared the over burdened work of the Anganawadi workers. The workers simply inform all pregnant and new born babies to come to center on Wednesday. Then the ANM organizes a meeting and tells them how to take care of themselves and their children. She also gives folliper, injection to both baby and the mother.

Mamata Maa - This is another programme for pregnant women by state government which started in September 2011. The women are given Rs.5000/- for first and second delivery. The Anganwadi workers organised a meeting in which pregnant women, lactating mothers and children between 0-5 years were weighed and given rice powder. But in past they used to get rice, dal, and other stuff.

Kisori Balika (Sabala Programme)

This is a programme for unmarried girls aged between eleven to eighteen years (11-18 years). They are given chattua, medicine, iron tablets and folliper. The ANM in meeting tells them the benefits of taking medicines. It is very essential in providing them with nutrition and strength which they do not get from their daily diet.

Every Saturday, the Anganwadi workers go to block and give report. This is called project meeting. Then on twenty eighth day of every month a sector meeting is organized. Every month they go to Neelanchal Bank and withdraw an amount of Rs.3000/ to buy eggs, dal, oil, rice for MDM programme.

Mission Shakti is a Self-Help Mission empowering women through promotion of women's SHG. A number of NGO's and fishery departments are involved in the programme of women empowerment.

Education

The constitution of India casts an obligation on the state to provide free and compulsory education to all children upto the age of fourteen. The literacy rate in Odisha during 1951 was 15.8 percent against the all India average of 18.3 percent which increased to 72.90 percent.

There has been a steady improvement in the literacy rates of the state over successive decades, which is a result of expansion of educational infrastructure both qualitative and quantitative.

There are different schemes implemented to upgrade the educational standards.

a) Mid Day Meal - It was introduced in the state in July 1995 to provide afternoon meals to to government school children of children Class I-V all over the state for 210 days a year. The objective of the scheme was to improve the nutritional status of students, increase enrollment and attendance and reduce the number of dropouts. Now this meal is provided every day. The meal includes rice, dal and egg.

In Arakhakuda village, there are two schools. One is the Project Primary School (Class I-V) in Harichandi Sahi and the other is UGUP School (Class I-VIII) in Mangala Sahi.

Arakhakuda UGUP School

Bidyadhar Jena – Head Master

Binayak Rath – Assistant Head Master

Kamini Behera, other teacher – Arakhakuda village

Ranjit Kumar Jena – other teacher

Chakradhar Jena – other teacher

Kanu Chandra Behera – other teacher – Arakhakuda village

Rabindra Kumar Behera – other teacher – Arakhakuda village.

Project Primary School

Duryadhana Ghadai – Head Master

Kailash Chandra Bebera – Assistant Head Master

UGUP School -

Total Student – 468

General – Boy – 3

General – Girl – 0

SC Harijan – Boy – 11

SC Harijan – Girl – 8

ST – 0

Nolia + Barik (OBC) – Boy – 225

Nolia + Barik (OBC) – Girl – 221

In the school they provide MDM to all students. All the female students and male students covered under BPL list get free school uniforms.

These grants are given once every year. Payment is given on the basis of inspection report. TL is given once in a month. All teachers are given Rs.500/- per head to buy all the necessary learning materials. The school has been renovated this year. For gardening, the Government gives Rs.55000-70000. There is plan to add classes nine and ten to facilitate further studies.

The need for education and the awareness for literacy are very poor among Nolias. That is why a person of that village named Pradipta Behera (37+) first started "Chilikashree Shikhyarthee Parishad". He could enroll only fifteen students and started giving private coaching in a shelter house. In 2008, for the first time, one of his students passed the tenth examination. The pass percentage has increased in the subsequent years.

Year	No. of Students
2008	1
2009	4
2010	10
2011	20

An interesting case is that most of his students are girls. Then Pradipta along with some other educated students of that village started campaigning. This helped to change the educational scenario of the village to a certain extent. Girls who passed tenth and enrolled in collegeare Deepa Behera, Sulochana Behera, Rupa Behera, and Banita Behera. State government provided cycle to the successful students.

Health

The definition of World Health Organisation states that health is a state of complete physical and social well-being and not merely the absence of disease or infirmity.

The state government is constantly making efforts to formulate and execute schemes to provide adequate health care services to the people of Odisha.

The main objectives are–

1. To provide adequate, qualitative, preventive, promotive and curative health care services to the people of Odisha.

2. To ensure equitable health care services for all in general and to disadvantaged groups like ST, SC and OBC in particular.
3. To provide affordable quality health care to the people not only through allopathic system of medicine but also through homeopathic and ayurvedic systems.
4. To ensure greater success in primary health care by bringing medical institutions as close to the people as possible, also through mobile health units to inaccessible areas.
5. To improve maternal and child health and reduce maternal and infant mortality and morbidity rates.
6. To impart training to doctors, nurses and other paramedical staff and to upgrade their skill and knowledge to meet the needs of varied healthcare cases.

National Anti-Malaria Programme (NAMP)

It is a centrally sponsored scheme with a fund and sharing pattern of 50:50 between centre and state. An awareness programme is organised for Nolia people about Malaria and the need for taking preventives.

The National Anti-Malaria programmes include maintaining cleanliness of inhabited areas, destroying mosquitoes by spraying DDT. The National TB control programme is to detect TB patients and take them under the supervision of peripheral health institutions. Free polio programmes for children under (0-5 years) are given in the Anganwadi center. This is combinedly given by ANM and ASHA members.

The irony is that the non BPL card holders are nearly as poor as the BPL card holders. The village has two PDS that opens once in a month. 90 percent villagers are illiterate and they do not follow what the PDS dealer does. My informant told that they are a landless community; fishing is their only source of livelihood. No catch means they have to sleep in an empty stomach. The government does not include them in harijan caste. They are included in OBC because of which they are not given the benefits of SC people. Ravi Narayan Behera, a small time fish trader is the only PDS dealer is hold a license for a record of fourty seven years running. He gives 12.5 kg rice per month which costs Rs.12.50 per kg. He cheats and keeps 2-3 kg rice per person as well and takes Rs.8.50 instead of Rs.6.50 per kg from people. But the fear of being denied rations by him forces most people to keep quiet.

Case Study - 26

Name: Banchanidhi Behera, Aged: 35, Village: Arakhakuda (Majhi Sahi)

Banchanidhi is a fisherman by profession who suffers from polio. He is one of the few lucky persons to get Rs.200/- per month under disability pension. This is his monthly budget. He said, "I have to manage on this money and whenever I can, I supplement it with extra work. But because of my disability no one is willing to offer me work". He is married and has a son and daughter. The only bread earner in his family is his wife who earns Rs.15 to Rs.20 per day by doing manual labour.

NREGA– This scheme promises villagers a minimum of hundred days of paid work a year and pay without work if no work is available to them. Arjun Behera, one of my informants told me that several families have reported that their NREGA job cards were being withheld, and they get Rs.25-30 for a day's work which should be Rs.58/-. There are other cases where job cards are paid for ten to fifteen days of work, when in reality it is only on two to four days of work.

Welfare Schemes for Fishermen of Odisha Matsyajibi Unnayana Yojana

Replacement of Wooden Country Craft with FRP Boat

About 7097 registered country fishing crafts are operated for marine fishing from Odisha coast. Frequent low pressure with cyclonic wind in the Bay of Bengal leads to loss of life and fishing accessories, and the major loss is in the form of boats and nets. The boats made of local wood are prone to destruction by wind and turbulent waves. So these country crafts were replaced by the FRP boat.

The cost of 30 feet long FRP fishing boat is about Rs.1 lakh. It is not possible on the part of fishing people to buy it. Therefore 50 percent subsidy is given to them. The budget required for this project is Rs.35.50 crore in five years for complete replacement of wooden boats. Annual fund required is Rs.7.10 crores.

Motorisation of Country Craft

To provide the marine fishermen's boat more speed, an inboard/ outboard engine was to the fishermen. The scheme will provide opportunity for the fishermen to earn more by catching more fish and arriving early at the fishing base with fresh fishes. In total, 3000 active fishermen are to be given 50 percent subsidy within the next five years. It is estimated to cover around 600 engines and the fund required is Rs.1.50 crore per annum.

Assistance for Fish Marketing Infrastructure for Fishermen

In order to sell and transport fresh fishes following assistance is proposed:

a. Provision for the purchase of a bicycle and insulated boxes with 50 percent subsidy, subject to maximum limit of Rs.2000/- per head.

b. 25 percent subsidy subject to a maximum of Rs.7500/- is proposed to be provided for purchase of two wheeler and insulated boxes. The beneficiary scheme can obtain balance amount as loan from financial institutions.

c. For quick transportation of fish in hygenic condition from fish landing centers to marketing places- 25 percent subsidy to a maximum of Rs.35000/- is proposed to be provided for the purchase of three wheeler auto rickshaw with insulated box by a group of 3-4 persons.

d. An ice box and three wheelers with ice boxes are provided.

Assistance for Net and Boat

Assistance is provided by the PFC to eradicate the role of money lenders. The unit cost for net and boat is Rs.25000/- under this scheme 60 percent subsidy is given to SC/ST fishermen and 50 percent for general category.

Netrajyoti Scheme

The marine fishermen are always exposed to adverse environmental conditions in the sea, which leads to opthalamic disorder. So the BPL people are provided financial assistance and free spectacles to genuine cases.

The scheme will benefit 1000 active fishermen every year. The budget required for the scheme is Rs.0.5 crore per annum at the rate of Rs.5000/- per person.

New scheme for fishermen for fatal diseases:

The assistance given for fatal diseases are:

a. Heart disease upto Rs.50000.00

b. Kidney transplant upto Rs.50000.00
c. Brain tumor upto Rs.50000.00
d. Cancer upto Rs.50000.00
e. Paralysis upto Rs.15000.00
f. Mental disease upto Rs.5000.00

The scheme will benefit 1000 active fishermen of the age group 18-65 every year. It needs Rs.0.5 crore per annum for its implementation.

Financial Assistance to SHG

It is proposed to provide Rs.10000/- for each group involved in fishing activities like marketing under this scheme. Under this programme it is proposed to cover one thousand women SHG per annum for the next five year. The fund required for it is Rs. One crore.

Reimbursement of HSD Oil Subsidy

The scheme is for reimbursement of HSD oil to registered boat owners of the 9thfive year plan period. The subsidy is Rs.1.50 per litre of HSD oil used for fishing purposes. The limit for mechanized and motorized boats are 33000 litres at 150 litres/day for 220 fishing days and 6000 litres at 25 litre/day for 240 fishing days respectively.

Janashree Bima Yojana

The scheme is operated by LIC for group insurance coverage of fishermen families involved in fishing activities. Minimum 25 beneficiaries must be in one target group. Each beneficiary of the group will deposit Rs.100/- towards the yearly premium and upon normal death, his family will get Rs.30000 and on accidental death or permanent disability he will get Rs.75000 and incase of partial disability he will get Rs.37500.

Savings-cum-Relief Scheme (CSP)

It provides lean and ban period assistance to fishermen and develops a saving habit among the fisherfolks. The beneficiaries will contribute Rs.70/- per month i.e. July/February and Rs.40/- in March. The beneficiary contribution is Rs 600. The state and central government match the fisherman's share on a 50:50 basis and give an assistance of Rs. 1200 (Rs.600 + Rs.600). The total amount of Rs.1800 is released in 3 equal monthly installments during the lean and ban period i.e. April to June. Under this scheme 2000 fishermen will be covered with financial requirement of Rs.2.5 crores per annum.

Group Accident Insurance Scheme for Fishermen (GAIS)

From 12 lakh fishermen of the state, 8 lakh have been extended insurance cover during the period of 2009-10 and 2010-11. The insurance beneficiaries are provided are Rs.1 lakh each for accidental death and permanent total disability while Rs.50000 is provided for partial disability. The scheme aims to cover 10 lakh fishermen 2011-12 onwards. The state share for this scheme is Rs.1.45 crore per annum.

House side for Fishermen under Vasundhara

The state government is likely to extend Vasundhara scheme for the fishermen communities. It is proposed to provide homestead land measuring 0.04 – 0.08 acres to the homesteadless fishermen families of the state. Under this scheme 5000 families may be covered every year.

Mo Khudia Scheme

The scheme provides house to homeless fishermen of Odisha. It is proposed to cover 10000 fishermen under Mo Kudia Yojana (2000/year) in five years by providing houses to the families under the scheme with unit cost of Rs.50000 each. The budget required for it ten crores per annum. Till yet there are only three people to get benefitted from this programme.

Programme	Name of beneficiary	Amount get in Rs.
Mo Kudia	Balaram Behera	45000
	Harihar Behera	45000
	Eruni Behera	45000

There is a target to include 50 more people in Mo Kudia Yojna. But those who have already been benefitted under IAY scheme are not eligible to avail the facilities of Mo Kudia Yojana.

Case Study - 27

Name: Bijuli Behera, Aged: 42, Village: Arakhakuda (Laxminarayan Sahi)

Bijuli Behera (aged 42 years) has two school-going children. She lived in a financial crisis inorder to provide education to her children.Bijuli and her husband tried hard to avail a house under IAY facilities but failed and requested their Sarpanch to help them in getting a house in the Mo Kudia scheme as the house they live in presently is in a broken state and a threat to their lives. But they are yet to be benefitted.

Development of Fishermen Villages

NWFF - This is marine society, which provides houses to 90 individuals from Arakhakuda village. It provides Rs.40000 in four terms.

The ultimate aim of this programme is to include those people under the beneficiary list who do not have any houses and provides houses to each poor fisherman. The houses are provided in clusters i.e. minimum 10 houses in a village. For more than 20 houses, there is a provision of one tubewell and for 100 houses or more in any village (one) community hall will be provided.

OMFRA Implementation

OMFRA is the Odisha Marine Fisheries Regulation Act and Rules. Under this act it was mandatory for all the fishing boats plying in the territorial waters of the state to register and get licensed. No mechanized fishing vessels are allowed to fish within 5 kms of the coast to protect the interest of traditional fishermen. To conserve the fish stock and biodiversity, there is a uniform ban on fishing activities from 15th April upto 31st May every year.

Table-26: List of NGOs involved in Social Training in Fisheries Sector in Puri district

<table>
<tr><th>Sl.</th><th>Name of NGO</th><th>Area of Operation</th><th>Activity</th></tr>
<tr><td>1</td><td>Coastal People's Development Association (CPDA)</td><td>Konark, Chandrabhaga of Puri district</td><td rowspan="4">Involved in training of fisher women/men in social sectors like family, hygine, mother and child care, sanitation, nutrition etc. Formation of SHG for both men / women.</td></tr>
<tr><td>2</td><td>People's Empowerment and Need based Community Development (PENCODE)</td><td>Penthakota area and Arakhakuda of Puri District</td></tr>
<tr><td>3</td><td>ICZMP – Integrated Coastal Zone Management Project</td><td>Arakhakuda, MOHO village of Puri district</td></tr>
<tr><td>4</td><td>United Artist Association</td><td>Ganjam District and Arakhakuda of Puri district</td></tr>
</table>

Contd...

5	International Handicap	Arakhakuda of Puri district.	Provide instruments to handicapped person. Besides that training to women and housing facilities are provided by them.

Integrated Coastal Zone Management (ICZMP)

Objectives - The project's description development objective is to assist the Government of India in building national capacity for implementation of the new integrated management approach for India's coastal zones and piloting the integrated coastal zone management approach in three states of Gujarat, Odisha and West Bengal. The project for Odisha will focus mainly in:

1. Gopalpur – Chilika
2. Paradip – Dhamra. The priority of it's inclusion
3. Conservation and protection of coastal resources
4. Environment and pollution management
5. Livelihood security of the coastal communities.

In the case of livelihood security of coastal communities it supports–

(i) livelihood improvement in 60 fishing villages in the periphery of the Chilika Lake and the Gahirmatha Wildlife Sanctuary to develop allied farming activities by the fisheries department,

(ii) support to fisher people groups in developing small scale tourism activities by the Tourism Department,

(iii) support to fishery communities in developing small scale industries and marketing activities, such as coir-making, by the industries department,

(iv) provision of cyclone shelters in the 14 remaining coastal villages where cyclone shelters were not constructed from earlier programmes by the disaster management authority and

(v) eco-tourism based livelihood security in restricted areas by wild life (Department of Forest and Environement, Govt. of Odisha).

ICZMP has formed different SHGs group in Arakhakuda village and nearby villages. The main aim of the SHGs is to provide the fishing people an alternate livelihood source. As the fish catch is decreasing, this it is an effort to provide the fishermen a means of livelihood from non fishing activities. They grant each group Rs.1.20 lakh in 4 phases.

United Artist Association (UAA)

It believes in community empowerment and provides support and strength to people's organizations– NGOs and CBOs in its area of operation. It was established in the year of 1964 by a group of like minded youths to help the people affected by natural calamities and start some educational institutions. Since then it has been working with the down trodden section of the society with focus on women and children. Its headquarters is at Ganjam district of Odisha.

Mission - its aim is to improve the socio-economic condition of the backward and weaker section of the society mainly the fisherfolk, tribal people and farmers by making them aware on various sustainable livelihood programmes.

Focus groups and partner -

UAA works with fisherfolk of SC and backward castes in six costal districts of Odisha. It has worked with government, UNICEF, and OXFAM for providing better quality of life for marginalized sections of the society. UAA has special skills in community organization and building people's organizations. People organizations like SAMUDRAM, SWOSTI, ANWESA, Rushikulya Rayat Mahasabha and Ganjam Zilla Adivasi Manch have emerged over the years and are functioning independently for the last 12 years.

In Arakhakuda village, UAA worked 10 years ago. Under its influence a Mahila Samiti has emerged and dry fish business is also running in this village. It provides training on fresh fish processing, grading, sorting and packaging to ensure better quality and improved self life. At first, there were only 10 women participants but later the numbers increased.

Peoples Employment and Need based Community Development Organisation

(PENCODE) – Pencode operated in Penthakota but recently it started its operation in Arakhakuda village. PENCODE has formed four new SHG groups in Harachandi Sahi and two new SHGs in Bhagabat Sahi. This group is to empower women, make themself sufficient and literate etc.

The organisation registered under the Societies Registration Acts and started in 1989 as Penthakota Community Development Project. The project objective was to improve the livelihood of the Telugu speaking fishermen and women living for decades on government owned land in the settlement of Pentakota of Puri.

PENCODE has played a vital role in motivating fisher women to organize themselves into fishing cooperative societies. It also gives training to members, secretaries and president of SHGs on leadership and group dynamics, fish marketing, fish drying and prawn pickles etc.

International Handicap

It was a Japan based organisation which established its headquarters at Delhi. Its main aim is to provide facilities to the physically challenged people so that they can lead a life of peace. In village there are three workers:

a. Pradipta Behera
b. Judistira Behera
c. Sundari Behera

This organisation gave training to Anganwadi workers, school teachers, ASHA members. Their work is to identify the physically challenged and give a detail to CDPO, so that they can be given an assistance of Rs.200 per month by the government. The number of physically challenged people in 2011 was 163.

It provides speech and hearing instruments for deaf, sticks to the blind and contigency plans for the disabled persons during cyclone. It also provides shelter modification for the disabled.

Case Study-28

Name: Monalisha Behera, Aged: 8, Sahi: Harachandi Sahi

Monalisha Behera is the daughter of Lalita and Indramani Behera. She is deaf from birth. She faces a lot of difficulties. Now she is eight years old. This organization has provided her with an instrument to be able to listen. She was also given pension for six years. Many others individuals have also been benefitted through this organisation.

The fishing communities have depended on Chilika for generations. They were never rich. They eagerly look forward to some improvement in their life. They dream of development through their trade. Hence their aspirations revolve round the problems and opportunities associated with fishing.

Some new programmes are implemented in the period 2020-2022).

Fishery Machinery/ Equipments/ Implements for Intensive Aquacutture

The schemes is to provide capital subsidy support to fish farmers for purchasing of machineries/implements like Aerators, Air Blowers with aero-tubes, bio-security nets, fishing nets are the integral part of enhancing the aquaculture production.

To increase the marine fishery production and to enhance incomes and livelihoods of coastal communities, support for purchasing new boat, engine and net, refrigerated van, insulated vehicles motor cycle with ice box coastal scheme is implemented.

Promotion of Intensive Aquaculture through Introduction of Bio-floc Technology

To promote sustainable intensification of the freshwater fish and brackish water shrimp farming and generating high income in a limited area farmers both fresh water and brackish water are provided with subsidy for Bio-floc tanks, poly lining, aerator and other implements.

For Marketing supports:

Capital Subsidy is provided for creation of morden fish market. Fish Kiosk

Reactivation of Fisheries Cooperative Societies

One-time revolving fund to eligible Primary Fishermen Cooperative Societies @ Rs.2.00 lakh each for improvement of the working capital of the society and socio economics status of the members.

Scholarship to meritorious children of the fisherman community

Education in fisherman community is always neglected. To generate interest among the children of the fishermen community cash award incentive are provided to pursue higher education who have scored >50% mark in HSC examination.

Livelihood Support to Marine Fishermen during Fishing Ban Period

Livelihood of fishermen solely based on sea fishing and the ban in fishing directly prohibits the profession over a long period of seven months in a year (1st Nov- 31st May), the scheme is to support the livelihood of marine fisher families in and around the turtle nesting and breeding areas of the state round the year in Bhitarkanika areas as no alternative is available, and an amount of Rs.7,500/- per family is given in support.

Establishment of Bio toilets in mechanised fishing vessels

To maintain the hygienic surrounding and cleanliness at the fishing points and encouragement of Swachh Sagar programme installation of bio toilets in mechanised fishing vessels, Jetty area fish landing centres financial assistance upto 60% of the cost is provided under PMMSY.

9

Changing Scenerio of Coastline Culture: Chilika

The rapid expansion of commercial aquaculture, particularly prawn culture, in Chilika lake is contributing directly and indirectly to the decline of the lake's fisheries and world-renowned bird population. Changes both in India's economic policies and in global markets have caused a rapid rise in the price of prawns and the abandonment of traditional fishing methods in favor of aquaculture.

Like many wetlands around the world, the Chilika lake is subject to a multiplicity of pressures, ranging from local to global in geographic scales, with impacts over short to very long periods, and with long-term effects on the socio-economic development of India. All these are driven partly by market forces and partly by socio-political situations. In the case of each type of pressure, different sets of root causes of biodiversity change are identifiable. With this backdrop of highly diversified possible root causes, it is important to study this wetland more closely, with a visionfor its conservation.

Changes attributing to causes of biodiversity loss are population dynamics, globalization, aquaculture technology, forest degradation and other ecological changes. The root causes for biodiversity loss in the lake lie in regional socioeconomic factors: Price changes, mix of fish in exports, tax and subsidy policy changes, demographic changes, literacy, mortality, fertility, migration, licensing, lease policy, natural ecological changes, deforestation, floods, changing lake mouth, technological interventions, aquaculture practices, dredging in the lake are all factors. We will focus more on socio cultural and economic changes that have impacted every day life of the Nolia people of Arakhakuda village.

Change is a universal factor in every society. Life is changing at each and every moment. Change occurs due tovarious natural and cultural factors. The Nolia people have undergone some changes due to the impact of education, modernization and local odia culture. Culture of a society consists of the values, orientations, attitudes, and beliefs of people about the system to which they belong. It may be the social system or the economic system or the political system. Starting with these changes and analyzing changes while looking at facts, we study the life, culture and occupation of Nolia people.

Changes are marked in their house pattern. A number of partially thatched and pacca houses are seen in Nolia village. The inter-connected muddy roads have been replaced with concrete roads as a part of government initiatives. For entertainment, most houses possess colour television, other electronics gadgets, modern sofa sets and bikes.

Changes are also visible in their family, marriage, kinship structures. They are now liberal towards pregnant women. Now, due to family planning methods and various awareness programmes by ANM; their family size has substantially reduced. Each family is nuclear with two to three children. The works they did together in the past have now become separated.

Now the dowry system is quite serious in the village. The people give television, radio, bi-cycle, and two-wheeler as dowry. In a case study, Gangei Behera (29+) daughter of Karun Behera was given a dowry of Rs.30,000 as cash in her marriage. These days, people are demanding Rs.1 or 2 lakh as dowry along with lots of gold ornaments. So the poor people are worried about their child's marriage. In the past the girl was married to the maternal uncle but now these customs are changing and girls are married to boys outside the Arakhakuda village. Kamini Behera (32+) of Arakhakuda village is married to a person in Seandi, Parikudamaluda. A number of brides like Malati Behera who is from Puri, Asini Behera from Khurda are now members of Arakhakuda village.

Changes are also seen in case of observance of different festivals and rituals. The Nolias who in the past, followed their Telugu tradition of worshipping Ganga Devi, Makar Sakaranti, Ammavairavi Budi Maa, Kali Maa, Sana Maa, Hara Chandi and Simanchal Devata etc., are now celebrating Durga puja, Kartika Purnima, Dola Jatra and following gods like Vishnu, Laxmi, and Shiva because of Odia culture's impact. The people celebrate all the festivals in Hindu way but only difference is that they give sacrifies of animals to their specific deities in their festivals.

The amount of sacrifice has reduced because of changing mentality and shortage of animals. The Nolia people admired "Aiguru" a lot in all their rituals. But now a day their importance is decreasing. The Nolia people give more respect to the Brahmin priests of their village. The importance of Kalisi remains the same. There are still a few people who believe in spirits but sorcery practice has stopped and there are no sorcerers in the village any more.

With the increasing rate of literacy, modern thoughts are increasing slowly in the evolutionary manner. In the village the people are taking Dikhya. The first mattha in Laxminarayan Sahi called Abhiram Baba mattha was started in the year 1954. Other Ashrams in Bhagabat Sahi are Purnananda Baba and Amma Bhagwan. The uncivilized Nolias who were very stubborn are transformed into adaptive beings and have taken up many religious paths. After crossing the age of 45 years, people are going to mattha for dikhya. Each mattha has some land on which they do worship and sit in meditation. Before doing any function or puja or ceremony, the dikshit people first come to the mattha and offer puja. Babaji Behera (58+) belongs to Bhagabat Sahi. He is a member of Purnananda mattha. He has taken dikhya at the age of 43. He has stopped taking liquor, taken a karna mantra and put sacred thread on body. He always does meditation to keep mind and body cool. He told me that his life was totally changed after taking dikhya. Now he has developed a positive attitude towards life.

Changes are marked in economic organization and economics of fishing. In past 100 percent villagers were engaged in fishing as primary occupation. They had no secondary occupation except some of them who worked as labourers in cashew field. But now 85 percent villagers are engaged in fishing and other 15 percent are engaged in service, business and workers etc. Numbers of cases are found in which people have left their traditional occupation and adopt alternate livelihood methods. Laxmidhar Behera who works in ICZMP project as a field worker has left his primary occupation. Kailash Behera and Arjun Behera are service holders. They do not go for fishing anymore. Besides fishing they are engaged in running small businesses. From 85 percent population, only 50 to 60 percent people are going for actual fishing and other people are engaged in net repairing, net binding, sorting etc. because of old age, and decline in catches. But now the scenario is changed. Due to economic upgradation the women are engaged in various activities. They are running SHGs which makes them self sufficient and literate enough to solve various problems on their own. Now drying fish is done by machine and is quite hygenic. The previous unhygenic methods of drying fishes had no market demand. Now the machine dried fishes are packed and exported outside the district and state. Different types of pickles and cutlet are also prepared. Marketing facilities are also provided by Fish FED and ORMASS. Bus services are available now as a communicable medium in the village.

The net used by earlier people like Kilumala, Katlala, Jagavala and different fishing lines are not used these days. The people use different nets like Chapada Jalo, Chingudi Jala, and Gheri Jala etc. All the nets are machine woven. These are zeromesh sized with nylon or plastic threads. The earlier nets are handmade. The people are mainly marine fishers. But now the government imposed more restriction on the marine fishing due to increase of large numbers of trawlers which caused the disappearance and decrease of special variety of fishes. Now the Nolia people are doing mainly lake fishing along with sea fishing. Earlier people used to catch fishes throughout the year. But now to save the Janala dispute the government has imposed restriction on Janala collection and ban on fishing from May 15 to June 15 every year. Earlier nets are heavy and lengthy and uncomfortable to carry but the present nylon nets are light and can be easily carried. The people are taking ice baskets along with them to store the fishes which are new.

The boats used are motorized. The relation of boat owner and crew has changed people. The people spend more money on rituals, education and liquor now. The loan givers are also easily available. So with a high interest rate the people take loan from money lenders of their villagers even from outsiders. Even after modernisation and technological advancement and more earnings, the people still dwell poverty and indebtness because of their lifestyle. The new generation has a little knowledge in navigational ethno-science. They only want to catch more fish by hook or crook methods to earn more money.

Recently the advent of Chingudi mafias has increased which has adversely impacted the economy.

Presently the Primary Fishermen's Cooperatives (PFCs) are not functioning actively not because of the organisation but because of internal dispute among members. Nobody respects anybody now-a-days. A new initiative taken up by ICZMP is to form SHGs for male members with an aim to make themselves self sufficient by providing alternate modes of livelihood.

The leadership pattern and political system of the village are seeing a new direction. The Pradhanpratha does not exist any more. The democratic system of village committee is established with a motto of development of village and villagers. Women are taking part in the sarpanch election. Both male and female have equal rights. Different government subsidies are provided to them. BPL card holders are provided various facilities under government schemes. The peoples are now aware of their rights. With the help of CDA a new Jetti is under construction. This will make the village more accessible.

Vast changes are marked in "women and empowerment". Fishing was their main occupation along with fish drying. They also helped in repairing nets in the off days. Some fisher women and girls were engaged in the prawn processing in the prawn godown of fish merchants. Now a fair amount of diversification has taken place in their occupational life. Fishing related activities continue to remain the core of their occupational life. But, besides this, they have moved to some other occupations. In recent years, many fisher women have been engaged in business of their male counterparts. As daily wagers, they are working in house building, road construction and cashew fields. In the morning they go the work place, and return home after nightfall.

Fisher women are very backward when it comes to education. Most men and women are illiterate. Traditionally they were averse to getting education. They have failed to positively respond to the educational initiatives of government and voluntary organizations. In Arakhakuda village, schools have opened since a long time. But interest of fishing boys and girls in getting education did not take off for a long time. However, the efforts of government and voluntary organizations to spread education among fisher women have not been a total failure. They have achieved some success. Many fisher boys and girls are now studying in colleges. The parents still think that there is no point in giving education to their daughters. The dropout in schools is much higher in case of girls than boys. Education is the only to ultimate development and fisher women need to be sensitized about this. Many women of this village are working as Anganwadi workers and ASHA members. The females of this generation are giving up their traditional occupation. The dress pattern of females is also changing. Earlier the people used to tattoo their bodies and wear a Noli shape in the ear and nose.This custom is not prevalent now. Female education is given more emphasis by the government and people have become aware by watching television. They know about the different programmes and aids given by the government. Now there are 38 tubewells in the villages, three ponds along with two schools and five Anganwadi centers. Various NGOs along with the government are trying to upgrade the economy and life of the village people.

In the developmental programme, it can be observed that a new image of the village and the Arakhakuda village of 19th century is quite different from the Arakhakuda village of the 21st century. Almost 50-60 percent people have a habitable house through IAY and Mokudia Yojna. Numbers of welfare programmes are implemented by the government for the betterment of the Nolia people. Tubewells supply fresh water to protect the villagers from contaminated diseases. MBPY is implemented through which people atleast get some money to buy their necessities. Under Employment Guarantee Scheme job cards are given, so that in the off season people can earn their livelihood. BPL cards are also given to eligible people. Numbers of initiative are taken to improve the education system. Everything is quite transparent. The roads are better; the village schools have a new face. Transport facilities are available to the village at all time. ICZMP is aiming to develop coastal villages by making them self-sufficient in all spheres of the life. Construction of a new jetty is going to benefit Nolias both directly and indirectly.

The result of globalization and the ecological degradation of the lake has resulted in a sharp decline in fish landings from Chilika and is posing a threat to the traditional fishermen's livelihood. If this trend continues, fishing in Chilika lake will soon be a thing of the past. Over fishing in the lake periphery partly explains the drastic reduction in fish and shrimp landings. In addition, very intensive fishing at the shallow and choked lake mouth makes it increasingly difficult both for mature prawns and gravid fishes to reach the sea and for juveniles to enter the lake. The fall in fish, shrimp, and crab landings over the years clearly indicates loss of fauna in Chilika Lake. Decline in these species has been reflected in the official statistics and equivalent loss of other aquatic species is highly probable. In response to a question on species loss in the field survey, 85.5 percent of people expressed their awareness of species extinction.

The most important local issue is the link between the unsustainable aquaculture practices and the neglect of lake biodiversity. This study found that it is through local socio-economic conditions that the ultimate effect of these practices is reflected on lake biodiversity. The starting point is the poverty of the people, which leaves them no choice but to over exploit Chilika's fisheries. Catching juvenile prawn and crabs, social conflicts, overexploitation of lake marine products, growth of weeds, declining salinity, and lake shrinkage have all adversely affected the biodiversity of the lake. The people of the region seem to understand these problems but are helpless to take conservative actions because of their poverty. Local fishermen are in perpetual debt because of loans taken from money lenders. As many as 72 percent of fishermen stated that they are unable to repay the loans on time, largely because of the declining fish catch. These fishermen have few other resources. Even among those fishermen with some education and exposure to the external world, almost 88 percent of the households reported that they have no participation in the onward fish trade. Ideally, vertical linkages with processing, marketing and sale, and distribution activities should be developed while maintaining fishing as the primary activity in this region. Such an expansion of economic activities might facilitate sustainable management of the lake.

Conclusion

Findings according to objectives are given below:

- To study the profiles of coastline culture, their socio-cultural life style, their situation in Odisha including topography, settlement pattern, ecology, administrative structure etc.

About 67 percent of fishing households are below poverty line. Socio-economic conditions of the people have deteriorated. Out of the 250 households surveyed, 62.5 percent have four to six members and 20.6 percent of families have seven to nine members. The average family size in the sample is 5.25. The predominant type is the lineally extended family followed by the nuclear family. Unlike other communities children in fishing communities do not normally inherit income or property from parents, and so they prefer to live separately after marriage. The people do not even own the house. 55 percent of sample households have their own house. 44 percent of the respondents' families have built houses through government programmes.

The conditions of the houses are not good. 318 respondents live in thatched and mud-walled houses, which do not provide protection during rains and cyclones. All the houses have a raised verandah, which is used to keep the net and other fishing equipments. Almost all houses have one or two rooms. Only few houses have three rooms. Even though electricity is available, people are not able to use it in their houses except few households. So far as the monthly income of the sample households is concerned, mostly it is low. The climate is also moderate and all seasons are properly felt.

- To know about the social organization specifically structure of family, patterns of marriage, kinship system and inter-personal relations and networks existing among Nolias.

Their traditional marriage rituals have undergone drastic changes. They have stopped child marriage. With the government regulation of required age for marriage of girls as 18 and boys as 21, they now follow this rule. Nolia people prefer easy and simple marriage. The dowry system is very minimal. Divorce cases are low. Now their marriage rituals are quite influenced by Odia tradition and culture. They also celebrate their marriage with a lot of fanfare and social gatheringin a grand way. The village has two Odia brahmin priests to perform their rituals.

A large numbers of divorce cases and remarriages are prevalent. In 70 percent cases the people have extra marital affairs and the village committee forces the people to keep one relationship stable and leave another one with some compensation.

- To study the traditional economy, occupational vis-a-vis modern economy they are adopting in catching, grading, drying, branding and selling of fishes. To enquire about the use of navigational ethno-science in catching of fishes now and in the past.

Nolia people have very limited assets. A few families have two boats and several nets. 60.56 percent of households do not have any productive asset. There are some families who share boats and nets. All household assets in the family are owned by the male members. Even though the fisher women are not directly engaged in sea-fishing, they participate in a number of related activities. Of the 254 respondents, 100 are regular fish vendors. Others go for fish vending occasionally. In fishing season (64.22 percent) fisher women spend nine to twelve hours per day in fishery activities, besides attending to the regular household activities. During the off season, the fish vendors work for five to twelve hours a day.

Boat owners give loans to poor fishermen through labor contract system. In this system the boat owner provides a lumpsum amount to few fishermen in April or May to work for him for the whole year on wage basis. This system ensures cheap and steady supply of labour to the boat owner. If they decide to discontinue the system, they have to pay the entire amount and in some locations there is requirement to find a substitute.

The money-lenders provide credit only after the fisherman mortgages some of his valuable assets like boat, house or gold as a security. The interest rate varies from 36 to 60 percent per annum. It has beenfound that about 89 percent of the households in the village are in debt. Besides everyday consumption, the men spend a lot of money on alcohol, which naturally forces them to borrow heavily. This binds them to the fish traders. The respondents feel that the moneylenders wish for the people to forever be in debt so that they always have a steady income from the interests received. The money lenders depend on the fisher people for progressive enrichment, whereas the latter's dependency on the former leads to their enslavement. In the process the fishing communities lose control over their resources, products and economic life. Cooperative societies of fisher people in the area are mostly controlled by the fish merchants themselves. They make groups of five or six, pool their resources and buy fish. They either divide the fish and sell it individually and take the profit or pool the profits together and divide it equally.

Economic inequality is a function of the distribution of debt, property and assets. Expenditure on the necessities almost equals or exceeds their income. The intensity of indebtedness is very high. The real income of the fisher people has fallen. The income of the fisher families are predominantly determined by the value of the fish products derived from the sea.Intrusion of modern modes of production is a threat to the marine ecosystem in general and the economy of the fisher people in particular. The community is gradually loosing control over the resources.

- To study the traditional political organization as well as modern political system including extend of women empowerment specifically in Nolia society.

The traditional Pradhanpratha does not exist any more. The democratic system of village committee established in the village has a motto of development now. The selection of the present village committee members is on the basis of life experience. Women are not allowed in the village meeting yet. But they are taking part in the sarpanch election. Both male and female have equal rights. But in case of females their role has changed. The emergence of SHG has helped the women to form a group and elect president and secretary among themselves. This is to solve the problems of the SHGs members and provide an economically self sufficient unit. But the political environment of these days is aggressive.

Women headed households are the poorest in the area. Very often the woman is the only earning member in these families. Of the total sample households, 50 houses are headed by women. Most of these women are widows. In a few cases the husbands are seriously ill and bedridden and the women have takenup the responsibility of the household. There is also a category of few women, who are staying alone. Their sons and daughters are separated from them and have their own families.

The division of labour within the fishing communities is such that the men go out on the seas for fishing while the women take care of distribution.

Whatever little gold and silver ornaments a woman brings at the time of her marriage is kept as a contingency plan for the off seasons and rituals like marriage and death. The people are very religious and spend a major share of their income in religious activities.

Some women sell fish in big markets and others at roadside markets. On an average, women spend 8-10 hours outside the home travelling and vending. Majority of fisher women sell fish outside their area of residence. Some of them sell fish in the neighboring villages. Others go to nearby rural as well as urban areas. The time of marketing depends on the landing of boats. In case of dry fish, the normal pattern is to hire trucks jointly and take the catch to the wholesale market at Humma. Expenses like transpotation, loading and unloading charges, market entry charges etc. reduce the total earnings. Apart from these activities girl children play a supportive role by cooking food and looking after the smaller children at home, making it possible for the parents to work outside for longer hours especially during the fishing season.

Nowadays lean fishing periods are extending in the region to nearly six months in a year. During the lean season men occasionally go for fishing. They usually stay at home and play cards rather than trying to seek work elsewhere. Women on the other hand work in the cashew fields and in construction works in order to save the family from starvation. The SHGs formed are not functioning properly.

In the entire village, unhygenic living environment, extreme poverty, lack of pure water and over-work has put the fisher people at a disadvantage. The prevalent social attitude, which favours male children, results in girl children getting less attention and care. Malnutrition among girls is more compared to males and leads to problem during pregnancy. In the sample, over-work, lack of nutritious food, worm infestation and continual delivery affect their health. Women fish vendors in this region suffer from severe back pain. High morbidity rate among fisher women has impacted the economic status of the family.

- To access the extent of success after the implementation of policies, plan and programmes by government for development of Nolias in Chilika lake.

Welfare programmes are implemented by government for the betterment of the Nolia people. Now peoples are not facing problems of water shortage. At least 10 numbers of tubewells are bored in the village. This was a major problem in the village earlier and forced them to carry usable water from long distances. MBPY is given to the beneficiary through which atleast 10 percent people are benefitted. Under Employment Guarantee Scheme 45 percent people have job cards. BPL cards have also been given to 40-50 percent people of the village. Government initiatives have been taken to improve the education system. The roads are bigger and better. The village schools have got new aids. The government has constructed a multipurpose jetty for Nolia people. But still people are complaining of not receiving all the facilities.

- To evaluate the impact of modernization and change on coastline culture in Chilika Lake particular and Odisha in general.

Culture includes customs, traditions, practices and people's beliefs and perceptions about themselves, their relations with others, their relationship with authorities, their place in the group or organization of which they are members and their attitude towards divine forces. Culture is a dynamic process, it is not static. Culture grows out of orientations, beliefs and attitudes etc accumulated for a long time and shared by a large number of people. Culture is a powerful binding force; it injects cohesion and unity into a system or group. A system may consist of people belonging to different religious, caste and other such groups with divisible potential. Regionalism and localism are other divisible forces. But, inspite of these differences and diversities; the system would remain united and strong, if it has got a well-established and integrated culture. Culture has another important function; it is a source of identity and self respects. It provides an identity to the members of society or community. Inspite of diverse roots and belongings, they have a common identity because of their culture. They are proud of their culture which distinguishes them from others. Culture constantly reminds the members of the system of their real roots and implicitly advises them to stick to their roots. There are now wide-spread fears that because of fast spread of communication and modernization, and high speed of mobility of people and ideas, the local cultures are in danger of being polluted or destroyed. Little traditions are vulnerable to invasion by great traditions. In order to defend itself from such invasions by foreign cultures, a culture needs to regularly re-enact itself. The strength and sustainability of a culture depends on how sincerely and regularly the individuals concerned observe their customs, traditions, rituals and festivals. The more regular and sincere they are in this respect, the stronger and more lasting their culture is, and vice-versa.

Testing of Working Hypotheses

- There is a narrow gap between coastal culture vs. other cultures in Odisha

The preceding discussion makes it clear that, coastline culture of the fishing people has been changing, even though the process of change is slow. However, during the last decade, the pace of change has increased and it is expected to continue with significant implications for the fishing society. The change represents a blending Telugu and Odia cultures. With the passage of time, they have adopted and internalized more and more of different elements of the Odia culture, which is the mainstream culture of the state. The change is more marked and substantial among Fisher women and girls than among middle aged and elderly women.

Fisher men represent two aspects of marginalization in India. Firstly, they (marine fishermen) are a backward community. For a longtime they have stayed illiterate and ignorant. They have been exploited and oppressed by local dominant castes on one side and by government officials and political leaders on the other side. They have been neglected by the government for along time. Though some policies have been made by the government for their welfare, these have not been properly implemented. Further, the government has not accepted their demand to be included in the category of scheduled castes. Some odia speaking fishermen have been accepted as scheduled caste. Fishermen are more backward than them, but their demand for scheduled caste status has not been considered. Therefore, they feel discriminated.

Secondly, fishermen have also been victims of various difficulties and disadvantages. Fisher people in Odisha suffer from a serious handicap. Though residents of Odisha, they are primarily Telugu-speaking. They had migrated here from Andhra Pradesh or old Madras in search of fishes. Some of them came to ferry men and goods between the beach and ships anchored near the shore of the old Gopalpur Port (during British Rule). They settled in the coastal part of Odisha. They live in small villages or hamlets near the beach of Bay of Bengal. They are afflicted with an identity crisis. With Telugu as their mother tongue, they are not fluent in Odia. Many of them speak Odia, but it sounds unnatural. To varying degrees, the fishing communities of sample village enjoy Oriya festivals, but they continue to observe most of Telugu festivals. They have not, as yet, been integrated into the main stream of Oriya culture.

- Major role played by women in economic activities do not enhance their traditional women position in Nolia society as compared to male society

Women are the main economic centre of their village. All the festivals and function are incomplete without them. Still they are not allowed to participate in the village meeting. Now some of them are competing in panchayat election but with the support of male persons of their family. They can not take a single decision on their own. This is not good for the future of both village and state. They only put their thumb impression wherever required. The women should be aware of the great responsibility imposed on them. Though they are empowered but the empowerment will achieve its success when the women realise it truly.

With the changing situation, the technology also changes. Scarce fish resources, strong competition, unhygenic environment, poverty, lack of good market, lack of pure water and over burden puts women at a disadvantage. Malnutrition among girls leads to problems during pregnancy. The fish-vendor women also suffer from joint pains and back pains. Due to dominance of males and patriarchal society, women are given less attention.Wife beating, lack of educational opportunities for girls, lack of control of fertility puts women at a miserable position. Due to modernisation of fishery sector women have become victims. The opening of new mouth (muhana) in Chilika is a great hinderance to sea fishing. This has caused decline in catch. The scarcity of fish has led women into an insecure future. An improvement in the fisher's economy alone cannot be taken as the symbol of development. Empowerment of the individuals, both male and female members should be assured to show any significant gain in the context of ever changing technological options in marine fisheries. There are numerous SHGs in the village. But still a need of capacity building for member and functionaries of SHGs with the help of NGOs and banks are required. The SHG are organised by female members and they have president, secretary and vice president. All of them are women. But they have little knowledge about the SHG income and various procedures. The main role is of their husbands who exploit them indirectly. In case of Anganwadi worker, they do not get any scope of pleasure or enjoy in their work. They are loaded with heavy work. Government should take step to provide assistance for them so that thewomen can manage both home and work smoothly.

- No relative improvement of quality of life even after adoption and application of modern technological devices in Nolias.

Though government provides a lot of schemes and subsidiaries for fishing craft and to build ice plant and cold storage along with landing centre, still the village has no cold storage centres. Attention was not given to production, processing and marketing. Though a large number (10-90 percent) of fish vendors are women still the market is controlled by men, who exploit the women in different ways. More efforts are needed towards filling the gaps in programme planning rather than programme implementation.

Suggestion:

- Special attention should be paid to the need of fisher women, towards their empowerment so that the community can develop through combined efforts of men and women through a holistic approach.
- Intervention of money-lenders or commission agent should be eradicated by taking different steps such as:
    i. Activating Primary Fishing Cooperative Society (PFCS) through supply of working capital to them and financial assistance to their members and marketing their products.
    ii. Various NGOs are working who formed different groups of Nolia people to guide them in fishing and provide fishing equipment to them.
    iii. SHG finance and various banking loan facilities need to be increased.
- Can provide them greater availability of fuel wood and make the villages self sufficient in fuel wood.
- Can include the fisher persons under scheduled caste category (presently they do not come under it although they have been one of the poorest and lowly castes for generations.)
- Can get better education and awareness facilities to facilitate livelihood methods related to education in the course curriculum.

Although attempts have been made to achieve convergence in the sector by various government departments and agencies, the possibilities of social and economic development can be achieved by incorporating maximum people participation.

Glossary

Aiguru - Who have done all the rituals of dead person

Anchal - A part of wearing saree

Anna - Rice

Arakha flower - A kind of flower specially given to Lord Shiva.

Bada-phanda - big hole

Bahania - Those who don't own net and boat are called

Bhauja - Wife of elder brother

Chaulia Mantra - The sorcerer's Mantra

Choro - Chief

Gadighara - Nolia people called their deity room

Gadighara - Where Gods are worshiped and form a mound shape in the corner of the room called Ishana

Ghanta - Instrument used in worshipping

Huluhuli - Madc by tongue during worship. It's sound.

Jalias - People who own net and boat

Jatra - Fair

Kanji - Liquid food prepared from watered rice and vegetables

Karbati - It is up to five days after the death of a person when they do "Gata Stala".

Khadi - Stick supporting net

Kirtan - Dancing with the tune of religious song

Mahuri - Musical instrument

Makar Chaula - A variety of offering which is prepared with raw rice, coconut, cheese, honey and milk etc.

Manasika - Praying God to fulfil wishes and promise to offer something for this fulfilment

Mandapithas	- Cakes
Mansika Khichdi	- Food prepared by the particular family for offerings
Muhana	- Opening of lake
Naga Medha	- A kind of decoration done during the village worship
Pala and kirtan	- Chanting of religious songs by group of people. They dance in group and used different musical instruments
Palinqui	- Instuments for carrying God/Goddess
Panahandi	- A pot filled with a drink prepared by some ingredients
Panji	- A religious book in which so many auspicious dates are mentioned
Parikrama	- Go round
Parswadevata	- Some smaller god nearby their main village deity
Patasaree	- Odisha special saree
Phagu	- Colour
Sataturigadabaiki	- The girl will take bath seven times during puberty.
Shradha	- It is given on every death anniversary.
Sirini	- Offering made up milk, sugar and banana
Solo	- Plastic
Suhagan	- Married woman
Suliapada	- Here, they leave the prasad which was offered by the villagers and sacrifice a goat. All these are later taken away by the Harijan people
Tadka	- Fry of mustard, ginger, garlic is given
Talapere	- Lower end
Uparapere	- Upper end

Bibliography

Acharya, Sabita (2000), *A Socio-economic Study of the Peripheral Villages of Chilika Lake, A Research Project of CDA*, Govt. of Orissa.

Ahuja, Ram (2001), *Research Methods*, Rawat Publication, Jaipur, New Delhi.

Behura, N.K. (1990), *Anthropological Theories,* Bidisa, Midnapur.

Chand, Oliver (1981), *The Discovery of Humanity,* Harper & Row of Publisher, (p. 341-391), New York.

Choudhury, N. (2009), The Question of Empowerment: Women's Perspective on Their Internet Use, *Gender, Technology and Development,* Delhi

Clark, Graham (1977), *World Prehistory,* Cambridge University Press.

Dawan, Subodh (2010), *On Being Women*, p.17-21, New Delhi.

Eliade, Mircea (1987), *The Encyclopedia of Religion*, McMillan Publishing Company (p. 380-391, 422-443), New York.

Fairbridge, R.H. (1966), *The Encyclopedia of Oceanography*, p.110, New York.

Galley Press (1975), *The Prehistoric World,* (p.34-35), England.

Ghosh, K Asish & Pattnaik, K. Ajit (2001), *Chilika Lagoon,* Odisha.

Goode, J William & Hatt K Paul (1952), *Methods in Social Research*, McGrawhill, New York.

Gulati, L. (1984), Technological Change & Women's Work Participation and Demographic Behavior: A Case Study of Three Fishing Villages, *Economic and Political Weekly*, Vol. XIX, No.4 9, pp.2089-2094, Mumbai.

Hornell, James, (1950), *Fishing in Many Waters*, Cambridge University Press.

Hunter, W.W (1877), *A Statistical Account of Bengal, Volume XIA*, Turner & Co, p.22-24, London.

Hunter, W.W. (1872) *Orissa*, pp.20-31, London.

Immanuel, S. N., Kumar S. Ashaletha, C. Ramachandran and V.P. Vipin Kumar, (2000), *Empowerment of Coastal Communities Through Fisheries Extension Project Report,* CMFRI.

Joshi, V. Mahesh (1996), *Economics of Fisheries*, APH Publishing Corporation, New Delhi.

Klause, A.M. (2001), *Kerala Fishermen and Indo-Norwegian Pilot Project,* Asian Publishing Gouse, New Delhi.

Krishna, G.R. (1990), *Caste and Tribes of Fishermen*, New Delhi.

Kumar, N. R. and R. Sathiadhas (2001), *Economics of Resource Management and Socio-Economics of Small-Scale Fisheries:Project Report,* CMFRI.

Madox, S.L. (1900), *Final Report on the Survey & Settlement of the Province of Orissa (1890-1900 A.D.) Vol.1*, Bengal Secretariat Press, Kolkata.

Malley, O' LSS, (1908), *Bengal District Gazzetters*, p.84-85, Bengal Secretariat Press, Puri.

Mitra G.N. (1946), *Development of Chilika Lake,* Orissa Govt. Press, Cuttack.

Mitra G.N. (1956), *A New Technique for the Construction of Dykes in Deep-Silted-Swamps,* Current Science.

Mitra, K. Subrata (2001), Making Local Govt. Work: Local Elites, Panchayati Raj and Governance in India, in Atul Kohli (ed), *The Success of India's Democracy,* Cambridge University Press.

Mohanty S. Mansingh, (2004), *A Study of Social Transformation of Arakhakuda: An Ethnic Coastal Village near Chilika Lake,* Bhubaneswar.

Mohapatra, P (1986), *Bay of Bengal Programme Development of Small Scale Fishery*, SIDA & FAO.

Mukherjee, B. (1969), The Fisherwomen of Puri and Their Sea Fishing Organization, *Bulletin of the Anthropological Survey of India,* 17:3, Kolkata.

Naik, Dibarker, *An Economic Analysis of Marine Fish Marketing in Odisha by OUAT,* Odisha.

Panigrahi, Rekha, Mishra, Manas & Rao, Giri (2001), *The Fisherfolk and the Lake, Changing Property Regime & Ecological Disaster in Chilika Lake,* Bhubaneswar.

Paramanik, S K (1993), *Fishermen Communities on Coastal Villages in West Bengal",* Jaipur, New Delhi.

Patro, S.N. (1988), *The Pride of Our Wetland Heritage,* Orissa Environmental Society, Bhubaneswar.

Pattnaik, Susmita, Baral, J.K & Dash, Manoj (2011), Socio-cultural Life of Fisherwomen in India: Continuity and Change; with special reference to Orissa State.)", in *International Journal of Sociology and Anthropology,* Vol. 3(10), pp.340-353.

Peter, Devasundaram M. (1954) *Report on the Fisheries of Chilika Lake,* (1948-1952), Superitendent, Orissa Govt. Press.

Peter, Devasundaram M. (1957), *Annual Administration Report of Fishery Section of the Industries Department for the Year1953-54*, Govt. Press, Cuttack.

Pradhan, Biswadayal (2011), Panchayati Raj and Tribal Development in Orissa: An Overview, in *International Journal of Current Research,* Vol. 3, Issue-1,Pondicherry.

Pritchard, Evans (1965), *Theories of Primitive Religion*, Oxford University Press *"Report on Fishing Gears & Methods*, (14-19 July 1991), FAO Fishery and Aquaculture, Victoria, British Columbia, Canada.

Sahu, B.N., *Chilika Lake is in Danger,* p.1-8, Bhubaneswar.

Sahu, N.C. (2009, *Economy of the Fisherwomen in Ganjam District of Orissa: Conditions for Environmental Governance and Sustainable Development,* Paper for Presentation in the Fifth Biennial Conference of the Indian Society for Ecological Economics (INSEE) on Environmental Governance, Ahmedabad.

Sahu, P. (2000), *Marine Fishery and Sustainable Development of Fisherman of Ganjam Distric,*. Berhampur University, Orissa.

Salagrama,Venkatesh (2006), *Trends in Poverty & Livelihoods in Coastal Fishing Communities of Orissa State*, India, Kokinada, A.P., FAO, Rome.

Samal, C. Kishore & Meher Shibalal (1999), Socio-Economic Survey of Villages in and around Chilika Lake: *A Report Research Project Sponsored by CDA, BBSR, N.B.C* for Development Studies, Orissa.

Sathiadhas (1997), *Production and Marketing Management of Marine Fisheries in India,* Daya Publishing House, Delhi.

Sekhar, C.S., Senthlnathan and S. Isabella Rani, (1993), *Marine Fish Production in Tamil Nadu,* pp. 29-32, Department of Agricultural Economics, Tamil Nadu Agricultural University, Coimbatore.

Srinivasan, A. (1981), *Small Scale Marine Fisheries of Tamil Nadu"* Bulletin 30-B, CMFRI, Cochin.

Tripati, Sila (1998), Traditional Boatbuilding & Navigational Technique, *in Journal of Indian Ocean Studies.*

Upadhayay, V.H. and Pandey, G. (2003), *Tribal Development in India, A Critical Appraisal",* Crown Publication, Ranchi.

Vidyarthy, L.P. (1998), *Applied Anthropology in India*, Kitab Mahal, New Delhi, 2001.

Wolford, John, Introduction to Cultural Anthropology, Lecture Notes for Chapter 12, *Political Organization and the Maintenance of Order* (324-359), Department of Anthropology, University of Missouri.

Index